Power Electronics

Thyristor Controlled Power for Electric Mot

Power Electronics

Thyristor Controlled Power for Electric Motors

RAYMOND RAMSHAW

Professor,
Department of Electrical Engineering
University of Waterloo, Ontario

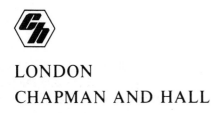

LONDON

CHAPMAN AND HALL

First published 1973
by Chapman and Hall Ltd
11 *New Fetter Lane, London* EC4P 4EE

Reprinted as a Science paperback 1975, 1978 *and* 1979

© 1973 *Raymond Ramshaw*

Printed in Great Britain by
J. W. Arrowsmith Ltd, Bristol

ISBN 0 412 14160 4

Distributed in the U.S.A.
by Halsted Press, a Division
of John Wiley & Sons, Inc., New York

Preface

The following pages are meant for those who wish to use thyristors. The details of the physics of semiconductor materials or the design of thyristors themselves are unnecessary here but a general description of the device may help to avoid pitfalls during electric circuit design.

Thyristor is the internationally recognized name for a particular semiconductor device. The name is derived from the Greek, the first part meaning switch and the second part an association with the transistor family. It has a trade name, viz. SCR (silicon controlled rectifier) and it got this name principally because it is a silicon device and it is used as a rectifier which can be controlled. As a controlled switch it forms a group together with the electromagnetic relay, the thyratron and the mercury arc rectifier. The advantages and disadvantages of the thyristor become apparent in the process of describing the device and its range of application. However, the present general interest, development and use of the thyristor, indicates that for many cases its many advantages make it superior to other devices.

Control of rotating electric machines is a major interest of the author so that in this book the applications of the thyristor are towards this end. Thyristors are used so much in connection with the control of machines that it is worthwhile to go into some details of both the electric drive to be controlled and the possible thyristor control units.

One text cannot cover all aspects of power electronics in detail. The important aspects of operation, protection and control are described carefully. However, the manufacturers' manuals must supplement this book, for example, with respect to rating specifications.

Special mention is made of the thyristor's place in technology. While much emphasis is paid to the power circuits for the control of a.c. and d.c. drives, the control circuits are not ignored. Care is taken in the practical and realistic worked examples to provide the design details of the logic circuitry which controls the behaviour of the electric drive.

Chapter 1 attempts to give an overall picture of electric drive control and the part that power electronics plays is established. A brief description of physical electronics in Chapter 2 establishes sufficient 'feeling' for the thyristor. Then the operation of the thyristor as a device is described in detail.

The next three chapters deal exclusively with the thyristor as a part of the many power circuits for the control of electric drives. Three of the most conventional machines, d.c., induction and synchronous motors have been chosen to illustrate the form of control. Special motors can also be controlled by the same power electronic circuits. An appendix is used to record the details of the logic circuitry so that there is no lengthy detraction from the main theme in the text.

The book is suitable for degree and diploma courses embracing electrical engineering as well as for practising electrical engineers in industry and research.

Waterloo, Ontario.   R. S. Ramshaw
June 1972

Contents

1 Power electronics and rotating electric drives

1.1. INTRODUCTION

Since the 1950's there has been a great upsurge in the development, production and application of semiconductor devices. Today there are well over 100 million devices manufactured in a year and the growth rate is over 10 million devices per year. These numbers alone indicate how important semiconductors have become to the electrical industry.

The control of large blocks of power by means of semiconductors began in the early 1960's. Large blocks of power meant kilowatts then, but now it means megawatts. Today the number of semiconductors capable of conducting over 7.5 A are manufactured at the rate of over 5 million units per year at a total cost of about £8.5 m ($20 m). The growth rate of the power semiconductors which are called thyristors follows that of the transistors.

Power electronics relates to thyristor circuitry, its design and role in the control of power flow in a system. The control of electric machinery is one of the major applications of power electronics. The power electronics interface between the supply and the rotating electric drive is the principal concern of this text. As such this book attempts to bridge a gap between the electrical and electronic equipment technologies.

1.2. POWER ELECTRONICS

The major component of the power electronics circuit is the thyristor. It is a fast switching semiconductor and its function is to modulate the power in a.c. and d.c. systems. All other components are to protect or to operate the thyristors. Modulation of power can vary from 100 W to 100 MW by turning the switch on and off, in a particular sequence.

The thyristor family is a group of four-layer silicon devices consisting of a number of diodes, triodes, and tetrodes. Most important of the controlled semiconductor switches for power applications are the silicon controlled rectifier (SCR), which is a unidirectional power switch, and the triac, which is a bidirectional power switch. Here the reverse blocking triode thyristor is just called a thyristor because there is no ambiguity.

Switches can perform the duties of rectification, inversion and regulation of power flow. It is not surprising that people become excited when a switch the size of one's fist has a power handling capability that approaches a megawatt. The thyristor is just such a switch. It is fundamentally an on-off device, but it can be controlled linearly if the output is averaged over time so it is useful to control electric drives. The ability to offer an ideal infinite or zero impedance at its terminals makes the thyristor an ideal element in a converter. A thyristor system can convert a source of power which is unsuitable, to one of the right kind. A d.c. supply can be obtained from an a.c. supply or a variable frequency supply can be obtained from a fixed frequency supply. Power electronics is versatile.

1.2.1. The thyristor

The thyristor is suitable for the control of large amounts of power because it is light-weight, reliable, fast acting, turns on with a small power and is free from mechanical difficulties because there are no moving parts. This switch does have some disadvantages. When the thyristor is turned on and conducts current there is a forward voltage drop of about 1.5 V. So these power devices are thermally limited. Ratings are important. There can be localized heating during turn-on because of the rate of rise of current. Heat transfer must be efficient if the silicon wafer conducts current at a density of 150 A cm^{-2} with 1.5 V across it. There must be protection against transient voltages. Turn-on is simple but turn-off can be complicated.

In spite of the disadvantages more and more installations are utilizing thyristors and larger and larger thyristors are being manufactured. Figure 1.1 gives an approximate illustration of the maximum voltage rating, the maximum current rating and the maximum safe power handling capability of individual thyristors developed over a ten-year period. There is a conflict in design procedures that makes it impossible that the thyristor with the highest voltage rating should have the highest current and hence the highest power rating. Power ratings are given as one-third of the product of the peak voltage and current ratings.

In 1968 the upper capability of production devices in the U.S.A. was 1200 V peak reverse voltage, 300 A average half-cycle current and 1 kHz switching frequency limit for fast turn-off thyristors (less than 15 μs). For slow turn-off thyristors, (greater than 15 μs) the ratings increased to 1800 V and 550 A. This was considered to be somewhere near the limit economically. Higher voltage and higher current systems could employ strings of thyristors in series and groups in parallel.

If a single thyristor is to control the system power level, the higher the current the greater must be the silicon wafer cross-section and the more the likelihood of imperfections and the lower the yield of thyristors. For higher voltages the wafer must be thicker, entailing a higher forward voltage drop, lower current and rate of change of current and higher gate currents to turn the device on. Compromise seems to be the lot of the device designer.

Since 1968 the Japanese have been at the forefront of design and have produced disc thyristors with a rating of 2500 V peak reverse voltage and 500 A average current. The forward voltage drop is less than 2.2 V. In 1970 the Japanese advertised a thyristor rated at 10 000 V and 400 A, which means that one device is capable of handling more than 1.3 MW of power.

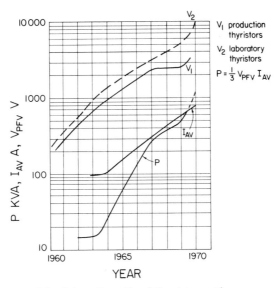

Fig. 1.1.   Growth of thyristor ratings.

1.3. ROTATING ELECTRIC DRIVES

One major application of power electronics is to control electric drives. There are other important areas of application such as general conversion of power, induction heating, light dimming and standby power supplies. Only the control of electric drives is described here.

Terminal voltage is the most common parameter to adjust in order to control a motor's characteristics. The most important characteristic is speed. Before the advent of the thyristor the conventional methods to adjust speed were to add resistance in the line or to use motor-generator sets. Commutator motors proved very satisfactory. Less often, frequency-change or pole-change systems were used. Mercury arc rectifiers and magnetic amplifiers also found a place in control systems. Now it seems that it is only in special applications that thyristor methods do not replace these older forms of control.

Thyristors are used to control electric drives ranging from the domestic application of hand drills, mixers, blenders and air-conditioning to the static variable frequency drives systems found in textile mills, 5 MW of power semiconductor controlled capacity to excite turbo-alternators and 50 MW installations in new steel mills.

1.3.1. The direct current drive

The d.c. motor is popular even though it has a commutator and is larger than the a.c. motor of equivalent rating. Its wide speed range by voltage control is the reason. Figure 1.2 illustrates how the d.c. voltage at the motor terminals can be altered if the supply is either direct current or alternating current when thyristors are used. The thyristor effectively switches the supply on and off in a discontinuous manner. Alteration of the ratio time-on to time-off adjusts the

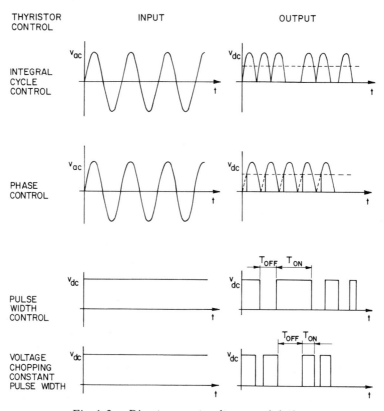

Fig. 1.2.   Direct current voltage modulation.

average voltage across the motor. The frequency of switching is rapid so that the motor only responds to the average voltage level and not to the individual pulses.

Four methods of modulating the average d.c. voltage at the terminals of the d.c. motor are shown in Fig. 1.2. The first two methods involve the conversion from alternating current to direct current by a rectifier bridge. Integral cycle control requires the thyristor to block the flow of current for one or more half cycles at a time. This is satisfactory if the a.c. supply operates at a high frequency. Otherwise the motor would oscillate about its mean speed. The load referred to the a.c. side has a high power factor. Phase control offers a much lower power factor but a greater range of voltage by allowing the thyristor to conduct only during part of the cycle.

The second two methods to adjust the motor terminal voltage when the d.c. supply voltage is fixed are alike. The thyristor is switched on and off rapidly to 'chop' the voltage. A train of pulses at the output of the thyristor 'chopper' provides an average voltage which is less than the input. Although each of the methods indicates that either the time the thyristor conducts, T_{ON}, or the time of the thyristor blocks, T_{OFF}, is constant, both can be varied.

An a.c. supply is most common and offers no problems for thyristor turn-off. Therefore, most d.c. drives operate with this kind of thyristor control. Only where fuel cells or conventional batteries provide the supply will chopper circuits be used. High-speed switching means fast turn-off and therefore special thyristors. In order to turn off a thyristor when it has a d.c. voltage across its electrodes there must be auxiliary circuits incorporated. Accordingly 'chopper' control is complex, but nevertheless it is used.

In rolling mills, adjustable speed d.c. motor drives have usually been controlled by motor-generator sets which provided the variable and reversible d.c. voltage. Motor-generator sets are being replaced by power electronic installations. It is said that the result is improved overall economy, higher efficiency, greater reliability, less maintenance and faster response. One disadvantage is that unlike motor-generator sets, where the motor is a synchronous machine, thyristors are not capable of producing a leading power factor.

In electric vehicles the single-phase a.c. commutator motors are being replaced by thyristor control and d.c. motors because of the commutation problems of a.c. machines.

An example of d.c. motor control by thyristor phase control is a recent thyristor converter in a 11.2 MW slabbing mill. Each main motor set is rated at 750 V, 4150 A, 35–70 rpm. There are four converter units which must be capable of delivering 275 per cent of the motors' rated current for 60 s so that each unit is rated at 3110–8560 kW, 750 V and 4150–11 400 A. Each converter has six legs for three-phase rectification. In each leg there are 13 thyristors which are all in parallel. The total number of thyristors is therefore 624. Every thyristor is rated at 2500 V peak forward voltage and 400 A average current. Disc type thyristors are used. These are pressed together under a force of about 100 kg on both sides by the cooling units which are made of copper. The silicon wafer is about 4 cm diameter. Each thyristor has a cooling unit, fuse, pulse transmitter for turn-on and resistor-capacitor protection circuit.

A combination of tap changer and phase angle controlled thyristors has given stepless control for locomotives operating from a 25 kV, 50 Hz power system which is transformed to 1150 V, 2800 A at the secondary. Rectification is by 96 diodes and 32 thyristors.

Another example of traction drive control by thyristors is a d.c. chopper for 1500 V railway equipment. A chopper unit is used for each pair of motors. There are two parallel strings of thyristors with six in series. The rating of each thyristor is 800 V to withstand the transient voltages. Frequency of switching varies from 100 to 400 Hz. The resultant control and drive operates at an efficiency of 95 per cent. Sixty-seven per cent was the efficiency of the system with resistance control of acceleration that the chopper replaced.

1.3.2. The alternating current drive

Speed control of a.c. motors by voltage adjustment at the stator or rotor terminals is confined to the induction motor. Many methods have been employed to this end. Whether it is resistance or a commutator machine success has only been moderate and the versatile d.c. motor has held its position in the market. Whatever was used as the instrument to adjust voltage, the thyristor can do equally well.

Variable speed a.c. motors have grown in importance, not through thyristor voltage control, but by thyristor frequency control. Inverters free the induction and synchronous motors from their inherent constant speed characteristic.

Variable a.c. voltage or variable frequency from a fixed voltage, constant frequency or d.c. supply is shown in Fig. 1.3. As in the d.c. case of Fig. 1.2 there is average voltage modulation by integral cycle control or phase control. In addition phase control of an a.c. input can simulate a lower frequency supply, although attempts are made to get higher frequencies by forced commutation. When the supply is a d.c. one the voltage is switched in a stepped manner so that current can alternate in the motor windings. The switching produces discontinuities but these effects can be minimized by reactive elements and wave shaping. If the supply is alternating, a variable frequency supply can be obtained by rectifying the supply and then inverting the rectified d.c. supply.

Induction motors and synchronous motors have no commutator so that they do not have the limitations of d.c. motors. Synchronous machines have an advantage over the induction motor for adjustable speed control because they run at a precise speed (i.e. synchronously), whereas induction motors run at a speed slightly less than synchronous speed and are load dependent. Feedback loops can overcome this difficulty but the open loop system with synchronous motors is more economic if there are a number of motors in cascade. Up to 100 motors have been run together in textile plants.

Applications of variable speed a.c. motors with inverter control include crane hoists, blowers, pumps and textile plants. These either require synchronized speed adjustment or a variable speed drive in an environment which excludes a commutator and brushes. Variation of frequency for power drives usually ranges from 20 to 120 Hz. A number of thyristor inverters may be operated in parallel if they are controlled from the same master frequency source. Parallel inverters are advantageous when regeneration is specified.

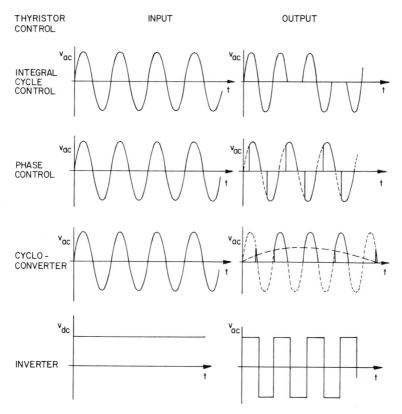

Fig. 1.3.   Alternating current voltage and frequency modulation.

1.3.3. Choice of drive and control system

Speed control can be obtained from a thyristor converter whose output is fed to a d.c. commutator motor. The mechanical commutator of the d.c. motor is a frequency changer whereby the d.c. input at the brushes becomes alternating current in the armature windings. Equally well the speed control can be obtained from a thyristor inverter supplying an a.c. motor. A thyristor converter and d.c. motor system is cheaper than a thyristor inverter and a.c. motor system. The latter is used in special circumstances where the environment does not permit the use of brushes and commutator, such as in aircraft or in mines.

It is more relevant to attempt to compare power electronics systems with other systems with the same adjustable speed features. Some attempts[1] have

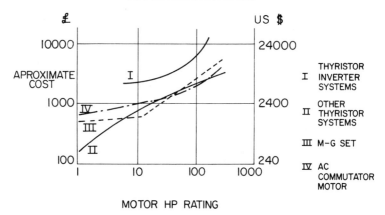

Fig. 1.4.   Drive system costs.

been published to show the differences of costs and efficiencies. These are shown in Figs. 1.4 and 1.5. The general conclusion is that the power electronics systems seem to be more expensive but more efficient than the older conventional systems. However, it is difficult to provide a general indication of the cost of thyristor drives compared with the cost of commutator motors or Ward Leonard sets. Costs are made up from the manufacturers' purchase costs, installation costs, maintenance costs and

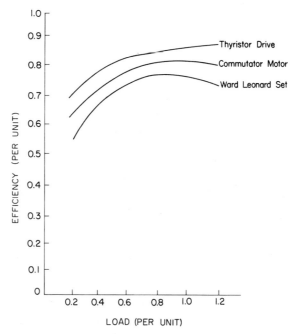

Fig. 1.5.   Drive system efficiencies.

running costs. Much depends on the type of supply, the environmental conditions, the control tolerances of speed and speed range and whether reversal and dynamic braking is required.

One thing is clear. More and more thyristor controlled drives are being used. There is also an indication that power electronics is becoming more standardized. The modular form of the thyristor and logic control circuits lends itself to the use of a simple motor and the choice of power electronics module to fit the load specification. It has not arrived yet.

REFERENCES

1. *Power applications of controllable semiconductor devices* (1965), IEE Conference Publication, No. 17.

BIBLIOGRAPHY

Special Issue on High-Power Semiconductor Devices (1967), *Proc. IEEE,* **55**.

Gutzwiller, F. W. (1967), 'Thyristors and diodes – the semiconductor work horses', *IEEE Spectrum,* **4**, 102-111.

Storm, H. F. (1969), 'Solid-state power electronics in the U.S.A.', *IEEE Spectrum,* **6**, 49-59.

Power thyristors and their applications (1969), IEE Conference Publication, No. 53.

Note
     Problems on page 207.

2 The thyristor

The thyristor is a switch. It can be switched on so that current may flow in a circuit. It can be switched off so that current ceases to flow in a circuit. The thyristor has no moving parts nor need there be any moving parts to operate it as a switch. It is constructed of four layers of semiconductor material. There are three terminals connected, two of which are used to switch on the thyristor and two of which are used to allow the passage of the load current.

How the thyristor operates as a switch, how it is turned on and off and how it is protected is described in this chapter.

Thyristors belong to a family of semiconductor devices. A brief description of some of these devices may aid the reader to understand the limitations of them and why the thyristor is foremost in the application of semiconductors to the control of power apparatus. Occasionally reference is made to a bidirectional switch, called the 'triac' because it is beginning to be used in low-power circuits, but, as manufacturing techniques improve, its use will increase and in many alternating current circuits it will replace thyristors. The triac can control the current flow in either or both directions in a circuit whereas the thyristor controls the current in only one direction.

2.2. SEMICONDUCTORS

The electrons important to the operation of semiconductors in electrical circuits are the valence electrons, which are the electrons furthest away from the nucleus. These electrons can take part in electrical conduction because they need only a small amount of energy to enable them to go to the next higher vacant energy level and escape from the attraction of the nucleus.

An electron, leaving the orbital path, leaves the atom as a positively charged ion which is rigidly held in the crystal structure. An ion, which is held in this way, is not available for conduction.

The two most important semiconductors are silicon and germanium, whose atoms each have four valence electrons (see Fig. 2.1). Four extra electrons are required to fill completely the valence energy subshell for a crystal or a solid.

Valence electrons of an atom and its four nearest neighbours are shared by one another to produce a covalent bond. Above the valence energy band there is a forbidden band. To make the electrons free for conduction they must be excited above this band into an energy range called the permissible band. Between the valence and permissible band the gap width at 300 °K for germanium is 0.72 eV and for silicon is 1.1 eV. So by the addition of energy, whether it is in the form of light, heat, nuclear radiation, an electric field or injection from a doped material, electrons can be established in the conduction band and holes in the valence band to create electron-hole pairs. These can move freely through the crystal for electrical conduction. The semiconductor is called intrinsic when only valence and conduction states are involved.

To change the electrical properties to give useful characteristics the pure silicon and germanium can be 'doped' with an impurity whose atoms can occupy the place of an intrinsic semiconductor's atoms in the crystal. Those

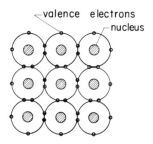

Fig. 2.1. A model of the atomic structure of a semiconductor material showing how valence electrons are shared.

impurities with three electrons in their valence subshells, as opposed to four for silicon and germanium, are called acceptor impurities, examples are boron, gallium, aluminium and indium. Donor impurities such as antimony, arsenic and phosphorus have five electrons in their valence subshells.

An intrinsic semiconductor has four complete electron-pair bonds. With acceptor impurities there are seven electrons to share among the four neighbouring atoms. Thus one electron is missing. The deficiency of an electron is called a hole and means there is a net positive charge, but an electron from a neighbouring atom can fill the deficiency and this causes the hole to move in the opposite direction. Acceptor impurities are so called because they accept electrons from the semiconductor crystal. The semi-conductors doped with such impurities are called p-type semiconductors.

Doping with donor impurities produces what are called the n-type semiconductors. There is one extra electron left over after the four nearest atoms have shared the required eight electrons to fill the valence bands.

The donor electrons and the acceptor holes are both available for electric conduction.

2.2.1. The diode (or p-n junction)

A p-type material joined to an n-type material, so that there is a perfect continuation of the crystal lattice, results in a p-n junction. This is the diode rectifier, symbolized in Fig. 2.2. When p- and n-types are joined, excess electrons on the n side diffuse into the p layer and excess holes on the p side diffuse into the n layer so there develops a small electrostatic potential across the junction to oppose further flow of charge.

To define some terms: the majority charge carrier in n-type materials is the electron, so that the hole is the minority carrier. Accordingly for p-type material the majority carrier is the hole and the minority carrier is the electron. Some majority carriers with enough energy can cross the junction barrier. Thus an electron may cross over into the p-region where it can combine with a hole, or a hole may cross into the n-region where it can

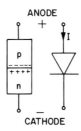

Fig. 2.2.   The structure and symbol of the diode rectifier.

combine with an electron. The recombination current is the sum of these two charge flows. Minority carriers also produce a current flow called the thermal current because with an increase of temperature some electron bonds in the crystal are broken to produce free electrons and holes. The potential barrier attracts the minority carriers in its vicinity, and accelerates them across the junction to become majority carriers. Of course, the total junction current, recombination and thermal, is zero since there is no external circuit.

A depletion layer capacitance is produced by fixed charges on either side of the p-n junction. Both the width of the depletion layer and the effective capacitance are a function of the voltage which is applied across the anode and cathode terminals. The applied voltage is sometimes called the junction bias voltage.

An external reverse bias voltage makes the cathode positive with respect to the anode. As the bulk resistivity of the semiconductor material is low, a reverse bias appears across the junction to decrease the recombination current, but the thermal current remains independent. The sum of the recombination and thermal currents increases as the reverse bias voltage increases but soon reaches a saturation level. Eventually, however, the reverse current will increase rapidly due to the increased energy of minority carriers to dislodge other minority carriers to add to the total current. Avalanche breakdown is the name given to this mechanism. This resulting constant voltage of a reverse biased p-n junction is a characteristic of the zener-diode (see Fig. 2.3).

With an external forward bias voltage such that the anode is positive, the junction barrier potential is decreased. Thermal current, that is, minority carrier flow, is unaffected but many more majority carriers with lower energies overcome the retarding electric field and flow in the external circuit. There is very little impedance to the flow of current with forward bias.

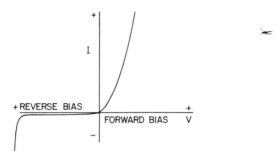

Fig. 2.3.   Voltage-current characteristic of the diode.

2.2.2. The transistor (n-p-n type)

Figure 2.4 shows the diagrammatic representation of the structure of the semiconductor wafer and its electrical circuit symbol.

If the emitter-base junction is forward biased, the net electrostatic potential V_{EB} reduces. More majority carriers can cross into the base region from the emitter. Not many holes pass from the base to the emitter because the base

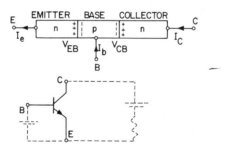

Fig. 2.4.   The structure and symbol of the transistor.

region has higher resistivity. If the collector-base junction is reverse biased, that is the collector terminal is positive with respect to the base, then V_{CB} increases so that there are less majority carriers to cross that junction. The base has collected a large number of electrons from the emitter so that if they reach the base-collector junction they are accelerated across to flow in the external circuit.

(a) Cut-off

Both junctions can be reverse biased so that the collector current is very small (see Fig. 2.5), and the total applied voltage is across the transistor. This part of the transistor characteristic is called cut-off.

An increase of reverse bias voltage widens the depletion layer until the minority carriers, which are accelerated across the junction, have sufficient energy to collide with and dislodge both minority and majority carriers in the crystal. Avalanche breakdown results. This determines the maximum collector

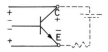

Fig. 2.5.   The transistor biased for no current flow.

voltage that can be tolerated. If the reverse bias voltage is great enough the depletion layers can touch and the transistor would be destroyed if the collector current were not limited by a suitable external resistance. The transistor is manufactured to have a narrow base region so that the recombination of electrons is minimized on their way from the emitter to the collector. Unfortunately the narrow base region signifies that a low collector-base voltage will destroy the transistor. The voltage at which the depletion layers touch is sometimes called the 'punch-through' voltage.

(b) Linear region

If the emitter-base junction is forward biased and the collector-base junction is reverse biased, current flows in the manner already described. The more positive the base potential, the greater the base current, the collector load current, and the voltage across the load, but the voltage across the transistor is less, until a saturation point is reached.

The biasing for this linear region is indicated in Fig. 2.6.

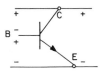

Fig. 2.6.   The transistor biased for controlled current flow.

(c) Saturation

Saturation occurs when the flow of current is limited only by the load resistance and happens when both the junctions are forward biased. At this condition the collector-emitter voltage difference is only about 25 mV. Figure 2.7 shows the bias for saturation.

It is possible to use the transistor as an on-off switch by utilizing only the cut-off and saturation parts of the characteristic. A positive step base bias on an n-p-n transistor will switch the device fully on without going through the linear region with its inherent higher losses. The voltage and power capabilities of the transistor are limited, but there is a similar semiconductor switch which has much higher voltage and power handling capabilities. This is the thyristor or silicon controlled rectifier.

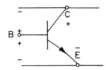

Fig. 2.7.   The transistor biased for saturation current.

2.2.3. The thyristor (p-n-p-n controlled rectifier)

The thyristor is a three-terminal, three-junction, four-layer semiconductor device made of alternate layers of p and n type silicon and its diagrammatic representation and electric circuit symbol is depicted in Fig. 2.8. The end p region is the anode, the end n region is the cathode and the inner p region is the gate. The anode to cathode is connected in series with the load circuit. Essentially the device is a switch. Ideally it remains off (voltage blocking state), or appears to have an infinite impedance until both the anode and gate terminals have suitable positive voltages with respect to the cathode terminal. The thyristor then switches on and current flows and continues to conduct without further gate signals. Ideally the thyristor has no impedance when it conducts. To switch off or revert to the blocking state, there must be no gate signal and the anode current must be reduced to zero. Current can only flow in one direction.

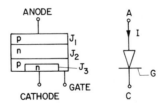

Fig. 2.8.   The structure and symbol of the thyristor.

Study the thyristor representation of Fig. 2.9. If there are no external bias voltages, the majority carriers in each layer diffuse until there is a built-in voltage that retards further diffusion. Some majority carriers have enough energy to cross the barrier produced by the retarding electric field at each junction. These carriers then become minority carriers and can recombine with majority carriers. Minority carriers in each layer can be accelerated across each junction by the fixed field, but as there is no external circuit in this case the sum of majority and minority carrier currents must be zero.

A voltage bias as shown in Fig. 2.9 and an external circuit to carry current allow internal currents which include the following terms.
The current I_1 is due to:

(1) majority carriers (holes) crossing junction J_1,
(2) minority carriers crossing junction J_1,
(3) holes injected at junction J_2 diffusing through the n region and crossing junction 1, and
(4) minority carriers from junction J_2 diffusing through the n region and crossing junction 1.

Similarly I_2 is due to six terms and I_3 is due to four terms.

The two simple analogues to explain the basic action of the thyristor are those of the diode and the two transistor models.

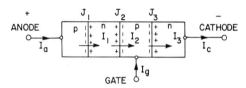

Fig. 2.9.   The thyristor: diagrammatic representation to show current flow and voltage bias.

(a) The diode model of the thyristor

The thyristor is similar to three diodes in series for there are three p-n junctions. Without gate bias, no matter what the polarity of an applied anode to cathode voltage, there is always at least one reversed biased junction to prevent conduction.

If the cathode is made negative by the supply voltage and the gate is biased positively with respect to the cathode, the p layer at the gate is flooded by electrons from the cathode and will lose its identity as a p layer. Accordingly the thyristor becomes equivalent to a conducting diode.

(b) The two transistor model of the thyristor

This analogue is illustrated in Fig. 2.10. The p-n-p-n wafer can be considered to be two transistors with two base regions. The collector of the n-p-n transistor provides base drive for the p-n-p transistor whose collector current plus the gate current supply base drive for the n-p-n transistor.

To turn the thyristor on the gate current is applied to the more sensitive n-p-n transistor component of the p-n-p-n structure. The first 10 per cent of the rise of anode current is then essentially the collector current of the transistor. The n base of the p-n-p transistor is charged by the collector current from the n-p-n transistor. Thus positive feedback is initiated by the collector current of the p-n-p transistor to add to the charge build up in the p base of the n-p-n transistor. Saturation level is rapidly reached and the current is only limited by the load impedance.

It is worth considering the different possible thyristor states more closely in order to describe its characteristics.

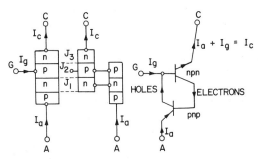

Fig. 2.10. The diagrammatic representation of the structure and the electric circuit symbol of the thyristor and its two-transistor model.

2.3. THYRISTOR CHARACTERISTICS

The device's characteristics must be known so that it can be adequately used and protected. The characteristics can be determined by considering the three main states of the device: that is under conditions of reverse bias, forward bias and blocking, and forward bias and conducting.

2.3.1. The thyristor reverse biased (cathode positive with respect to the anode)

Junctions one and three are reverse biased and junction two is forward biased so, just as with the single p-n junction, only a small leakage current flows from cathode to anode.

A positive gate drive to the thyristor, while the anode is negative, causes the thyristor to behave like a transistor and the reverse anode leakage current will increase up to a value comparable with the forward gate current so that appreciable power dissipation can occur in the thyristor. Junction overheating can cause thermal runaway.

The anode current is equal to the reverse saturation current of junction one plus a fraction of the gate current. Saturation current depends on temperature so a rise in junction temperature increases the saturation current which further increases junction heating. The maximum gate voltage during conditions of reverse bias is often specified by the manufacturer so that its heating effect is limited.

An increase of reverse bias voltage causes the depletion layers of junctions one and three to widen. Junction one normally blocks most of the anode to cathode voltage so the junction one depletion layer is usually wide. To accommodate this the centre n region is made wide so that there is no voltage 'punch-through' caused by depletion layers of J_1 and J_2 overlapping.

2.3.2. The thyristor forward biased and blocking (anode positive with respect to the cathode)

Junctions one and three are forward biased but junction two is reverse biased. The anode current is still small since one p-n region is reverse biased and it equals the saturation current at junction two plus a fraction of the gate current. The gate current increases the anode current during this mode of operation, although the gate current must be small.

2.3.3. The thyristor forward biased and conducting

There are four ways to switch the thyristor on but once it is on it offers almost zero impedance to the flow of current so that the overall voltage/current characteristic is as shown in Fig. 2.11. While the thyristor conducts,

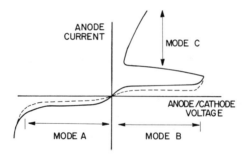

Fig. 2.11.   Steady-state thyristor characteristic.

the voltage drop between the anode and the cathode is about 1 to 1.5 V and remains substantially independent of anode current.

The four ways of triggering the thyristor are by gate signals both by (1) electrical signals or (2) light activation, by (3) the high magnitude of forward bias voltage and by (4) the rapid rate of rise of forward bias voltage. The first mentioned is the most important and the most usual, while the latter is to be avoided because of its spurious nature.

(a) Light turn-on

A beam of light directed at the gate to cathode junction, J_3, can produce sufficient energy to break electron bonds in the semiconductor and bring about the necessary additional minority carriers to switch on the device.

(b) Gate turn-on

Additional minority carriers can be injected into the gate region through the gate lead to switch the thyristor on. If the gate current is large enough the thyristor will switch on as soon as the anode becomes positive with respect to the cathode. With increasing size of thyristor this gate current will vary from a few mA to 250 mA or more.

Some time is required for the thyristor to attain full conduction when the device is turned on at the gate. The property of dynamic plasma spread, which determines the maximum frequency of device operation, refers to the rate of increase of area of the semiconductor through which conduction is taking place. The spread properties are adversely affected by increases in device thickness, and inhomogeneities increase as the silicon area increases. Thickness and area increase as higher voltage and higher current thyristors are developed so that plasma spread becomes increasingly important.

Turn-on time is defined as the time from the initiation of triggering, when the thyristor offers infinite impedance to the flow of anode current, to the time when an equilibrium charge distribution is established throughout the device together with a steady state forward voltage drop. The turn-on time is about 1 to 3 μs for the thyristors readily available commercially. There are thyristors which are manufactured especially for radar-pulse modulators. These can have anode current rise times of 300 ns.

There is a minimum gate current below which the thyristor will not turn on. Fast turn-on times are achieved if higher currents than the minimum are injected at the gate, because anode conduction begins after a certain charge has been injected into the gate region; the higher the magnitude of the gate current, the less time it takes to produce the necessary minority carriers to switch on the device. The switching speed is reduced for an inductive load in the anode circuit, if the final current is the same as a resistive load, but the power dissipated in the thyristor is also reduced.

The best shape of a gate signal is one with a sharp leading edge, and the shorter the signal duration the greater must be its magnitude for reliable turn-on. Once the thyristor is on, the gate current is no longer required to flow for the device to remain conducting, so a gate pulse is enough. For thyristors which are used for general industrial applications, a gate pulse with a rise time of 10 A μs^{-1} may turn on a thyristor in 0.1 μs, although a pulse length less than 0.2 μs is usually ineffective. Thyristors for applications such as pulse modulators may require gate signals with a rise time of 40 A μs^{-1}.

If the gate signal is reduced to zero before the rising anode current reaches the latching (or pick-up) current, the thyristor will turn off again. Once the latching current has been exceeded the thyristor remains on until the anode current is reduced below the holding current, which is lower than the latching current (this is electrical backlash). For low-load currents, a capacitor discharge circuit or bleed resistor may be used to ensure exceeding the holding current at turn-on. Latching current increases slightly with larger gate currents.

During the initial interval of turn-on, only a small area near the gate electrode conducts anode current. An appreciable rise of anode current in a short time, that is, large di/dt, before conduction spreads across the junction, may give rise to local heating sufficient to damage the thyristor. This heating limits the maximum di/dt during turn-on to between 3 and 30 A μs^{-1}, although a specially fast thyristor may have a capability of 10^3 A μs^{-1}. An inductance in series with the anode will reduce the di/dt and, as a refinement, once the thyristor is conducting fully it is possible to have the inductor saturate to allow a larger di/dt up to full load current. This inductance also reduces the turn-on and off losses but it can also give rise to large reverse

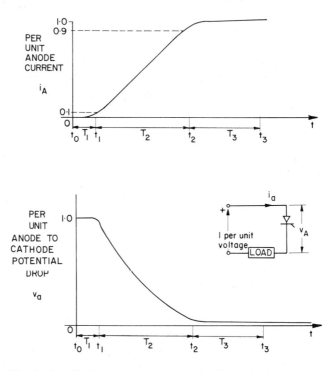

Fig. 2.12.   Variation of current and voltage during turn-on.

voltage transients which could be damaging. Higher gate current also tends to increase the anode di/dt withstand capability.

   Figure 2.12 indicates the form of current rise during the transition from the non-conducting to the fully conducting state. The time t_0 indicates the initiation of turn-on which is produced by a step function of voltage applied at the gate terminals. The period T_1 is the delay time between the front of the gate pulse and the beginning of a rapid rate of increase of anode current. A gate pulse would have a duration of at least T_1 seconds. Power dissipation in the thyristor is greatest during the period T_2 because the current rises rapidly over a small area while the voltage drop is still appreciable. The period

T_3 is the conductivity spreading time and also the time during which the voltage decay stabilizes.

(c) Breakover voltage turn-on

An increase of the anode to cathode forward voltage increases the width of the depletion layer at junction two and also increases the accelerating-voltage for minority carriers across the same junction. These carriers collide with the fixed atoms and dislodge further minority carriers until there is an avalanche breakdown of the junction. This makes junction J_2 forward biased. The anode current would be limited only by the external load impedance in this case.

At this forward breakover voltage, V_{BO}, (see Section 5.1) the thyristor changes its characteristic of having a high voltage across the device with low leakage current to a low voltage across the derive with large forward current. At the voltage V_{BO} the thyristor turns on.

Surface effects of the silicon wafer may locally constrict the space-charge layer and depress the breakdown voltage. This effect is normally non-uniform around the junction periphery so the entire avalanche current may flow through a minute area and the p-n junction can be destroyed by overheating. The periphery defects are prevalent on high-voltage structures. A suitable contour, or bevel, at the edge of the wafer, where the diffused junction meets the surface, permits the efficient manufacture of reliable, high-voltage thyristors.

The breakover voltage is greater than the reverse voltage rating and is only used as a method of turning on four-layer, p-n-p-n diodes.

(d) dv/dt turn-on

A rapid rate of increase of forward anode to cathode voltage can produce a transient gate current, which is caused by anode to gate and gate to cathode capacitances. This can turn on the thyristor and is to be avoided. Thyristors are limited to 20 to 200 V μs^{-1} at the anode, although there are high-voltage devices (1600 V) with dv/dt performances greater than 500 V μs^{-1} in which, however, gate sensitivity is low. Practically, the dv/dt for switching is increased by using a low external gate to cathode resistor, by internally shorting the gate to cathode junction over part of its periphery or by gold diffusion at the final stage of manufacture.

2.4. THYRISTOR TURN-OFF

Turn-off means that all forward conduction has ceased and the reapplication of a positive voltage to the anode will not cause current to flow without there being a gate signal. Commutation is the process of turning off the thyristor and the commutation circuit comprises the additional components to facilitate turn-off.

2.4.1. Ways of turn-off

There are three ways to switch off a thyristor. There is natural commutation, reverse bias turn-off and gate turn-off.

(a) Natural commutation

When the anode current is reduced below a minimum value called the holding current the thyristor turns off. However it must be noted that rated anode current is usually greater than 1000 times the holding value. Since the anode voltage remains positive with respect to the cathode in a d.c. circuit, the anode current can only be reduced by opening the line switch, increasing the load impedance or shunting part of the load current through a circuit parallel to the thyristor, that is, short-circuiting the device.

(b) Reverse bias turn-off

A reverse anode to cathode voltage (the cathode is positive with respect to the anode) will tend to interrupt the anode current. The voltage reverses every half cycle in an a.c. circuit so that a thyristor in the line would be reverse biased every negative cycle and would turn off. This is called phase commutation or a.c. line commutation.

To create a reverse biased voltage across a thyristor, which is in the line of a d.c. circuit, capacitors can be used. The method of discharging a capacitor in parallel with a thyristor to turn off the thyristor is called forced commutation.

In power electronic applications one advantage of using thyristors is that they are compact. The control equipment is also compact if integrated circuits are employed. There has also been at attempt to miniaturize capacitors[1] used for forced commutation and for filtering. The former use is important because the currents can be high and thermal dissipation takes high priority in design considerations. Small sizes of capacitors are at present being achieved by the use of metallized plastic film or a plastic film and aluminium foil.

(c) Gate turn-off

In some specially designed thyristors the characteristics are such that a negative gate current increases the holding current so that it exceeds the load current and the device turns off. The current ratings are presently below 10 A and this type will not be considered further.

2.4.2. Thyristor turn-off time

Turn-off time is the time during which the charge present in the silicon structure decays to a level near its equilibrium off-state. If, during this interval of decay, a forward bias voltage is reapplied the device will conduct. Turn-off time is temperature sensitive, doubling between 25 °C and 125 °C. For natural commutation it takes between 10 and 100 μs to switch off the thyristor, while for forced commutation it can be between 7 and 20 μs, but this does not take into account special purpose thyristors. To be a little more specific: turn-off times are about:

10 μs for low-voltage, low-current thyristors,

>20 μs for 500 V ratings

>35 μs for 800 V ratings

>50 μs for 1200 V ratings

and

100 to 200 μs for 1500 to 2000 V ratings.

The action of turn-off is as follows. A reverse bias voltage which is applied to turn the thyristor off, allows moving charges to flow in the direction from cathode to anode voltage. This reversal of charge flow may result in a large reverse anode current, where the di/dt is determined by the external circuit. This current must flow until most of the carriers of junctions J_1 and J_3 (see Fig. 2.9) have been removed, at which state the junctions revert to a blocking state and the current is zero. The thyristor blocks the reverse voltage because J_1 and J_3 are reverse biased. However, the junction J_2 is still forward biased and has many charges which are trapped. The thyristor blocks forward voltage when the excess carriers at junction J_2 have recombined, but this recombination is independent of the external circuit. Turn-off time increases with junction temperature because recombination takes longer at higher temperatures. The amount of charge near junction J_2 depends on the forward current. So large currents mean increased turn-off times. A reverse current decreases the turn-off time because junctions J_1 and J_3 become reverse biased in a shorter time.

2.5. THYRISTOR RATINGS

Voltage, current and power ratings are interrelated but each will be treated singly.

2.5.1. Voltage ratings

There are three voltages to consider.

The peak forward voltage (*PFV*) is the limiting positive anode voltage above which the thyristor may be damaged.

The forward breakdown voltage (V_{BO}) is the minimum anode to cathode voltage to cause turn-on when no gate signal is applied. To specify this value, the gate is in the open circuit condition and the junction temperature is at its maximum permitted value, although V_{BO} is still a function of dv/dt. In general *PFV* is greater than V_{BO} so that there is some inherent protection for the device. However, if there is a voltage transient with an amplitude greater than the transient rating of the thyristor, although it is unlikely to damage the thyristor, it may lead to circuit malfunction if it causes the thyristor to switch on at the wrong instant. If the junction temperature is low, it is possible that the *PFV* is less than V_{BO}.

Peak reverse voltage (*PRV*) is the maximum repetitive voltage that can be applied to the thyristor so that the cathode is positive with respect to the anode. If the *PRV* is exceeded there may be avalanche breakdown and the thyristor will be damaged if the external circuit does not limit the current.

For large power applications in 1967, thyristors with *PRV* ratings up to about 1600 V were available commercially. These high-voltage thyristors had current ratings of up to 250 A half cycle average forward current. In 1968 Japan developed thyristors rated at 2500 V and 400 A. At the same time it was stated that with a more accurate control of the diffusion process during the manufacture of the four layer silicon wafer it would be possible to develop 4 kV thyristors. However in 1969 thyristors capable of handling 10 kV and 400 A (4 MVA) were produced for use in prototype interrupters and static converters.

High voltage ratings are obtained at the expense of fast turn-off times and low forward voltage drops. For high voltage design the silicon wafer is thick and for high current and high di/dt the silicon wafer is thin. The designer has a conflict when thyristors are to handle large powers and must make a compromise.

2.5.2. Current ratings

In order to make the thyristor with the best possible current rating the active crystal area should be large, the thickness small and there should be good external heat transfer. Small crystal thickness, however, means low voltage capabilities and large silicon area means a reduced yield of high-voltage thyristors due to increased density of imperfections and an uneven resistivity distribution. One definition of current rating is achieved by employing a defined cooling medium temperature and then establishing the current at which the junction approaches the maximum permissible temperature.

There are thyristors capable of conducting currents up to 500 A half cycle average forward current. These commercially produced thyristors can have ratings up to 7000 A peak one cycle surge current. There are limited production models for use in radar pulse modulators for high-current amplitude, short duration pulses. An example of a manufacturer's specification for pulse application is:

> 1000 A peak current (30 A average current),
> maximum repetitive di/dt—1200 A μs^{-1},
> current rise time to 300 A—300 ns,
> applied voltage—400 V,
> gate current—4 A with 0.1 μs rise time.

2.5.3. Power rating

This is strictly associated with current conduction and the forward voltage drop, so that cooling or power loss is a better consideration. A silicon device has a maximum temperature at the junction between 120 °C and 180 °C. As the ambient temperature increases, the amount of power dissipated by the thyristor must be reduced, thus decreasing its rating.

Thyristor power losses can be divided into five parts, specified by the manufacturers.

(a) Load current forward conduction loss

The mean anode current multiplied by the forward voltage drop across the thyristor (1.2 to 1.5 V) is the average power dissipated in the thyristor. The 10 kV, 400 A encapsulated thyristor rests comfortably in the palm of the hand. At rated current the average forward conduction loss is about 600 W. To maintain the silicon temperature well below 120 °C the heat generated in the thyristor must be removed quickly. Large heat sinks and efficient cooling are necessary.

An example of cooling is the 120 A rms continuous current a.c. switch. Two thyristors mounted in inverse parallel between water-cooled heat exchangers require about one gallon of water per minute to maintain the temperature at 40 °C when the maximum average power dissipation is 1800 W.

(b) Forward leakage power loss

When the thyristor is blocking and has a positive voltage applied to the anode there is a leakage current. This loss, which is the integration of the vxi product waveforms, is small compared with the conduction loss.

(c) Reverse leakage power loss and turn-off loss

It is possible during rapid turn-off for the reverse current to rise to a value comparable to the forward current. When the thyristor impedance starts to increase, dissipation occurs as the current falls and the reverse voltage builds up. To limit the rate of change of current at turn-off, and hence the energy to be dissipated, circuit inductance is used. This also limits the rate of rise of forward current which is an advantage but the inductance can give rise to high reverse voltage transients during turn-off.

(d) Gate power loss

The loss is small if pulse signals are used to turn on the thyristor. The product of gate voltage and current for continuous signals gives the loss.

(e) Turn-on loss

This loss is rather higher than turn-off loss. Because the switching process takes a finite time there is a relatively high voltage across the thyristor while a current flows. For example, by the time the current has reached 90 per cent of its final value, there may still be 10 per cent of the supply voltage across the device (see Fig. 2.12). Accordingly, appreciable power may be dissipated during this turn-on interval. Above 400 Hz switching, additional circuitry is used to reduce switching losses or else some derating of the normal forward current is made to allow for the extra dissipation.

The thermal time constant of the thyristor is short so ratings are not exceeded and flat-plate heat sinks attached to the device stud are large compared with the device. Heat sinks have free convection and can have forced air or water cooling.

2.5.4. Intermittent ratings

Because the thyristor has a short thermal time constant, there is no difference between continuous and intermittent ratings above a few seconds conduction period. Over short periods, if the heat sink does not heat up fully to its rated steady state value during the first 'on' period, some rating increase is possible. This information is given in the manufacturers' specification of each type of thyristor.

An example of an intermittent rating is afforded by the thyristors used in radar pulsed modulators. The maximum peak repetitive current is 1000 A whereas the mean current is only 30 A.

In order to obtain the maximum rating of a thyristor the manufacturers' suggested methods of cooling must be followed closely.

2.6. THYRISTOR MANUFACTURE

One manufacturing technique is to begin with a thick inner n-type material. The two p layers are formed simultaneously by solid diffusion using either gallium or aluminium as the diffusant. The cathode junction and anode contacts are formed by alloying, using gold-containing antimony as an n-type impurity, and aluminium respectively (see Fig. 2.13).

A tungsten or molybdenum plate is soldered to each side of the structure when it is in its molten state. This is to help compensate for the different coefficients of thermal expansion of the materials. The gate contact is attached to the p base before mounting the assembly on a copper base with hard solder and hermetically sealing the container. Some devices have the mechanical contacts made by compression bonding to eliminate fatigue problems of solder mounting. However, pressure contact bonding has its own design problems.

For high-power devices a second cathode connection is made near the gate to provide a special terminal for gate signals in order to minimize any unbalanced pick up on the gate and cathode gating leads. Unbalanced voltages induced in the leads by stray fields could give rise to spurious thyristor triggering.

Also for high power devices, double sided encapsulation of the silicon cells, called the 'button' thyristor is a recent development. The integral heat sink on both sides of the cell provides thermal mass in good contact with the wafer. Short-term overloads are increased especially when the heat sinks are water cooled.

During the manufacturing process of high-voltage thyristors it is a problem to control the silicon surface properties so that premature surface breakdown does not occur. Conventionally a double bevel is used to combat this problem and this is shown in Fig. 2.13. The double bevel reduces the conduction area so that the current rating is low. This low current rating is avoided by bevelling the surface near the junction only. For example a 2° level has been found satisfactory for 3 kV thyristors.

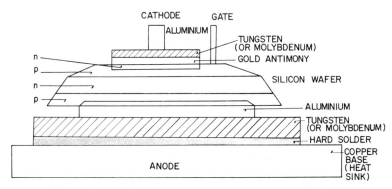

Fig. 2.13. Schematic cross section of a thyristor assembly.

2.7. THYRISTORS IN CIRCUITS

The way in which the thyristor works has been briefly described. Before an examination of the individual control circuits for electrical machines is made, there are still some general details common to all applications to be made known. These are the arrangements for increasing power handling capabilities, the gate circuits for turning thyristors on and the important subject of protection.

2.7.1. Thyristors in series

When the supply voltage is greater than the thyristor voltage rating, a number of thyristors can be connected in series to share the forward and reverse voltage. Care must be taken to share the voltage equally. For steady-state conditions, voltage sharing is forced by using a resistance or a zener-diode in parallel with each thyristor. For transient voltage sharing, a low non-inductive resistor and capacitor in series are placed in parallel with each thyristor (see Fig. 2.14). Since the capacitor C can discharge through the thyristor during turn-on, there can be excessive power dissipation, but the switching current from C is limited by the resistance R. This resistance also serves the purpose of damping out 'ringing', which is the oscillation of C with the circuit inductance during commutation.

All thyristors, which are connected in series, should be turned on at the same time when signals are applied to their gates simultaneously. Circuit elements can be added in order to delay the rise of anode current until all the units are on and the anode to cathode voltages have dropped to the minimum value. This prevents a voltage spike across the thyristor with the longest turn-on time.

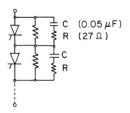

Fig. 2.14.   Sharing voltage.

2.7.2. Thyristors in parallel

When the load current is greater than the thyristor current rating, operation is still possible if a number of thyristors are connected in parallel to share the load current. The forward voltage drops across the thyristors vary, so current division can vary unless matched thyristors are used, but the current ratings are reduced.

The number of thyristors required to be connected in parallel is not altogether determined by continuous load conditions but also by the number of devices required to carry current over a given short-time overload duty cycle, or to carry a fault current limited only by supply impedance and for a period determined by the clearing time of the protective devices.

Matched thyristors need only about 20 per cent derating to allow for the tolerances and thermal effects, and the paralleled thyristors are usually mounted on the same heat sink to maintain equal junction temperatures.

The gate signals must be applied until the latching currents of all thyristors have been exceeded, because, once one unit conducts, the voltage drop across it reduces to a value just above 1 V, and this is then the voltage across the others.

To attempt to get equal current sharing external balancing resistors or reactors can be used. The voltage drop across balancing resistors would be comparable with the anode cathode voltage drop across the thyristor. Reactors can be connected in the anode circuit of two thyristors as shown in Fig. 2.15 so that the ampere turns of the two circuits are equalized. If thyristor *TH*1 carries a changing and larger current, the net induced emf in the series reactor will tend to oppose that current. Because of the coupling and winding direction the reactor induced voltage in series with *TH*2 aids an increase in current, so there is a balancing action. Currents can be equalized to within about 10 per cent of each other.

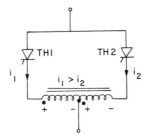

Fig. 2.15.   Current sharing by reactor equalization.

2.7.3. Circuits to Turn on Thyristors

The circuits described below provide the necessary gate to cathode signal to turn the thyristor on. The gate requirement is that the gate voltage should be between 2 and 10 V to cause current between 100 μA and 1500 mA to flow. High gate currents are needed for thyristors of high power capacity. The characteristic provided by the manufacturer will be somewhere within the cross-hatched area of Fig. 2.16. This shows that there are minimum values of gate

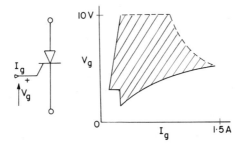

Fig. 2.16.   Thyristor gate characteristics.

voltage and current, below which the thyristor will not turn on. The odd shape near the origin is to take into account the higher gate power needed at low-junction temperatures. There are also maximum limits set for the gate signal. A signal in excess of this limit will cause damage. Signals within the cross-hatched area will always turn on the thyristor.

There are so many possible gate circuits that only a few will be described in this section, but others will be discussed in the detailed examples of motor control. Three basic types can be categorized. They are d.c. firing signals, pulse signals and a.c. phase signals.

(a) Direct current firing signals

A continuous gate signal is not normally desirable because of the associated power dissipation in the thyristor, but in applications where the thyristor may turn off before the time required this extra dissipation must be tolerated.

Figure 2.17(a) illustrates a firing circuit. The switch S could be a single-pole mechanical switch or it could be a relay, reed switch, transistor switch, or another thyristor if only a very small switching signal can be obtained from the source of control. Figure 2.17(b) is a modification which needs no extra power supply. When the anode is positive and S is closed the gate current is limited by R. When the anode is positive and the thyristor is on, then the gate current is much reduced because the voltage to produce the gate current is now only the thyristor forward voltage drop of about 1 V. The

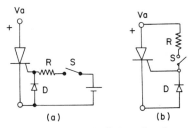

Fig. 2.17. D.C. firing signals.

diode is in the circuit to prevent a large reverse voltage across the gate and cathode terminals when the current is interrupted. The diode limits this voltage to about 1 V although up to about 5 V can be tolerated.

Another common method to produce d.c. firing signals is the use of a bistable multivibrator. All the multivibrator family is manufactured in modular form so that the logic elements and actual firing circuits can readily be built up without it being necessary to design the individual circuits. When a small pulse from the control circuit arrives at the input of the bistable it changes state and either a voltage appears at the output, as a gate signal, or is removed if it appears at the output terminals before the application of a signal.

(b) Pulse firing signals

There are major advantages to be had by using pulse firing signals rather than continuous d.c. signals. Thyristor gate coupling by transformer is possible and this gives isolation from the gate control power source. Hence many gate circuits can be fed from that source. Power dissipation in the gate circuit is either reduced or individual pulse powers may be higher to ensure a more rapid and reliable turn-on when pulses are used instead of continuous signals.

If a continuous firing signal is required then a continuous chain of pulses at high frequency can be used. Accordingly, pulse signals can be categorized into single or multiple pulses, which can be controlled in time, or simple on-off pulses.

On-off pulses can be obtained from a transistor monostable multivibrator. Every small signal input pulse to the multivibrator provides a large pulse output of defined magnitude and duration. Figure 2.18 shows a circuit, which employs a saturable core transformer to give an on-off pulse. When the anode is positive the thyristor will turn on if the transformer is unsaturated. The

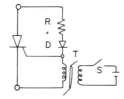

Fig. 2.18. On-off pulses.

transformer T becomes saturated when the switch S is closed and the thyristor will not fire because the gate is by-passed by the low-impedance secondary winding.

Single or multiple pulses can also be obtained from unijunction transistor (*UJT*) circuits, one of which is depicted in Fig. 2.19. It has a simple manual control. The capacitor C charges up until the *UJT* breaks down and a pulse then appears across the transformer. The time it takes for the pulse to appear depends on the RC time constant.

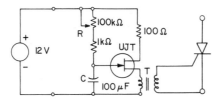

Fig. 2.19. Unijunction transistor firing circuit.

The astable of free running multivibrator is another of the family that can provide a train of high frequency pulses. This is a reliable form of gate signal when the supply is alternating current and loads are inductive so that the latching current may not be reached until well after the anode becomes positive. This method of firing can be operated from a d.c. signal.

(c) Alternating current firing signals

Phase control is a common way to alter the a.c. power supplied to a load. The power is modulated by varying that part of the voltage cycle during which the current is allowed to conduct (see Fig. 2.20). This means that the pulse to turn on the thyristor at the correct part of the cycle is synchronized with the a.c. supply and its phase with respect to the supply voltage is controlled.

(a)   (b)   (c)

Fig. 2.20. Anode to cathode voltage during phase control: (a) no conduction; (b) $90°$ firing; (c) $150°$ conduction.

A simple method to give up to a $90°$ conduction angle is an extension of the circuit shown in Fig. 2.17 which is redrawn in Fig. 2.21 with a variable resistance R. An increased R delays the time, or phase, in the cycle that the voltage is positive enough to drive sufficient gate current to turn the thyristor on.

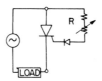

Fig. 2.21. $90°$ phase control.

A more precise firing circuit is shown in block diagram form in Fig. 2.22. The a.c. supply gives the synchronized signal which is converted to a ramp waveform and this in turn is fed to the schmidt trigger of the multivibrator family. The latter is the pulse shaper for firing the thyristor. When the signal input to the schmidt trigger reaches a particular level there is an output signal with a steeply rising wavefront. When the input signal drops below a certain level the output of the pulse shaper reduces to zero. A sawtooth waveform enables the output of the pulse shaper to fall to zero at the same instant in every cycle but the pulse rise is phase shifted by altering the d.c. level of the sawtooth waveform and hence the time when the pulse shaper switches on. This phase shift covers nearly the whole $180°$ range of the cycle.

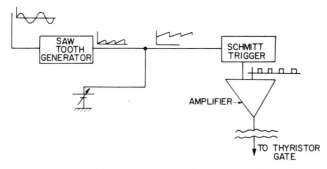

Fig. 2.22.   Phase control firing circuit.

2.7.4. Circuits to turn off thyristors

The general methods of turn-off have already been described and classified into two forms: current interruption and forced commutation. The former is accomplished by opening a switch in the load line or closing a switch in parallel with the thyristor to starve it of current. The latter is accomplished by many means. The simplest method is phase commutation; that is, when the supply is alternating, over one half cycle the thyristor is reverse biased and will turn off. Turn-off will not necessarily occur 20 μs after the cathode becomes positive. The thyristor switches off when the forward current reduces

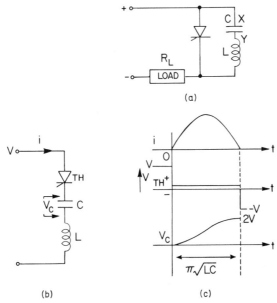

Fig. 2.23.   Self-commutation. (a) Parallel resonant turn-off; (b) series resonant turn-off; (c) waveforms.

to zero and this depends on the load reactance. If the load is capacitive the current reduces to zero before the voltage and this suggests itself as a means of forced commutation through resonance when the supply is a d.c. one.

Capacitors are mainly used in forced commutation circuits. One circuit which does not require a capacitor is that which uses an external pulse from a transformer for turn-off. Four examples of capacitor turn-off are described, but the method chosen is often dictated by the thyristor application.

(a) Self commutation by resonance

An *LC* resonant circuit is shown in Fig. 2.23(a). Plate *X* of capacitor *C* is positive as the thyristor *TH* turns on to conduct load current. Once the thyristor is on, *C* discharges through the resonating circuit of *C, TH* and *L* so that the capacitor changes polarity. The resonating current will reverse after one half cycle. The thyristor will turn off if the resonating current is greater than the load current. An implication of this is that if the load were short-circuited the resonating circuit could not provide a current high enough to turn off the thyristor.

For all loads

$$C > t_{\text{off}}/R_L \ \mu\text{F},$$

where t_{off} is the commutation time in μs and R_L is the load resistance. In practice C would be reduced from this value to the minimum which would give reliable commutation.

A similar circuit, in which the reverse voltage is from resonance derived from induction in circuits supplied with direct current, is shown in Fig. 2.23(b). The corresponding element waveforms are shown in Fig. 2.23(c). The waveforms describe the action of turn-off. That is, when the capacitor has charged up the resonant circuit tries to make the current reverse so that the thyristor turns off. The conduction period is fixed by the values of L and C.

(b) Auxiliary resonant turn-off

Figure 2.24 illustrates how the instant of turn-off can be controlled by an auxiliary thyristor *TH2* together with the resonating *LC* circuit. Thyristor *TH2* must be fired first to charge *C*. Thyristor *TH2* turns off when the current falls

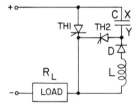

Fig. 2.24.   Controlled resonant turn-off.

below the holding value. Thyristor *TH1* can then be turned on to carry both load current and the resonating current of *C* and *L*. When *C* has changed polarity, that is when the *Y* plate is positive with respect to the *X* plate and at a voltage nearly twice that of the supply, the diode prevents further change. At the instant, when *TH2* is fired a second time the capacitor voltage reverse biases *TH1* and turns it off. Again

$$C > t_{\text{off}}/R_L \ \mu\text{F}.$$

Due to discharge leakage of the capacitor through both *TH1* and *D* the turn-off time from the initiation of *TH1* conduction must not be long if reliability is to be ensured. Accordingly the application is usually for a case which requires a variable average direct current. This is obtained by rapid *TH1* switching and altering the ratio of the time on to the time off.

(c) Parallel capacitance turn-off

Figure 2.25 is one of a number of parallel capacitance turn-off methods. Operation is as follows: thyristor TH2 is off and thyristor TH1 conducts the load current. This means that plate Y of capacitor C is almost at ground potential and plate X is positive at almost supply potential because C was charged via the R, C, TH1 path. If the stored energy in C is great enough when TH2 is fired, C discharges to reverse bias TH1 for a longer period than its turn-off time. This system is repetitive. Switching one thyristor on will switch the other thyristor off.

If R is not another load then it must be chosen carefully, to minimize the power loss in it, to ensure the RC time constant is not long compared with the switching rate and to make it small enough so that the current through it is greater than TH2 leakage current, otherwise C would not charge up with plate X positive.

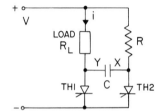

Fig. 2.25.   Parallel capacitance turn-off.

In order to find the value of C to ensure turn-off, it is necessary to find the time it takes for TH1 to become forward biased again after TH2 has been turned on. While TH1 is reverse biased, C carries the full load current so that if V is the applied voltage the load current is

$$i = \frac{2V}{R_L} e^{-t/CR_L}.$$

The voltage across TH1 is

$$V_{TH1} = V - iR_L$$

i.e.

$$V_{TH1} = V(1 - 2e^{-t/CR_L})$$

and the time it takes for this voltage to become zero, that is just before TH1 becomes forward biased, is

$$t = 0.7CR_L.$$

This must be greater than the turn-off time t_{off} of TH1 so that

$$t_{off} < 0.7CR_L$$

or

$$C > t_{off}/0.7R_L.$$

It is advisable to use a larger capacitance than the calculated value and reduce C in practice until its value is just above that at which commutation fails. When the load contains inductance the value of C reduces so that the above criterion can be used whatever the load.

(d) Series capacitance turn-off

Figure 2.26 exemplifies this method in an inverter circuit which has a square-wave voltage output. If $TH2$ is off and $TH1$ is on, current flows in the load. If $TH1$ is off and $TH2$ is on, load current flows in the reverse direction.

It is often desirable to have a sine wave output so that a filter is inserted to give zero regulation at the fundamental frequency and high attenuation at the other unwanted frequencies. If the filter presents a capacitive load to the inverter this would cause the current to reverse before the voltage reverses. The reverse current can flow through a diode and creates a reverse bias voltage

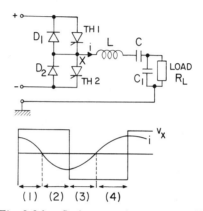

Fig. 2.26. Series capacitance turn-off.

across a thyristor and turns it off. It will be noticed that in this case the reverse voltage is no more than the forward voltage drop across the diode, that is, about 1 V.

The elements LC resonate at the fundamental frequency, and offer zero impedance between the inverter at the required frequency. The elements LC, act as a low-pass filter to attenuate the unwanted frequencies. The element C_1 also serves to make the load appear capacitive so that the current will lead the voltage and provide the turn-off facility.

There are four modes of operation as depicted in Fig. 2.26 with

(1) $TH1$ conducting and $TH2$ off,
(2) $D1$ conduction, $TH1$ and $TH2$ off,
(3) $TH2$ conducting and $TH1$ off, and
(4) $D2$ conducting, $TH1$ and $TH2$ off to complete the cycle.

There are never two thyristors conducting at once to short-circuit the supply.

2.8. THYRISTOR PROTECTION CIRCUITS

The thyristor is sensitive to high voltage, overcurrent and any form of transients (both in magnitude and rate of change). Because protection can become both complex and expensive, there are design engineers who have the philosophy that it is best to keep protective components to a minimum and use thyristors whose ratings are about three times the steady-state load requirements.

2.8.1. Overvoltage

High forward protection is inherent in thyristors. The thyristor will breakdown and conduct before the peak forward voltage is reached so that the high voltage is transferred to another part of the circuit, which is usually the load. The thyristor turn-on causes a higher current to flow so that the problem becomes one of overcurrent protection.

2.8.2. Overcurrent

High currents in any circuit are generally limited by fuses or circuit breakers. Thyristor circuits are protected in the same way, but there are reservations to their use. The fuse must have the specification of high-breaking capacity and

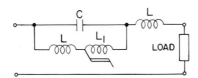

Fig. 2.27.   Overcurrent protection.

rapid interruption of the current. There must be a similarity of thyristor and fuse $I^2 t$ rating without producing high overvoltage transients which endanger those thyristors in the off or infinite impedance condition. These are contradictory requirements necessitating voltage protection when fast acting fuses are used. Fuses are not always used, but when they are their arc voltages are kept below 1.5 times the peak circuit voltage. For small power applications it is pointless using high-speed fuses for circuit protection if the fuse costs more than the thyristor. Current magnitude detection can be employed and is used in many applications. When an overcurrent is detected the gate circuits are controlled either to turn off the appropriate thyristors, or, in phase commutation, to reduce the conduction period and hence the average value of current decreases.

If the output to the load from the thyristor circuit is alternating current, LC resonance provides overcurrent protection as well as filtering. Figure 2.27 illustrates a current limiter[2] which employs a saturable reactor. At permissible currents the saturable reactor, L_1, offers high impedance and C and L are in series resonance to offer zero impedance to the flow of current of the fundamental harmonic. At overcurrent levels L_1 saturates and so has negligible impedance. There is LC parallel resonance and hence infinite impedance to the flow of current at the resonant frequency.

2.8.3. Voltage surges

There are many types of failure due to voltage surges because the thyristor does not really have a safety factor included in its rating. A slight excess of energy can cause damage. Protection is afforded by immediate storage of the energy in L or C elements followed by slow dissipation or immediate dissipation of that energy as heat in non-linear resistors, surge suppressors or avalanche devices.

External voltage surges cannot be controlled by the thyristor circuit designer. He can just try to protect his equipment against them. Figure 2.28 shows some methods. When main contactor switching-off occurs on no-load the magnetic field energy in the transformer core in the supply can be transferred to C_1. C_1 also protects the thyristor against the magnetic energy

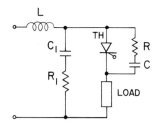

Fig. 2.28.   External surge protection.

in the same transformer leakage field or in the smoothing choke L when the load reduces. The capacitor C absorbs the electrostatic energy produced by the transformer interwinding capacitance when switching-on occurs at no-load. But this operation can produce oscillations in the protective LC_1 circuit so that R_1 is added as a damping resistance, because a voltage twice the supply peak value could appear on C_1.

The energy associated with internal voltage surges, which are produced by switching individual thyristors, is small. This requires only small components for protection. R has been added in series with C in Fig. 2.28 to help prevent damage caused by minority carrier storage during commutation oscillations. Capacitor C provides a path for reverse current when the thyristor suddenly blocks at the end of the minority carrier storage time, but charges with opposite polarity during forward blocking and then discharges rapidly through the thyristor at turn on. The resistance R limits the initial forward current when TH turns on and damps oscillations due to carrier storage effects when the thyristor is reverse blocking.

To protect against local burnout in the thyristor junction due to high di/dt

at turn-on, both L and R limit the rise of anode current. There can be a discharge from the surge suppression capacitor C_1 and the hole storage capacitor C greater than 30 A μs^{-1}.

High forward dv/dt can produce thyristor turn-on when it is not required and can subsequently produce overload damage. If the supply is a d.c. voltage then a high dv/dt is unavoidable when closing the mains contactor, for ideally it is a step change. In a converter, part of which is shown in Fig. 2.29, when *TH2* is switched on *TH1* receives the full d.c. voltage which has been measured to have an initial rise of 400 V μs^{-1}. All the elements L, R and C in Fig. 2.28 help to protect the thyristor against dv/dt. Letting V be the applied d.c. voltage and V_c the voltage across the capacitor C, the voltage equation is initially

$$\frac{dv}{dt} = \frac{V - V_c}{L/R}$$

where L/R is the inductance time constant.

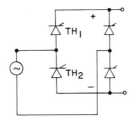

Fig. 2.29.   High dv/dt.

If a diode is connected in parallel with the resistance R it allows R to be by-passed for forward step voltages in order to keep down dv/dt, but switches in R to control the initial current at turn-on. The capacitor across the thyristor does not allow the voltage to change suddenly just as an inductor opposes any change of current. If the diode is used, a small capacitor may be connected in parallel with it to absorb the high-frequency oscillatory voltages to which the RC product of Fig. 2.28 cannot respond.

Gate circuits also need protective elements because of the low voltage and power. Rapid voltage and current changes produce unwanted induced voltages in the gate leads so that careful screening, grounding and filtering are essential. It is also helpful to keep the leads together, and preferably twisted together, so that any pick-up will be balanced in the two leads and cancel. Some possible forms of protection are shown in Fig. 2.30. A clamping circuit in Fig. 2.30(a) is formed by R_2 and $D2$ to attenuate the positive gate signals whenever the anode is negative. The reverse dissipation is thus limited. In Fig. 2.30(b) diode $D4$, which must have a lower reverse blocking current than *TH1*, will take a greater share of reverse voltage. Since the gate should never be negative with respect to the cathode by more than a limited amount (about 5 V), diodes $D1$ or $D3$ or zener-diodes Z_1 and Z_2 in Fig. 2.30(d) prevents this. Diode $D1$ will limit the negative bias voltage to its forward voltage drop, which is about 1 V, and the zener-diodes will clip voltages to any desired value so are useful for a.c. gate signals. In Fig. 2.30(c) capacitor C_2 is only used in low power thyristor circuits where d.c. triggering is used and affords protection against line transients. Resistance R_3 is used to limit the anode to cathode dv/dt.

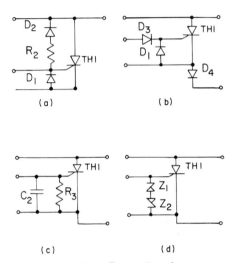

Fig. 2.30.   Gate Protective elements.

Use of a line inductor for smoothing or an inductive load means that high voltage-transients can be expected when the load current is interrupted rapidly. Free-wheeling diodes as shown in Fig. 2.31 allow the energy stored in the inductances to be dissipated elsewhere rather than within the thyristor. Inspection of Fig. 2.12, which shows the turn-on characteristic of voltage across the thyristor and current through it, indicates that the forward energy dissipation should be kept low by fast turn-on times which means gate current rise times of several A μs^{-1}. This does not mean added elements for protection but good design procedures for the firing circuits.

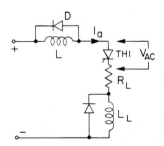

Fig. 2.31.   Stored energy dissipation through free-wheeling diodes.

2.9. RELATIVE MERITS OF THYRISTORS

Thyristors, transistors, thyratrons, mercury arc tubes and electromagnetic relays are all electric switches. What determines the choice?

Relays are simple and cheap to manufacture. They will not rectify but they do have easily controlled switching characteristics. There are mechanical moving parts to produce both wear and contact bounce. The power handling capability is low if the device is to be simple. Because of the coil inductance there is delay between input and output to cause switching speeds in the millisecond range.

Thyratrons and mercury arc tubes are both switches which carry uni-directional current. Both are bulky and fragile. They have large power losses between electrodes, due to the forward conducting drop of 10 V for the former and about 50 V for the latter. A.C. sources can only be used because of the difficulty to turn off. Turn-off can only occur when the positive anode voltage is reduced to zero.

Thyristors and transistors, which are both semiconductor devices, have no moving parts, weigh little, occupy a small volume and their turn-off times are several orders of magnitude faster than the previous switches. This is almost enough to accept them for all switching applications, but the mercury arc tube does have the great advantage of a much higher withstand voltage capability.

Consider the choice between the thyristor and the transistor. The transistor has two points of merit: it has a lower voltage drop, 25 mV compared with 1 V for the thyristor, and it needs no turn-off circuit although, while on, a continuous base current is required, whereas only a pulsed gate current is required for the thyristor. The thyristor has a better voltage rating because of the wide, inner n-layer of silicon and a higher current rating because the current is more uniform at the junctions. Both these give the thyristor a better power handling capability. In fact the thyristor can be used from milliwatts to megawatts although it is predominantly used at the higher power levels where the transistor cannot compete.

Although thyristors were first developed in 1957 they were not accepted immediately for application. At first their power handling ability was not great and they had unstable characteristics in the sense that parameters changed easily with time, temperature and use and varied widely from sample to sample. This has now changed to the extent that the stability is good, thyristors with uniform characteristics are high and power levels are in the megawatt range.

2.10. THE BIDIRECTIONAL TRIODE THYRISTOR (TRIAC)

The thyristor conducts current in one direction only. It is a controlled rectifier. To control alternating current in a load with power semiconductor

devices requires the use of two thyristors back to back. This is depicted in
Fig. 2.32(a), which shows the circuit configuration. The schematic structure of
these two thyristors in parallel opposition, as in Fig. 2.32(b), suggests that as
there are similar layers in common (p-n-p), it should be possible to fabricate a
single device to perform the same duties. A resultant structure is schematically
shown in Fig. 2.32(c). Its performance is similar to the pair of back-to-back
thyristors but it does have its own special characteristics which give some
disadvantages and some advantages over the thyristor pair. In some cases the
thyristors can be replaced by this single structure device but not in all cases.

This new switch has been given a circuit symbol, shown in Fig. 2.32(d), and
the trade name 'triac', 'Tri'—indicates that there are three terminals, T_1, T_2 and
G in the figure, and '-ac' means the device controls alternating current or can

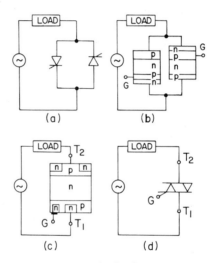

(a)   (b)   (c)   (d)

Fig. 2.32.   Back-to-back thyristors and the triac.

conduct current in either or both directions. The terminals T_2 and T_1 represent
the anode and cathode of the thyristor but it is not possible to differentiate the
conduction direction with the same terminology for the triac. The terminal G
represents the same gate electrode, but with the gate attached to both a p and
n layer there is only need for a single pair of terminals GT_1 whereas the
thyristor pair needs isolated pulses to feed two pairs of separate terminals.

To operate the triac a current pulse of a few milliamperes is introduced at
the gate. If terminal T_2 is positive with respect to T_1, the triac turns on (the
device changes from the ideal infinite impedance condition to the zero
impedance condition) and conventional current will flow from T_2 to T_1. If
terminal T_1 is positive with respect to T_2 and a signal is applied to the gate
then current flows this time from T_1 to T_2. Therefore the triac can be used
as an a.c. contactor or, by phase control of the a.c. voltage, it can be used to

adjust the power transferred from the source to the load. The triac's characteristic is shown in Fig. 2.33. When the triac is switched on, the voltage drop across the triac is about 1 V and remains roughly independent of the magnitude of the current.

Whereas the thyristor will switch on only if the gate signal is positive with respect to the cathode and the anode is also a positive potential, the gate signal to the triac may be of either polarity. This is an added advantage because the pulse circuits are simpler if polarity need not be considered.

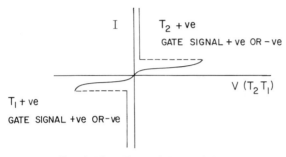

Fig. 2.33. Triac characteristic.

However, it is a characteristic of the triac that, when T_1 is positive with respect to T_2, a negative pulse requires less charge than a positive pulse at the gate to turn the triac on. For maximum sensitivity a negative pulse would be used.

Without a gate signal or even without a gate electrode the device can be turned on by avalanche. Just as the thyristor or the two terminal p-n-p-n device will turn on safely by the application at the anode of a high enough voltage (V_{BO}) or if the rate of change of applied anode voltage (dv/dt) is above a critical value, the same applies to this composite structure of the

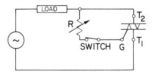

Fig. 2.34. Simple triac circuit.

triac. For the triac the voltage V_{BO} or a high dv/dt can be applied to either of the terminals T_1 or T_2 to turn it on. This passes on the need for protection of the device to the rest of the circuit. The two terminal device without a gate electrode is called the bidirectional diode and has the trade name diac.

The turn-on procedure is more versatile than that of the thyristor. The simplest possible arrangement for switching the triac on every half cycle is illustrated in Fig. 2.34, where it will be seen that the gate receives the more sensitive negative signal when T_1 is positive. Compare this with the simplest gate circuits needed to trigger the thyristor back-to-back arrangement to control a.c. power. Another circuit which allows current to flow in either direction or both directions by manual phase-control utilizes the unijunction transistor and two, low-power thyristors (see Fig. 2.35). Thyristor $TH2$ is on when the triac is required to conduct when rail A is positive, and $TH1$ is on when the triac is required to conduct when rail B is positive. Otherwise $TH1$ and $TH2$ are off and no current flows through the load via the triac. If rail A is positive and $TH2$ is on, the capacitor will charge up at a rate depending on the value of R. At a particular voltage level the UJT breaks down and the transformer primary receives a pulse the energy which is transferred to the triac by means of the transformer secondary. The gate is negative with respect to T_1. When the triac conducts it short-circuits the gating circuit. This ensures that the capacitor is at the same initial conditions at the end of every half cycle. The same firing pulse is obtained when B is positive and $TH1$ on.

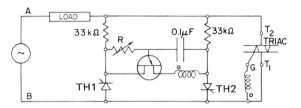

Fig. 2.35.   Bidirectional d.c. or a.c. control.

The triac is less versatile than the thyristor when turn-off is considered. Because the triac can conduct in either direction, forced commutation by reverse biasing cannot be employed. A sudden reverse bias voltage across the triac while it conducts in one direction would only avalanche conduction in the other direction. Accordingly, turn-off is either by current starvation, which is generally impracticable, or else by a.c. line commutation. The current is allowed to come to zero, at which point the triac recovers its blocking state naturally, to await a gate signal for the next conduction period, whichever direction is chosen.

There are two limitations enforced on the use of the triac at the present state of commercially available devices (200 A and 1000 PRV). The first is the frequency handling capability produced by the limiting dv/dt at which the triac remains blocking when no gate signal is applied. This dv/dt value is about 20 V μs^{-1} compared with a general figure of 200 V μs^{-1} for the thyristor, so that the limitation of frequency is at the power level of 60 Hz. The same dv/dt limitation means the load to be controlled is preferably a resistive one. If the load is inductive it means that the voltage across the load becomes negative, to a value depending on the power factor of the circuit, before the current reduces to zero. At current zero the triac turns off and goes into the blocking state. That is, the triac changes from zero impedance to near infinite impedance in a time of a few microseconds. In this same time the reverse voltage which was across the load now appears across the triac. The short time involved produces a high dv/dt which may turn the triac on again when it should be required to block. An RC circuit has to be connected across the triac to absorb some of the energy associated with this dv/dt. There are 25 A triacs whose dv/dt limit is 200 V μs^{-1}.

The triac has a much more limited application than the thyristor and is at this time being used to control heating, lighting and motor drive units. When high frequencies and high dv/dt are involved then the back-to-back thyristors cannot be replaced by the triac. Accordingly in the application of semi-conductor power devices to the control of electric drives, triacs are mentioned only occasionally.

2.11. SUMMARY

The thyristor is a bistable switching device; it is either on or off. That is, it is either saturated and fully conducting offering zero impedance, or it is blocking, offering an infinite impedance to the flow of current. It is principally used as a controlled rectifier. With a forward bias voltage no appreciable current flows. With a forward bias voltage and a small pulse across the gate to cathode, current flows from anode to cathode and is limited only by load impedance in series with the anode. If the thyristor is on, no further gate signal is required to maintain conduction. Current can be extinguished to turn off the thyristor by:

(1) increasing the load impedance to reduce the current below a specified holding value, or

(2) making the cathode positive with respect to the anode. The anode current which flows during the blocking state is called the leakage current and is usually neglected.

Although thyristors can in many ways be said to be better than the other switches there are limitations regarding the ratings of semiconductor devices so that protection forms a necessary part of a thyristor circuit. If the forward current rise, di/dt at turn-on is too rapid, local burnout near the gate can occur. Failure by burnout may occur if there is undesired turn-on by the forward dv/dt being too high, if there is overload, or if excessive reverse voltage is applied and there is a local concentration of reverse current.

Although the triac can be made to conduct in either or both directions by the application of positive or negative pulses to its gate and hence can be considered as a pair of thyristors back to back in one device, its low dv/dt withstand capability limits its application at present.

WORKED EXAMPLES

Example 2.1. A load, whose resistance is 550 Ω, is to have current pulses of about 1 ms duration. The time between current pulses may be large in comparison. Analyse a thyristor circuit to satisfy these conditions if the d.c. supply voltage is 120 V.

Consider the parallel resonant circuit of Fig. 2.23(a). The purpose of analysing the circuit is to determine the values of C and L so that the thyristor will remain on for about 1 ms and will be reverse biased long enough in order that it will turn off.

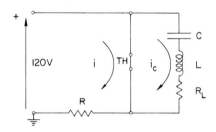

Fig. 2.36.   Self commutation by oscillation circuit.

Analysis may begin at the point after the thyristor has been turned on and the capacitor has changed polarity to reach the maximum voltage V_c. This is the reference time $t = 0$. The equation describing i_c of the equivalent circuit in Fig. 2.36 is

$$\left[\frac{1}{Cs} + Ls + R_L \right] I(s) = \frac{V_c}{s}$$

or

$$I(s) = \frac{\dfrac{V_c}{L}}{\left(s + \dfrac{R_L}{2L} \right)^2 + \left(\dfrac{1}{LC} - \dfrac{R_L^2}{4L^2} \right)}$$

where s is the Laplace operator.

Transforming this into the time domain provides the solution

$$i_c(t) = \frac{V_c}{L} \cdot \frac{1}{A} \, e^{(-R_L/2L)t} \, \sin At,$$

where

$$A^2 = \frac{1}{LC} - \frac{R_L^2}{4L^2}.$$

The maximum value of the discharge current is

$$i_{c\ max} = \frac{V_c}{L} \left(\frac{4L^2C}{4L - CR_L^2} \right)^{1/2}$$

The resistance of the inductor has very little effect on the magnitude of the first current maximum so that if

$$R_L \simeq 0$$

then

$$i_{c\ max} \simeq V_c \sqrt{\frac{C}{L}}.$$

The capacitor discharge current $i_{c\ max}$ must be greater than the load current i for the thyristor to turn off. If it were less, the thyristor current would never reduce below the holding value. Let

$$i_{c\ max} = i$$

for the limiting case of turn-off. The period T of the resonant circuit is

$$T = \frac{2\pi}{A} \simeq 2\pi \sqrt{LC}.$$

These last three equations allow the problem to be solved for any case, because from the time the thyristor turns on to the time it turns off is $0.75T$. The capacitor continues to discharge through the load once the thyristor blocks. A new response should be calculated but to a first approximation the pulse of current through the load can be said to terminate when the thyristor turns off. If the duration of the pulse is t_p then

$$C = 2t_p/3\pi R \simeq 0.4\ \mu F$$

and

$$L = 2t_p R/3\pi \simeq 120\ mH.$$

It has been assumed that the voltage across the capacitor reaches a peak value whose magnitude is the same as the supply voltage.

The gate pulse to turn on the thyristor must have a duration a fraction of a millisecond. A continuous gate pulse prevents the thyristor from recovering to its blocking state. Voltage waveforms are shown in Fig. 2.37 for the practical case of a continuous gate signal.

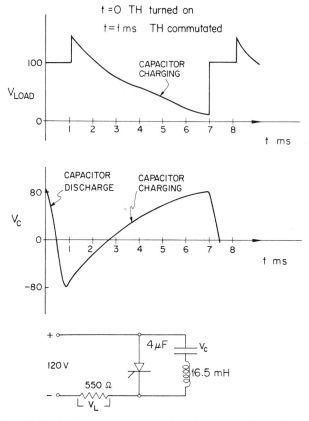

Fig. 2.37.   Voltage waveforms of self-commutation circuit.

Example 2.2. Investigate the forced commutation circuit of Fig. 2.38 to determine the minimum duration t_{min} of a load current pulse for a range of loads.

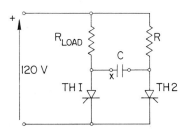

Fig. 2.38.   Forced commutation.

In order that the capacitance may store sufficient energy to turn off thyristor *TH*1 the value of the capacitance is given by

$$C > t_{off}/R_{LOAD}$$

where t_{off} is the thyristor turn-off time. The value of the resistance R determines the time for capacitor charge-up and it is this charge-up time that determines how quickly $TH1$ can be commutated after it has been turned on. For safety R should be of such a value that the current through R and $TH2$ should be limited below the holding value. In this way $TH2$ always turns off after C has charged. If R were too low and if $TH1$ where not turned off by turning on $TH2$, both thyristors would continue to conduct. Consequently C would not charge up and neither thyristor could be commutated.

The resultant data is as follows:

R_L, Ω	R, kΩ	$C, \mu F$	t_{min}, s
60	1 M	4	2
60	150 k	4	0.5
13	330 k	4	5
13	33 k	4	0.5
10	150 k	4	5
10	33 k	4	0.5
8	150 k	15	5
8	12 k	15	0.2
6	150 k	15	5
6	5 k	15	0.1

REFERENCES

1. Yates, W. J. and Stevens, R. S. (1969) 'Selecting the correct capacitor for use in thyristor circuits', *Power Thyristors and their Applications,* I.E.E.E. Conference Publication, No. 53, 140-145.
2. Watabe, S. (1969) 'A 3ph 250 kVA no break power supply with current limiting filter', *Power Thyristors and their Applications,* I.E.E. Conference Publication, No. 53, 216-224.

BIBLIOGRAPHY

Gentry, F. E. *et al.* (1964), *Semiconductor Controlled Rectifiers,* Prentice-Hall.

Bedford, B. D. and Hoft, R. G. (1965), *Principles of Inverter Circuits,* John Wiley and Sons Inc., London and New York.

Griffin, A. W. and Ramshaw, R. S. (1965), *The Thyristor and its Applications,* Chapman and Hall, London.

S.C.R. Manual, General Electric Co., U.S.A.

Silicon Controlled Rectifier Designers Handbook, Westinghouse Electric Co.

Power Applications of Controllable Semiconductor Devices (1965), I.E.E. Conference Publication, No. 17.

Gentry, F. E., Scace, R. I. and Flowers, J. K. (1965). 'Bidirectional Triode P-N-P-N Switches', *Proc. I.E.E.E.*, 355-369.

Howell, E. K. (1964), 'The Triac-Gate-Controlled Silicon A.C. Power Switch', *I.E.E.E. Int. Conv. Record*, **12** (9), 86-91.

Power Thyristors and their Applications, (1969), I.E.E. Conference Publication, No. 53.

PROBLEMS

2.1. The circuit shown in Fig. 2.24 can be used as a lamp dimmer by altering the average voltage across a bank of lamps. For any value of inductance between 2 and 30 mH, find the maximum load currents that may be switched off when capacitors of 1, 4, 7, 8 and 10 μF are used in the circuit. Find the complete circuit response.

Note how long the capacitor holds sufficient charge to turn off *TH*1 when *TH*1 is triggered on. The maximum voltage across the load is 120 V.

(Answer. Practical values 4.4, 6.2, 8.3, 10 and 11.2 A.)

2.2. Figure 2.39 illustrates a thyristor circuit whereby commutation is accomplished by resonance. The values of *C* and *L* are high to give a long

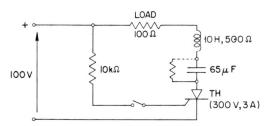

Fig. 2.39.   Self commutation.

period of conduction. Determine the response of the circuit and compare the practical voltage waveforms across each element both when the gate current is a pulse (1 ms) and when it is continuous.

(Answer. $i(t) = 0.4 \, e^{-30t} \sin 25.3 \, t$. Measured duration of current flow, 150 ms.)

2.3. Find the values of the elements in Fig. 2.27 to limit the current through a resistive load of 240 Ω to 0.5 A. The inverter supplies power to the load at a frequency of 60Hz.

(Answer. $L = 43.5$ mH, $C = 161.5 \, \mu\text{F})^2$

2.4. By empirical means, find the elements needed to protect the thyristor in the simple circuit of Fig. 2.28 against external surges

(*Answer.* $R_1 = 11$ to 47Ω; $C_1 = 0.01$ to $0.5\ \mu F$)

An empirical formula for C_1 is

$$C_1 = \frac{VA}{31\ f(V_p)^2}$$

where C_1 is in F, VA is the voltampere rating of the supply transformer, f is the supply frequency in Hertz, and V_p is the peak transient voltage rating of the thyristor. Also

$$C = \frac{10\ I_f}{V}$$

where C is in the μF, I_f is the current flowing through the thyristor immediately preceding commutation, and V is the maximum continuous PRV rating of the thyristor.

NOTE
Additional problems on page 208

3 Induction motor control

A rotating mechanical load has to be brought up to speed from rest. The load duty cycle may comprise a change of speed, a reversal of speed, a change of position and perhaps a return to an initial condition in the shortest possible time. The cycle can be controlled by the adjustment of power fed to the electric motor which drives the load.

Induction motors are relatively cheap and rugged machines because they can be built without slip-rings or commutators. Consequently much attention has been given to the study of induction motor control, for starting, braking, speed reversal, speed change and position control.

At present the thyristor is tending to replace the conventional elements for the control of induction motors because of the longer life and lack of moving parts. Not only is the thyristor being used for commercial drive control but the methods of use are under intensive study. One of the important applications receiving much attention is the electric car.

An electric drive to replace the internal combustion engine would reduce air pollution drastically so there have been many attempts to make the conversion economically feasible. Much depends on the method of stored energy. The large, heavy and expensive lead-acid batteries have to be replaced by fuel cells to match the controller and electric drive which could be an induction motor. One example which appeals to the imagination is an electric drive running at 100 000 rpm and controlled by a thyristor unit. The volume of a motor is roughly proportional to the rated torque. Since the power output is proportional to the torque and speed, the higher the speed the smaller the motor. Problems at these speeds become those of rapid heat transfer from small volumes and, of course, the transmission to the wheels.

This chapter concerns the different methods of induction motor control by thyristor units with some practical examples described at the end.

3.2. INDUCTION MOTOR STARTING

To see clearly that there is a problem associated with starting an induction motor by applying the supply voltage directly across the motor terminals, it is only necessary to consider an equivalent circuit of the induction motor and find the current in terms of the slip and the machine impedances. Very little

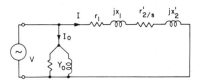

Fig. 3.1. An equivalent circuit of the induction motor.

error will be introduced if the approximate equivalent circuit is used. This is shown in Fig. 3.1 on a single-phase basis where

Y_0 is the magnetizing admittance of the motor,
r_1 is the resistance of the stator winding,
r_2' is the resistance of the rotor winding referred to the stator,
x_1 is the leakage reactance of the stator winding,
x_2' is the leakage reactance of the rotor winding at the supply frequency and referred to the stator, and
s is the slip.

The current per phase I for any slip s is

$$I = \frac{V}{\sqrt{\left[\left(r_1 + \frac{r_2'}{s}\right)^2 + (x_1 + x_2')^2\right]}} \tag{3.1}$$

and the power factor is

$$\cos \theta = \frac{r_1 + r_2'/s}{\sqrt{\left[\left(r_1 + \frac{r_2'}{s}\right)^2 + (x_1 + x_2')^2\right]}}$$

$$= \frac{1}{\sqrt{\left[1 + \left(\frac{x_1 + x_2'}{r_1 + r_2'/s}\right)^2\right]}} \cdot \tag{3.2}$$

The gross mechanical power output per phase is

$$P_m = I^2 \, r_2' \left(\frac{1 - s}{s}\right) \tag{3.3}$$

so that the electromagnetic torque per phase is

$$T = \frac{p}{\omega} I^2 \frac{r_2'}{s} \tag{3.4}$$

where p represents the pole pairs and ω is the angular frequency ($2\pi f$).

The ideal conditions for starting a motor would be to have a low inrush current for the sake of good supply voltage regulation, a high torque so that the load may be rapidly accelerated to its stable operating speed and a high power factor to limit the voltamperes for a given power requirement. Inspection of the above equations for starting, when $s = 1$, shows that the current is a maximum, the power factor is a minimum and, although the high current tends to increase the starting torque, the maximum value of slip in the denominator of the torque equation tends to reduce the value of the starting torque for a constant rotor resistance. These are not ideal starting characteristics, but for small motors of only a few horsepower they can be tolerated. These poor characteristics only present themselves when the supply is switched directly across the terminals of the motor, that is 'direct-on-line' starting, and can be altered by adding some circuit element to give varying degrees of control.

Starting small motors direct-on-line does have some advantages. It is a cheap method, and the high starting current means that there is a minimum delay running up to speed. Direct-on-line starting for large motors could have a number of undesirable effects. The extremely high currents drawn from the supply could produce a supply voltage drop and the associated light dimming or flicker might not be tolerable to local domestic and industrial consumers. The current, if, for example, a number of motors were started together, might even be too large for the rated capacity of the supply cable, so that the protection devices would operate to trip or switch off the supply. Also, the high starting current for large motors would tend to persist longer than for small motors because of the greater moments of inertia. The starting current can easily be greater than six times the full load current. If this high current flows for any length of time the heating may well damage the winding insulation, which is the most vulnerable part of this type of machine.

To overcome these disadvantages, produced by high surge currents, current is limited either by reducing the applied voltage or by adding impedance to the circuit for the period of starting.

Starting methods are:

(1) Direct-on-line starting
(2) Stator resistance starting
(3) Autotransformer starting
(4) Star-delta starter
(5) Cage induction motor (shaped rotor conductors or double cage)
(6) Rotor resistance starting
(7) Thyristor starting control.

The first six methods are conventional and descriptions of these methods are to be found in standard electric machine texts.[1] However, the thyristor can be used so that the starting current is not excessive and the starting torque is high.

3.2.1. Thyristor starting

The thyristor is a switch, which can be turned on and off using very small powers and which has no moving parts. Its use in a contactor or inverter for high-power switching becomes apparent. Its high efficiency is a major advantage.

The ideal situation would be to have an induction motor which did not require any special starting equipment and yet had no starting currents reaching over six or seven times full load current. It is quite uneconomic to have thyristor circuits deal with such high currents for short periods, although the use of thyristors could be to limit currents to an acceptable level. A system requiring no extra starting equipment would be one which required speed control over a large range so necessitating the use of a variable frequency inverter. At starting the frequency would be set as low as possible and as the running speed is proportional to the frequency, this synchronous speed would be low. Control of the increase of frequency would control the run-up speed and limit current surges. However, if the application of the induction motor is for a constant speed drive, then a simple thyristor contactor offers a good method to control starting.

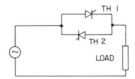

Fig. 3.2. Single-phase voltage regulator.

An a.c. voltage regulator for starting an induction motor is shown in a single-phase circuit in Fig. 3.2. Because the thyristor will only allow current to flow in one direction, two thyristors are placed back to back in parallel opposition for the passage of alternating current. The input voltage is fixed. The output voltage is adjusted by controlling the conduction period of the thyristors, which are fired alternately and symmetrically with respect to the supply waveform. The triggering occurs at some adjustable point in the voltage cycle as shown in Fig. 3.3. This is known as phase commutation. The phase angle of firing, α, decreases from nearly $180°$ to give a low voltage as the motor starts up to $0°$ at full speed and rated voltage at the motor terminals. The main purpose of this thyristor contactor is to limit the current by controlling the average fundamental voltage amplitude. Acceptable levels of current can be maintained without any appreciable loss of energy, and some general three-phase circuits are shown in Fig. 3.4. For a four-wire, three-phase system, back-to-back thyristors are required, but for the three-wire case diodes can replace one of a pair, or only three thyristors need be used.

Two thyristors in back-to-back opposition can be regarded as a variable impedance. Alone they change from zero to infinite impedance when the

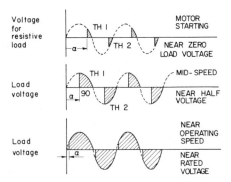

Fig. 3.3.   Voltage variation by phase commutation.

phase angle α is altered from $0°$ to $180°$. These extreme impedances can be adjusted with the addition of other elements. For example Fig. 3.5 depicts a circuit configuration whose equivalent impedance can be varied smoothly from R_1 to $(R_1 + R_2)$. This circuit structure may be connected in series with the stator winding for stator resistance starting. For better torque control the same circuit would be placed in the induction motor rotor circuit. The latter method of starting produces greater difficulties than the former to fire the thyristors accurately at some definite point in the cycle because the slip frequency cycle must be detected.

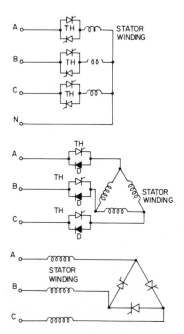

Fig. 3.4.   Voltage control configurations.

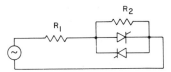

Fig. 3.5. Variable non-linear impedance.

There is waveform distortion when the thyristors are not fully conducting. The greater the firing angle α, the greater is the percentage of harmonics. This produces extra heating in the load without any increase in mechanical energy conversion, and the power factor is poor even with a resistive load, decreasing with output voltage reduction. A method of having very little distortion is to use regulators fully with the autotransformer method, as in Fig. 3.6. where only one phase is shown. Induction motor starting is accomplished at a low voltage with a good sinusoidal waveform if only $TH1$ and $TH2$ are allowed to conduct fully. With speed as the switching criterion, thyristors $TH3$ and $TH4$ can be turned on in order to apply the higher voltage to the winding and to turn off $TH1$ and $TH2$.

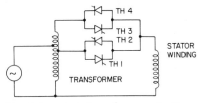

Fig. 3.6. Autotransformer starting.

Figure 3.6 demonstrates the basic principle. Two practical examples[2] illustrate two ways in which the thyristors are used to affect a transformer tap change in order to adjust the voltage for starting. One example is to employ a conventional mechanical tap changer and to use thyristors only during the tap change. Arcing can be eliminated this way because the thyristors can divert the current from the contacts during the make-and-break procedure. A second example is to replace the mechanical tap changer by thyristor units so that there are no moving parts.

A mechanical switch is shown in Fig. 3.7. To start the induction motor the switch will short circuit the contacts $22'$. The lower of the two voltages will

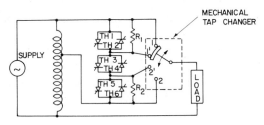

Fig. 3.7. Mechanical tap changer.

be applied to a stator phase winding so that the starting current does not exceed an acceptable level. Once the induction motor has run up to speed the switch is moved to contacts 11′, through 2′, 2′1′ and 1′, to apply the higher voltage so that the load may be driven at the full rated power of the machine.

While the contacts 22′ are short-circuited only thyristors TH5 and TH6 have signals applied to their gate terminals. During the sequence of switching contact 2 becomes open circuit and the switch is only in contact with 2′. Current continues to flow in the load through the path provided by TH5 and TH6 which minimizes the arcing when 2 becomes open circuit. The gate signals to TH5 and TH6 are removed at this stage so that at the first current zero these two thyristors block and load current is diverted through R_2. Gate signals are applied to TH3 and TH4 so that when contacts 2′ and 1′ are short-circuited there is minimum arcing (contacts 2′ and 1′ are at different potentials before the switch connects the two together). The leakage impedance of the autotransformer between taps, made up of R_2 and R_1, limits the circulating current. As contact 2′ becomes open circuit, TH3 and TH4 reduce the arcing to a minimum. After contact 2′ is open circuit the gate signals to TH3 and TH4 are removed so that these thyristors block at the next current zero. The switch, at this stage, is connected only to contact 1′ so that load current flows through R_1 from the higher voltage tapping. Thyristors TH1 and TH2 are turned on to carry the load current, then to minimize arcing as the switch short circuits 1′1. Current finally flows directly from the higher voltage tapping through contact 1 but the gate signals are applied continuously to TH1 and TH2 in preparation for another tap change.

Little thyristor protection is required because the mechanical switches take the fault currents and overvoltages during normal operation. However, an RC network must be connected to cope with the transient dv/dt and the peak tap voltage which is switched mechanically.

The second practical example does not have a transformer employing conventional tap changing gear. The secondary winding comprises a number of isolated and hence independent coils. Any number of the coils may be connected in series to provide a required voltage. Connections are made by turning on the correct thyristors. The five secondary coils of the binary sequence in Fig. 3.8 can provide 31 different voltage levels. Consequently the output voltage varies from V to 31 V in steps of V. In order to obtain 17 V volts, thyristors 1, S2, S3, S4 and 5 would be on and all others would be off for the positive half cycle and 1′, S2′, S3′, S4′ and 5′ would be on and all others would be off for the negative half cycle.

The pairs of conducting thyristors in series with the coils enable the voltages to contribute to the output while the pairs of conducting thyristors in parallel with the coils allow the voltage sources to be non-contributory. None of a series and parallel pair of thyristors of the same coil would conduct at the same time.

A triac or a single thyristor across a diode bridge could be used in place of a pair of thyristors. The use of the triac depends on the magnitude of the switching transient dv/dt and the diode bridge depends on the comparative cost.

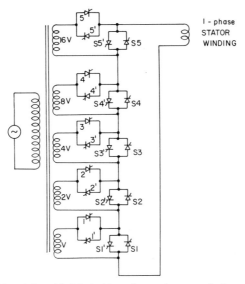

Fig. 3.8. Multiwindings for voltage variation.

3.3. INDUCTION MOTOR SPEED CONTROL

The induction motor is a common drive because it is robust and relatively simple and cheap to manufacture. The torque-speed characteristic illustrated in Fig. 3.9 is typical for a high efficiency machine which is supplied from a constant voltage, constant frequency source. A speed range from no-load to a load which would produce stalling is only within about 10 per cent of synchronous speed. Consequently the machine is inherently a constant speed motor. However, both because of the induction motor's simplicity and special applications, numerous methods have been found to enable the speed of the induction motor to be adjusted.

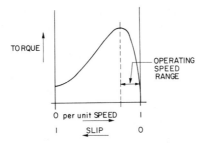

Fig. 3.9. Torque-speed characteristic of an inductor motor.

Principles associated with speed control are concerned with stator and rotor voltage adjustment, pole changing and frequency variation. Speed control methods are extensions of starting methods but can be listed conventionally as:

(1) Supply frequency
(2) Pole changing (pole amplitude modulation)
(3) Supply voltage variation (or additional stator impedance)
(4) Rotor injected voltage
(5) Rotor resistance
(6) Cascading
(7) Commutator motors
(8) Thyristor systems.

The first seven methods can be classified as conventional methods whose descriptions will be found in standard texts on electrical machines. The thyristor systems described in this chapter offer alternative methods of speed control but the overall principles remain conventional.

3.3.1. Thyristor systems for speed control

Thyristors have become important elements in the control of induction motors. The ways they have been used are many. Initially many of the thyratron circuits were adapted for the same purpose but utilization of semiconductors has been so great that the differences have produced many circuits in their own right.

There are similar patterns between some of the starting methods and some of the speed control methods so that it is not surprising that thyristor circuits used for one can be extended to the other.

(a) The alternating current switch

A semiconductor a.c. switch for power applications may consist of two thyristors connected in parallel opposition, or a single thyristor connected across a diode bridge, or a single triac. The purpose of the switch is to enable the voltage across the induction motor terminals to be adjusted in a controlled manner. There are two ways that the switch controls the voltage. One way is by phase control of the switch turn-on and the other is to switch the motor terminal connections from one group of windings of a transformer to another, as in tap-changing.

The starting torque of an induction motor is proportional to the square of the applied voltage. Typical torque-speed curves for rated voltage and half-rated voltage, as in Fig. 3.10, illustrate the speed variation for a particular load. The variation is not great, but the method for obtaining the speed change is simple.

The thyristor a.c. regulators described in the Section 2.1 on induction motor starting can equally well be used to alter the value of the steady-state speed. The circuits shown in Figs. 3.2 to 3.8 are used with the same effect as

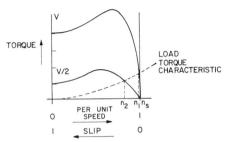

Fig. 3.10. Torque-speed curves for different applied voltages.

altering the supply voltage, adding impedance to the stator or adding impedance to the rotor. The circuit of Fig. 3.6 does alter the motor voltage but only in magnitude and acts as a contactless tap changer. The voltage waveform remains sinusoidal whereas, for the phase angle control regulator, power factor and harmonic contents vary with the phase triggering angle α in a way illustrated in Fig. 3.11(a), (b), (c) and (d) if the load impedance is

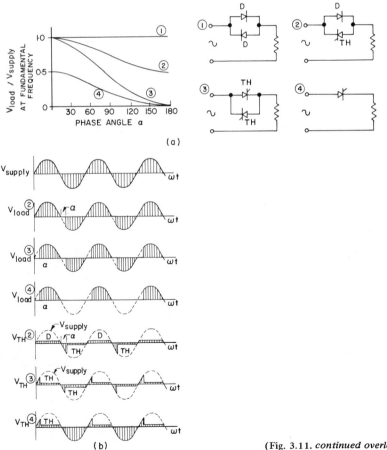

(a)

(b)

(Fig. 3.11. *continued overleaf*)

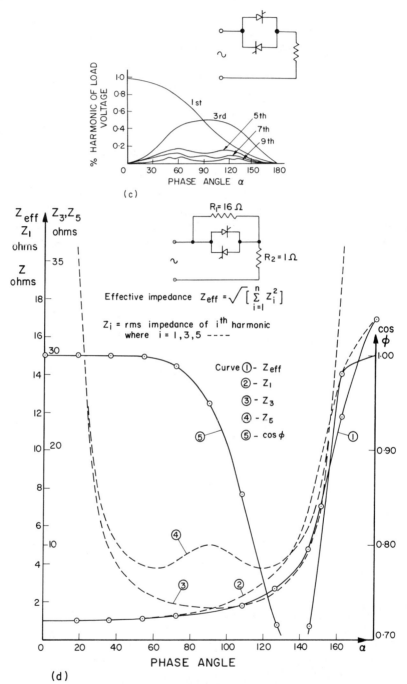

Fig. 3.11. The a.c. regulator characteristics. (a) Fundamental load voltage for different regulator configurations; (b) voltage waveforms; (c) harmonics for the full regulator; (d) effective impedance and power factor variation.

resistive. These figures indicate the losses to be expected from the higher harmonics but simplicity and cost give this method advantages over others for a small speed range. Typical circuits for three-phase induction motors with wound rotors are shown in Fig. 3.12 where the circuit (a) is easily adapted for

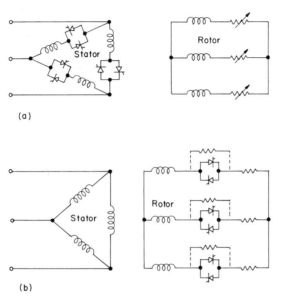

(a)

(b)

Fig. 3.12. Typical speed control circuits.

the cage motor. Torque-speed curves could be illustrated as in Fig. 3.13, but they depend on rotor resistance and where the regulator is in the circuit.[3]

The regulator phase control in the rotor circuit is more difficult than in the stator circuit because of the need to have a reference sinewave at slip frequency for the trigger circuits. However, the same result could be obtained from a slightly different system without the need for sensing slip frequency

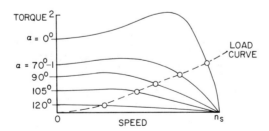

Fig. 3.13. Typical curves for different phase angles (α).

sinewaves. Figure 3.14 illustrates this system in outline. The slip power from the rotor is converted to direct current by rectification. The average resistance across the rotor slip rings will vary from zero to R depending on the rate of switching of the rapidly pulsed thyristor. There is need only for one main thyristor plus an auxiliary thyristor for turn-off. The fact that there is only one resistance is another advantage and this also provides perfect circuit balancing between the three phases, although the loss of any resistance control method would mean limiting the motor drive to, say, 100 kW. Low voltage is a problem for thyristor turn-off because of low-energy storage in a commutating capacitor. Special care is needed in the design stage.

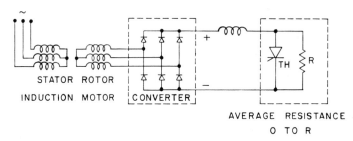

Fig. 3.14. Variable rotor resistance by pulse control.

Worked example 3.1. Design a simple thyristor a.c. regulator for a 220 V, $\frac{1}{4}$ hp, single-phase induction motor and determine the speed characteristics.

A single phase induction motor could have its terminal voltage, and hence to a certain extent its speed, controlled by any of the regulators described above. An outline of one method with the simplest gate circuit is shown in Fig. 3.15. The motor characteristics are:

220 V, 2.25 A, $\frac{1}{4}$ hp, 4 poles, 50 Hz
Starting current 8 A
Centrifugal switch opens at 900 rpm.

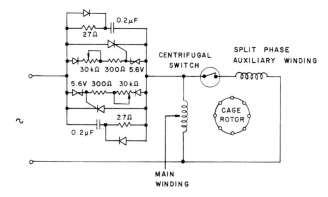

Fig. 3.15. A simple voltage regulator. Motor: 220 V, 2.25 A, $\frac{1}{4}$ hp, 4 pole, 50 Hz. Starting current 8 A. Centrifugal switch opens at 900 rpm.

Phase control is limited to $90°$ of each half cycle but this is quite adequate for a small machine which relies on an auxiliary winding for starting and a single main winding for running. Torque-speed characteristics for this particular example are shown in Fig. 3.16.

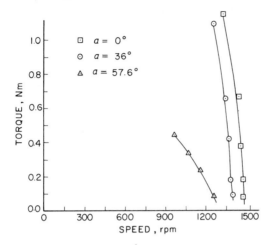

Fig. 3.16. Speed variation of a $\frac{1}{4}$ hp, single-phase induction motor.

The example illustrates that the phase angle for conduction need not be greater than $90°$. The speed range is only between 900 and 1450 rpm because of the split phase winding and this is accommodated within a phase angle of $60°$.

(b) Inverters (Direct current to alternating current conversion)

Inverters enable a supply of direct current or alternating current of one frequency to be converted to a supply of alternating current at some other frequency or frequencies. The conversion of power from mW to MW can be accomplished with thyristor inverters which have replaced most rotating electrical machinery manufactured for frequency changing.

The synchronous speed of an induction motor is the speed of the mmf waveform rotating in the air gap, that is,

$$n_s = \frac{f}{p} \text{ rps}$$

where f is the supply frequency (c s^{-1} or Hz) and p is the number of pole pairs. The actual rotor speed of a motor with a characteristic like that in Fig. 3.9 is just less than the synchronous speed and does not alter much with variation of load. Accordingly, for a fixed number of poles, a change in the supply frequency would bring about a proportional change in the synchronous speed and the actual speed would follow in roughly the same manner.

An induction motor is designed to work at a particular flux density, and as the electromagnetic torque is proportional to the magnetic flux, it is necessary to have a high value of flux density without going too far into the saturation region. It is usual to work at the knee of the magnetizing curve to get the highest torque for low losses. If the applied voltage can be said to be almost equal to the induced emf, then from the induced emf equation.

$$V = k\Phi f \tag{3.5}$$

where

$\quad k$ = constant involving the form factor, the winding factor and the number of turns on the winding,

$\quad \Phi$ = maximum flux per pole, and

$\quad V$ = rms voltage applied to the motor terminals.

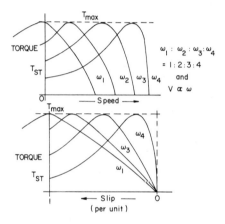

Fig. 3.17. Torque-speed and torque-slip characteristics of the induction motor for adjustable frequency.

In order that the magnetic flux is kept constant for any frequency, the applied voltage to the induction motor must be adjusted in proportion to the frequency. In other words, Equation (3.5) shows that the ratio of applied voltage to frequency should be a constant.

The inverter frees the cage induction motor from its inherent limitation of a single speed. There are further advantages in that this machine is relatively cheap to manufacture and there is no need for sliding contacts on slip-rings or commutators. Induction motors, which have a variable frequency inverter to supply power to the stator, have the ideal characteristics of Fig. 3.17 if the voltage is adjusted in proportion to the frequency.

Large induction motor units with inverters now compete more favourably with d.c. units or a.c. commutator units from the aspect of cost, efficiency, maintenance and versatility. These are generalities and there must be many examples of special applications where one of the three types has special advantages over others. But because of its rugged simplicity the induction motor can be placed almost anywhere while the inverter (the equivalent of the commutator) can be placed in its stationary cubicle wherever it is convenient, and this is a great advantage over the commutator machines. Large units were stressed simply because the power electronic equipment is costly relative to small motors, but as the motor size increases the inverter cost does not increase in proportion and becomes a smaller fraction of the total cost.

Not only can inverters be placed in the stator lines but they can also be used in the rotor circuit to replace the rotary frequency changers. The system can then perform duties to provide constant torque or constant horsepower during the adjustable speed operation by a two way controlled flow of power between the rotor circuit and the power supply.

There are many kinds of thyristor inverter circuits, classified both by basic thyristor circuit configuration and also by the method of thyristor commutation. There are more than enough to fill a book. A short and broad description will be given here followed by a discussion of design procedures and different ways of using similar inverters to achieve the variable voltage, variable frequency drive for induction motors.

(i) Inverter classification. Four basic configurations of the inverter are illustrated in Fig. 3.18. Only in the single-phase bridge, configuration number 3, is there need for more than two thyristors per phase. By sequentially switching the thyristors on and off the voltage across the load can be made to change polarity cyclically to produce an alternating current. Even where an a.c. supply already exists, it is necessary to convert to direct current first except in the case of the cycloconverter (described in the section on synchronous machine control) for variable frequency conversion.

With each of these configurations of Fig. 3.18 there are at least six

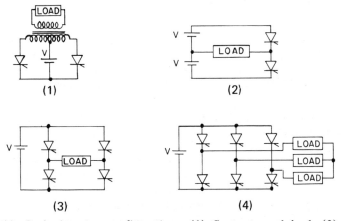

Fig. 3.18. Basic inverter configurations. (1) Centre-tapped lead; (2) centre-tapped supply; (3) single-phase bridge; (4) three-phase bridge.

different methods of commutation, which have been described in Chapter 2 on thyristors and which are repeated in Fig. 3.19. Twenty-four different inverters have now been mentioned and there are many variations of these. For each inverter application there is an optimum design, so the choice can be different. However, the broad range of application becomes apparent in the

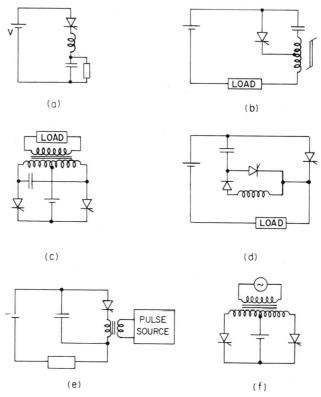

Fig. 3.19. Types of commutation. (a) self-commutation by resonating load; (b) self-commutation by an *LC* circuit; (c) charged capacitor switched by another load thyristor; (d) charged capacitor switched by an auxiliary thyristor; (e) external pulse source; (f) a.c. line commutation.

following examples, the first being a type *C*1 inverter. This has type *C* commutation of Fig. 3.19 and type 1 inverter configuration of Fig. 3.18.

(ii) A C1 inverter for a single-phase induction motor. This *C*1 inverter is the only one which must require a transformer for its operation, and, although the average thyristor current is only half that of the supply, each thyristor must be capable of blocking twice the supply voltage. Because of phase shifting difficulties it is not suitable for three-phase operation. It is used for powers up to about 10 kW.

The basic form of the converter is shown in Fig. 3.20. The only difference between this and the C1 inverters dipicted in Figs. 3.18 and 3.19 is the added commutating reactor, L. It has the functions of orientating the voltage on the capacitor for determining the length of time for commutation and for limiting di/dt.

To get an alternating current in the load the two thyristors are made to conduct alternately, but, as the supply is direct current, a capacitor C is connected across the transformer primary winding to provide the energy to turn off one thyristor when the other begins to conduct.

For operation, initially no current is allowed to flow, because the thyristors are in their blocking state. A pulse of current from the frequency generator is then applied to the gate of TH1 to make the thyristor conduct. The full

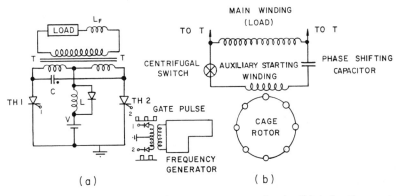

Fig. 3.20. C1 type inverter. (a) Basic C1 inverter circuit; (b) induction motor load (single phase).

supply voltage V is now across half the transformer primary winding so that by induction (or transformer action) there is $2V$ across the whole of the primary winding. Capacitor C then becomes charged up to twice the supply voltage, positive at the dot. Thyristor TH2 has to withstand this voltage until a second pulse of current, this time to the gate of TH2, turns on the second thyristor. This allows C to discharge, reverse biasing TH1 and thus effecting commutation (or turn-off) of TH1. Also, the voltage applied to the primary winding, due to TH2 being on, results in a change of polarity so that the winding sees alternating current. A change of polarity has also occurred at the plates of the commutating capacitor so that when the third pulse is applied to TH1 the cycle begins to repeat itself.

The load frequency and so the speed of the motor is the frequency of the winding current reversals. Therefore, it is the repetition rate of the gate signals to one of the thyristors that governs the load frequency. A free running multivibrator could well act as the gate control unit to give an adjustable switching rate.

Depending upon the circuit parameters the ideal load waveform could be either square (if the transformer could handle square waves) or sinusoidal. The latter is obtained by using the resonating nature of the circuit and never allowing steady-state conditions to be reached in the primary circuit.

The diode across the inductance, L, enables stored energy to be dissipated during commutation intervals without generating high reverse voltage spikes.

The circuit elements need to be chosen to produce reliable operation which means continuously successful commutation. A circuit analysis will provide the design relationships.

This inverter is sometimes referred to as the basic parallel inverter because the commutating capacitor is effectively in parallel with the load. One fault is that if the trigger signal is lost the supply is short-circuited.

Analysis of a C1 inverter with a resistive load. Inspection of Fig. 3.20 with its unilateral elements shows that relationships are non-linear. However, if only ideal elements are considered, and that includes the thyristor to be a

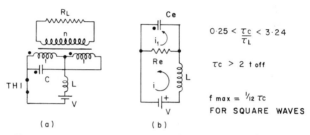

$$0.25 < \frac{\tau_C}{\tau_L} < 3.24$$

$$\tau_C > 2 \, t \text{ off}$$

$$f \text{ max} = \frac{1}{12} \tau_C$$

FOR SQUARE WAVES

Fig. 3.21. Equivalent circuits over one-half cycle with *TH*1 on. (a) Circuit in operation; (b) equivalent circuit of (a).

perfect switch, then over a half cycle the system is linear and the Laplace method can be used to solve the transient equations. During the half cycle that *TH*1 conducts the circuit is as in Fig. 3.21(a). It is assumed that *TH*2 conducted previously in order to charge C. With the primary bifilar winding having a ratio 1:1, the capacitor can be referred to one side of the primary by the ratio of the turns squared, that is, the equivalent capacitance is

$$C_e = \left(\frac{1+1}{1}\right)^2 \cdot C = 4C \tag{3.6}$$

If the primary to secondary turns ratio is $1:n$ then the load resistance referred to the primary is

$$R_e = \left(\frac{1}{n}\right)^2 R_L \tag{3.7}$$

and the equivalent circuit is as in Fig. 3.21(b). There are also initial conditions to consider. Just before *TH*1 was triggered a steady state current,

$$I(0+) = \frac{V}{R_e} \tag{3.8}$$

was flowing in *TH2* and hence in *L*. Further, the capacitor *C* was charged up to a voltage $2V$ so that the voltage across C_e would be

$$V_{ce}(0+) = \left(\frac{1}{1+1}\right) V_c(0+) = \frac{V_c}{2}(0+) = V \tag{3.9}$$

The differential equations describing the transient performance of Fig. 3.21(b) circuit are

$$Vu(t) = (Lp + R_e)i(t) - R_e i_1(t) \tag{3.10}$$

and

$$0 = \left(R_e + \frac{1}{C_e p}\right)i_1(t) - R_e i(t) \tag{3.11}$$

where

$u(t)$ is the unit step function, 0 at $t \leqslant 0$, 1 at $t \geqslant 0$,

$p = \dfrac{d}{dt}$, and

$\dfrac{1}{p} = \displaystyle\int_{-\infty}^{t} dt.$

Performing the Laplace transform, whose operator is s, Equations (3.10) and (3.11) become

$$\frac{V}{s} = [LsI(s) - LI(0+)] + R_e I(s) - R_e I_1(s) \tag{3.12}$$

and

$$0 = R_e I_1(s) + \left[\frac{I_1(s)}{C_e s} - \frac{Q(0+)}{C_e s}\right] - R_e I(s) \tag{3.13}$$

where $Q(0+)$ is the initial charge on C_e, shown positive at the dot in the figure; and so from Equation (3.9)

$$\frac{Q(0+)}{C_e} = V_{ce}(0+) = V. \tag{3.14}$$

From Equation (3.13)

$$I_1(s) = \frac{VC_e}{1 + R_e C_e s} + \frac{R_e C_e s}{1 + R_e C_e s} I(s) \tag{3.15}$$

and substituting this in Equation (3.12)

$$\frac{V}{s} + \frac{LV}{R_e} + \frac{VR_eC_e}{1 + R_eC_es} = \left[\frac{R_e + Ls + LR_eC_es^2}{1 + R_eC_es}\right] \cdot I(s). \qquad (3.16)$$

Let the time constants

$$\frac{L}{R_e} = \tau_L \qquad (3.17)$$

and

$$R_eC_e = \tau_c \qquad (3.18)$$

and rearranging Equation (3.16)

$$I(s) = \frac{V}{R_es} \frac{[\tau_L\tau_cs^2 + (\tau_L + 2\tau_c)s + 1]}{(\tau_L\tau_cs^2 + \tau_Ls + 1)}. \qquad (3.19)$$

Using Murphy and Nambiar's[4] dimensionless factor

$$Q = \left(\frac{\tau_c}{\tau_L} - \tfrac{1}{4}\right)^{1/2} \qquad (3.20)$$

the inverse transform of equation (3.19) is

$$i(t) = \frac{V}{R_e}\left[1 + \frac{2}{Q}(Q^2 + \tfrac{1}{4})\exp(-t/2\tau_c)\sin\frac{Qt}{\tau_c}\right]. \qquad (3.21)$$

For real Q then one condition arises from Equation (3.20), that is,

$$\frac{\tau_c}{\tau_L} \geqslant \tfrac{1}{4} \qquad (3.22)$$

or

$$4R_eC_e \geqslant \frac{L}{R_e}. \qquad (3.23)$$

In the limiting case of equality in Equation (3.23),

$$Q = 0 \qquad (3.24)$$

and Equation (3.21) shows that the current $i(t)$ is the invariant value

$$i(t) = \frac{V}{R_e}. \qquad (3.25)$$

If

$$4R_eC_e < \frac{L}{R_e}, \qquad (3.26)$$

that is, if Q were imaginary, then the supply current would go on rising exponentially until the reactance saturated.

As Q increases the supply current becomes more oscillatory as shown in Fig. 3.22. Not only is there a minimum value of Q there is also a maximum value too. If Q were too high the current oscillations would be such that in the second half cycle the current would be negative. Any attempt for the current to go negative makes $TH1$ block and conduction ceases. This must never happen. The limiting case is where the current becomes zero as shown in Fig. 3.22 for the case of Q_3. To determine this value of Q is to give the

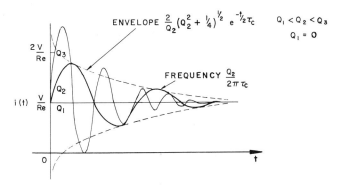

Fig. 3.22. Supply currents for different time constants.

maximum value possible. The abscissa axis would be a tangent to the function $i(t)$ after three quarters of a cycle, that is when

$$\frac{Qt}{\tau_c} = \frac{3\pi}{2} \tag{3.27}$$

from the sine term of Equation (3.21), and since

$$i(t) = 0 \tag{3.28}$$

at this point, substitution in Equation (3.21) gives

$$0 = 1 - \frac{2}{Q}(Q^2 + \tfrac{1}{4}) e^{-3\pi/4Q}. \tag{3.29}$$

Solution of this equation yields

$$\frac{\tau_c}{\tau_L} < 3.24. \tag{3.30}$$

Together with the other condition

$$0.25 < \frac{\tau_c}{\tau_L} < 3.24. \tag{3.31}$$

This is not sufficient for design purposes. The final condition must be that thyristor $TH2$ must be reverse biased long enough after $TH1$ has been turned on (at $t = 0$) to revert to its blocking state. By continuing the analysis in the same way the voltage across the load (also $TH2$) is

$$v_{R_e}(t) = V\left(1 - 2\exp\left(-t/2\tau_c\right)\cos\frac{Qt}{\tau_c} + \frac{1}{Q}\exp\left(-t/2\tau_c\right)\sin\frac{Qt}{\tau_c}\right). \quad (3.32)$$

This waveform looks like that in Fig. 3.23, more or less damped, but the less damped the greater the value of τ_c/τ_L. By the time this voltage becomes zero $TH2$ must have turned off otherwise, after time t_1, $TH2$ becomes forward

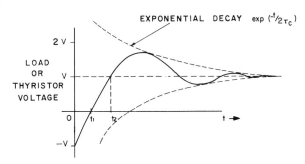

Fig. 3.23.   Load voltage.

biased and will conduct again. This cannot be tolerated, so if we assume the slope at time zero remains the same until time t_1 we can find t_1 in terms of the circuit parameters.

$$\left(\frac{dv_{Re}}{dt}\right)_{t=0} = \frac{2V}{\tau_c}. \quad (3.33)$$

But up to t_1 the slope is assumed to be

$$\frac{dv_{Re}}{dt} = \frac{V}{t_1}. \quad (3.34)$$

Therefore

$$t_1 = \frac{\tau_c}{2}, \quad (3.35)$$

but

$$t_1 > t_{\text{off}}$$

where t_{off} is the turn-off time of the thyristor, so

$$\tau_c > 2t_{\text{off}}. \quad (3.36)$$

This whole analysis has assumed that steady-state conditions are reached before the next switching operation takes place. Otherwise the initial conditions for the operational Equations (3.15) and (3.16) would be incorrect.

The steady-state mode implies square wave operation neglecting the initial commutation pulse. Steady-state can be roughly defined as that reached when the exponent of Equation (3.32) has arrived at within 5 per cent of its final value, that is

$$\exp(-t/2\tau_c) = 0.05 \qquad (3.37)$$

or

$$t = 6\tau_c \qquad (3.38)$$

This time represents the minimum time of one half cycle of the square wave, so that the maximum frequency of the load alternating frequency is

$$f_{max} = \frac{1}{2t} = \frac{1}{12\tau_c} = \frac{1}{12C_eR_e} = \frac{n^2}{48CR_L}. \qquad (3.39)$$

Actually the initial conditions are approximately met if switching occurs at time t_2 shown in Fig. 3.23. The waveform would then be approximately sinusoidal.

For a particular design, choose the maximum frequency of operation and apply the relation

$$f_{max} \leqslant \frac{1}{12\tau_c} \qquad (3.40)$$

so that

$$\tau_c < x_1 \quad \text{(say)}. \qquad (3.41)$$

Next, determine the thyristor turn-off time and apply

$$\tau_c > 2t_{off} > x_2 \quad \text{(say)}. \qquad (3.42)$$

This gives the tolerance

$$x_2 < \tau_c < x_1. \qquad (3.43)$$

The load resistance must be known and the value of C_e and C follows. Equation (3.31) gives the limits for L.

If there is an inductive load in place of R_L in Fig. 3.21(a), after commutation, C provides the only path for the inductive load current so C must be large to prevent excessive voltage rise after commutation and to cancel L_L.

In a typical practical arrangement[5], shown in Fig. 3.24(a), the class B chopper with a filtered output supplies power at a variable voltage to the class $C1$ inverter whose basic operation has already been described. The class A chopper provides the external source for commutation for the inverter. If the inverter produces a rectangular waveform then this arrangement is suitable for pulse width modulation, a technique for both harmonic elimination and for a constant voltage per cycle per second. Fig. 3.24(a) shows added feedback diodes, *D* and *D*2, to accomodate reactive loads. When the current lags the voltage and the thyristor has been commutated the diode provides an alternative path for the load current because the thyristor newly turned on is not appropriate. If *TH*1 is turned off, lagging current has a path through the right-hand primary winding, the supply and *D*1. *D*2 is used during part of the next half cycle. Accordingly the diode allows reactive power, stored in the

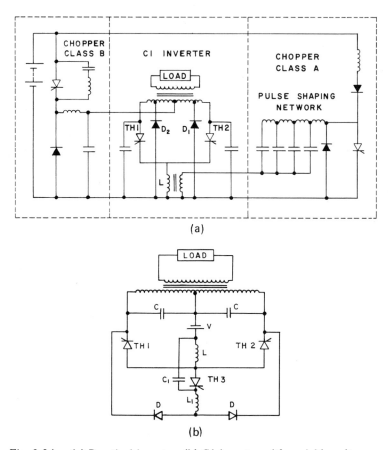

Fig. 3.24. (a) Practical inverter; (b) C1 inverter with variable voltage.

load inductance during the latter part of the half cycle, to be returned to the d.c. supply during the first part of the next half cycle. The diodes also transfer the reactive power of a capacitive load back to the supply. This is perhaps simpler to understand if the inverter role is reversed and it is used, as in the case of reactive energy, as a converter with the same rails positive and negative only with the aid of the diodes. When the reverse voltage across the thyristor exceeds the supply voltage, current flows through the diode. A continuous firing signal to the gate of the conducting thyristor is necessary for reactive loads. To obtain maximum efficiency, two diodes are connected to a tap on the inverter transformer about 10 per cent from the end of the windings.[6] If the diodes were connected to the ends of the transformers then none of the energy trapped in the inductance L during commutation could be returned to the supply.

Figure 3.24(b) is basically the same $C1$ inverter where the firing sequence of $TH1$ and $TH2$ determines the frequency. The other two circuits of Fig. 3.24(a) are constant voltage inverters. With the addition of $TH3$, C_1, L_1 and two diodes, D the average voltage is now an adjustable parameter. At any point in the half cycle, triggering $TH3$ reverse biases whichever load thyristor is conducting and turns it off. $TH3$ itself turns off after a short time because of the LC_1 oscillating circuit.

(iii) A class 4 inverter for a three-phase induction motor. The class 4 inverter is a bridge configuration, and its form can be seen in Fig. 3.18.

Ideally the thyristor is a switch. It is on or it is off. If the supply were direct current and neglecting C and L switching transients, a thyristor in the line would produce a rectangular voltage wave across the load. For a three-phase load such as an induction motor, whose three windings are displaced in space by 120 electrical degrees, it is necessary to have a switching configuration to produce three-phase line voltages which are also displaced by 120°, but in this case with respect to time. The basic and elementary arrangement is displayed in Fig. 3.25.

By triggering the thyristors cyclically without or with varying degrees of overlap a quasi three-phase supply is produced. The winding voltages with the triggering pulses are indicated in Fig. 3.26 for no voltage overlap.

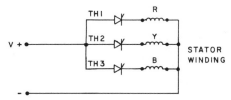

Fig. 3.25.   Half wave bridge inverter.

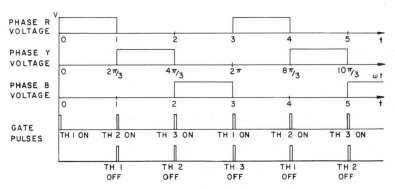

Fig. 3.26.   Load voltage waveform and triggering sequence.

Figure 3.27 illustrates the behaviour of the mmf pattern in the air-gap of the motor as a function of time. Over interval 0 to 1 (in Fig. 3.26) current flows only in phase *R* and produces an mmf as in Fig. 3.27(a). During the next interval 1 to 2, only phase *Y* conducts and, as seen in Fig. 3.27(b), the mmf retains the same magnitude although its direction has changed through a

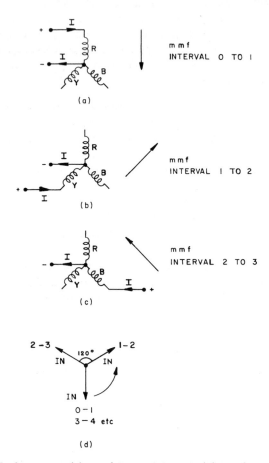

Fig. 3.27.   Mmf pattern. (a) mmf interval 0 to 1; (b) mmf interval 1 to 2; (c) mmf interval 2 to 3; (d) mmf phase relations for each interval.

step of 120 electrical degrees. During the interval 2 to 3 the mmf changes through another 120° until interval 3 to 4 when it is back to its original direction having rotated through 360 electrical degrees and completed a cycle. This stepping mmf produces a quasi rotating magnetic flux which is required for the induction motor operation. Alteration of the magnitude of the sequential time intervals will alter the frequency and hence the speed of the machine.

There are a number of ways to provide a stepped and rotating mmf pattern. For example, current flowing through R and B together, then through B and Y of Fig. 3.25 uses the windings more efficiently and produces a higher mmf although the step is still 120°. At the other end of the scale, without the star connection and with current flowing in either direction through each winding a 30° step is possible. This entails a switching arrangement $(+R)$, $(-B)$ and $(-Y)$ followed by $(+R)$ and $(-Y)$, etc. as in Fig. 3.28. The magnitudes of the mmf alternate with each 30° step so there is imbalance. For the most efficient use of the windings and following as close as possible to a

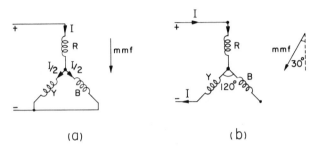

(a)   (b)

Fig. 3.28. A 30° mmf step change. (a) Current through $+R$ $-B$ $-Y$; (b) current through $+R$ $-Y$.

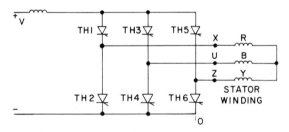

Fig. 3.29.   Class 4, three-phase bridge inverter.

three-phase sinusoidal supply, a full three-phase bridge is used so the current can alternate in the windings. Figure 3.29 shows the general arrangement of the bridge without any details of the commutation circuits. Figure 3.30 shows the winding voltages and Fig. 3.31 shows the mmf pattern for the 60° stepped rotation.

The rectangular voltage wave produces an ideal steady current, which is nevertheless bidirectional and so the mmf is stepped. However a harmonic analysis will produce a strong fundamental sine wave plus higher harmonics of lesser magnitude. It is the fundamental wave whose energy does useful work and the higher harmonics create losses. Neglecting the higher harmonics the fundamental wave will produce the mmf which rotates at this constant speed around the air-gap of the motor. That speed is under the control of the thyristor circuits and they are under a programmable control, either in open or closed loop depending on what regulation is required.

The induction motor line voltages shown in Fig. 3.30 are not far from sine waves. There are no even harmonics because of positive and negative half cycle symmetry. There are no third or multiples of the third harmonic

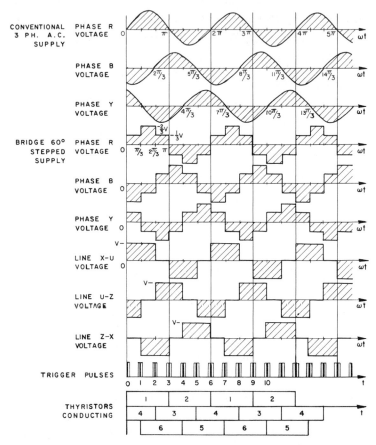

Fig. 3.30. An example of one set of inverter waveforms and conduction periods.

because of the 60° dwell between the positive and negative waves. There are, however, fifth, seventh, eleventh, etc. harmonics which produce energy loss and torque ripples, although the mechanical dynamics will not respond to the eleventh and higher harmonic torques.

Also in Fig. 3.30 the turn-on, turn-off period of any one thyristor is shown to be one whole half cycle each. In practice, switching would occur every 1/6th of a period. That is, starting at *TH*1 in Fig. 3.29 *TH*1, 4, 5 would be turned on. At the end of 1/6th of a period *TH*1, 4 5 would be turned off. As soon as this is accomplished, *TH*1, 4, 6 would be turned on. They would be on for 1/6th of a period before being extinguished so that *TH*1, 3, 6 could all conduct. This would continue as shown in the time and space sequential steps of Fig. 3.31. Lower harmonics are reduced a little this way.

This form of forced commutation chosen for the basic bridge inverter of Fig. 3.29 can take many modifications of the six already illustrated in Fig. 3.19. Some of these have already been described so new ones will be introduced in the next section.

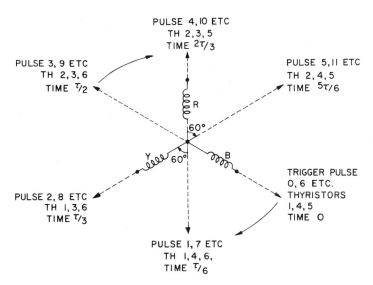

Fig. 3.31. Stepped mmf axes: mmf in space with respect to the windings and the thyristor switching sequence. The six steps are displaced in space and time by $\pi/3$ radians (i.e. θ and ωt). The frequency is $1/\tau$.

(c) Inverter commutation

Three different types of commutation within the classes of (c) and (d) of Fig. 3.19 are described in the next three sections. These are the commutation methods involved in the McMurray inverter,[7] the improved McMurray-Bedford inverter[8] and the inverter with an auxiliary commutating supply.[9] The design procedures and choice of the components L and C are given in the references cited.

(i) The McMurray inverter. The McMurray inverter is an impulse commutated inverter which relies on an LC circuit and an auxiliary thyristor for commutation in the load circuit. The impulse is derived from the resonating LC circuit and is applied to turn off a thyristor carrying the load current. Only the single phase bridge form is shown in Fig. 3.32.

The inverter behaves by alternately allowing *TH*1 and *TH*4, then *TH*3 and

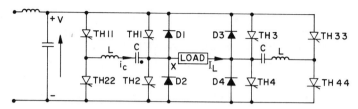

Fig. 3.32. The McMurray impulse commutated inverter with auxiliary thyristors.

*TH*2 to conduct. All the other labelled elements are to facilitate a successful turn-off, and the diodes conduct for a part of each half cycle to return power to the supply if the load is reactive.

Assume *TH*1 and *TH*4 to be conducting and *C* to be charged to +*V* at the dot by a previous action. Figure 3.33 depicts the operation after *TH*11 has been turned on to initiate commutation at time t_0. When *TH*11 has been turned on, *C* discharges and current i_c rises taking part of the load current from *TH*1. At time t_1 the capacitor current begins to be greater than the load current so that *TH*1 no longer carries current. The difference between the capacitor current and the load current flows through diode *D*1 so that *TH*1 becomes reverse biased and turns off.

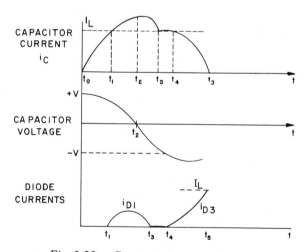

Fig. 3.33.   Commutation waveforms.

Because of the load inductance, which keeps the load current sensibly constant during commutation, I_L continues to flow after the commutation of *TH*1. Further, the capacitor current starts to decrease at time t_2, when its polarity changes, and starts to charge up. Current stops flowing in diode *D*1 at time t_3 when the capacitor current becomes equal to the load current once again. The load sustains I_L until the load is clamped by the diode *D*2 to −*V* at X. Stored energy in L is transferred to C in the form of excess charge proportional to the load current flowing in L, C, load, D_3 and $TH11$. Thyristors $TH3$ and $TH2$ can be fired when i_c reduces to zero and the stored energy in the inductance of the load has also been reduced to zero. When the capacitor current drops below the load current then $D2$ carries this excess to return energy to the supply. The fact that the capacitor charge increases with the load current is an aid to reliable commutation.

A disadvantage of this circuit is the high dv/dt which can be applied to the commutated thyristor when the capacitor current falls below the load current and $D1$ blocks and $D3$ conducts to supply the deficiency in current. If the dv/dt is too great then care must be taken to protect the thyristors.

A multiple circuit arrangement provides a polyphase inverter with the load generally being fed from a transformer.

Worked example 3.2. Design a commutation circuit for a McMurray inverter to supply a $\frac{1}{2}$ hp, 60 Hz, 208–360 V, 1800 rpm three-phase induction motor which has a rated current of 2.33–1.34 A. The available thyristors have a forward breakover voltage of 400 V.

The induction motor stator should be connected in delta to accommodate the 208 V, three-phase supply and the low-voltage rating of the thyristor. The thyristors for inverters are required to have fast turn-off times because of the frequency of switching. Fast turn-off also reduces the requirements of the commutation circuit. A suitable turn-off time would be 12 μs.

A thyristor with a current rating of 7.4 A would not be adequate for 'on-line' starting of the induction motor. However, low-voltage starting to provide current-limited acceleration would mean that low current, easily available and hence inexpensive thyristors can be used.

General purpose 12 A, 400 V diodes can be used for the feedback bridge. The current ratings of these diodes must be higher than the thyristors. Under no load conditions the diodes must carry a peak commutation current which is greater than the maximum load current.

The thyristors are cheap so that the fuses to protect them must be cheaper. Fast acting fuses are therefore not considered. If the motor current is to be limited to about twice the rated value then a 5.0 A slow fuse could be chosen. Since the current rating of the fuse is only 70 per cent of that of the thyristors, its thermal destructive value (i^2t rating) must be below that of the thyristors (40 A^{2}s).

The commutation capacitor and inductor determine the shape of the commutation pulse. The pulse must exceed the maximum load current for a period greater than the turn-off time of the thyristor. A minimum amount of energy* is available when the peak commutating current is 1.5 times the

---

* See section 7.1 of Reference 6.

maximum design load current. This means that 7.5 A is the optimum peak height of the commutation pulse for this inverter. The value of the capacitor is given by

$$C = 0.893 \frac{I_L t_0}{E_c} \text{ F.}$$

where

I_L is the maximum design load current,

t_0 is the time during commutation when the thyristor is reverse biased, and

E_c is the minimum supply voltage

A minimum value for the supply voltage may be 20 V. Below this value it is doubtful whether the motor would operate. In order to ensure reliable commutation t_0 can be given a value of 20 μs. Therefore

$$C = 0.893 \times \frac{5.0 \times 20.0 \times 10^{-6}}{2.0} \text{ F}$$

$$= 4.46 \ \mu\text{F}$$

To be sure of commutation a 10 μF capacitor would be chosen.

The corresponding value for the inductor is

$$L = 0.397 \frac{E_c t_0}{I_L} \text{ H.}$$

$$= 31.76 \ \mu\text{H.}$$

The calculated figures do not account for losses.

A simple RC network across each thyristor is necessary because of the high dv/dt across the thyristor immediately after commutation. Values of 220 Ω and 0.1 μF are usual. The maximum d.c. supply voltage is applied across a thyristor. This maximum voltage is determined from the amplitude of the fundamental component of the inverter's square wave output. That is,

$$E_{max} = \frac{2\sqrt{3}}{\pi} (208 \times \sqrt{2}) \simeq 260 \text{ V.}$$

This gives the worst case rise time of

$$\frac{E_{max}}{RC} = \frac{260}{220 \times 0.1 \times 10^{-6}} \text{ V s}^{-1},$$

that is 12 V μs^{-1}.

See Appendix 1 for the logic control circuits for the sequential thyristor gate signals and protection.

(ii) The McMurray-Bedford inverter. The circuit of Fig. 3.32 needed many thyristors. The number can be reduced to four for a single-phase bridge and only six for a three-phase bridge if the class (c) form of commutation is used. That is, a complementary load thyristor can be used to turn off the conducting thyristor just as in the parallel inverter of Fig. 3.20. This form of inverter, where the two legs can be quite independent, is illustrated in Fig. 3.34.

Briefly, with *TH*1 and *TH*4 on, *C* charges up positively at the dot. Triggering *TH*2 on only, to show independence, L_2 becomes nearly zero volts at the *TH*2 anode, but because *C* is at *V*, then the voltage across L_2 is *V*,

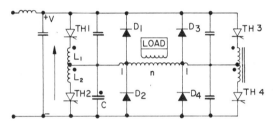

Fig. 3.34.   The   McMurray-Bedford   complementary   impulse   commutation inverter.

positive at the dot. If there is close coupling between L_1 and L_2 and they are equal, *V* will be induced in L_1 by transformer action, making 2*V* at the dot since *V* exists at the junction of L_1 and L_2. *TH*1 is now reverse biased and turns off, but what happens to the energy trapped in L_1 due to the act of supporting the voltage during commutation? The energy is fed back by means of diodes connected to taps on the primary of the transformer.

During commutation the inductance of the load maintains constant current which is supplied from *C*. *C* also provides the current in L_2 and *TH*2, and when the voltage across L_2 is zero the current is at a maximum. When the tapping point reaches the potential of the negative bus (OV) then *D*2 carries the current of L_2 and instead of this energy being trapped, the auto-transformer action transfers the energy back to the supply via the diodes. Since *D*2 clamps the main primary winding to OV, after the trapped energy in L_2 has reduced to zero, *D*2 continues to conduct the load current which continues to flow because of the much larger inductance and this energy is returned to the supply via *D*3. During this latter interval the voltage induced at the end section of the transformer winding appears as reverse voltage across *TH*2, which turns off and remains so unless its gate signal is a train of pulses.

The action of the discharge of one capacitor, *C*, is representative of the action of any of the four and of whichever thyristor is used for turn-off. Thyristors *TH*1 and *TH*2 are complementary, that is, one will turn-off the other, Thyristors *TH*3 and *TH*4 are also complementary.

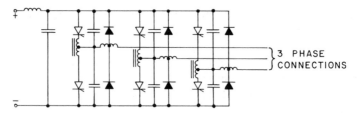

Fig. 3.35. A three-phase McMurray-Bedford inverter.

It is possible to have the three-phase version as in Fig. 3.35, but this has limitations regarding the method of obtaining a variable voltage output.

(iii) Auxiliary commutating supply. If the d.c. bus voltage is being varied to suit a desired inverter voltage-frequency characteristic, then commutation of thyristors can become unreliable. At low voltages and high currents, the capacitors cannot acquire enough energy from the d.c. bus to oppose effectively the charge flow through a thyristor when required. With the aid of an auxiliary supply this difficulty can be overcome. Figure 3.36 shows such a system.

The converter is shown to be controlled to provide a variable d.c. source voltage for the inverter and the three-phase inverter has fly wheel diodes so that reactive energy from the load can be returned to the d.c. bus. Care must be taken here that if there is no inverter to feed the reactive energy back into the a.c. source and if there is no other load on the d.c. bus to absorb it then some energy storage device must be added. A large capacitor as shown would serve this purpose.

Operation of the commutating circuit is as follows. After a commutation, with $TH1$ still on, the capacitor C charges up with the dot positive to a voltage slightly in excess of the d.c. bus voltage, say V_1. This is due to energy stored in the inductances, L. Thyristor $TH1$ will commutate naturally, after which $TH2$ is triggered. After one resonating half cycle of L_2C, the capacitor will have charged up so that the voltage is $E + V_1$, this time negative at the dot, and $TH2$ will have commutated naturally.

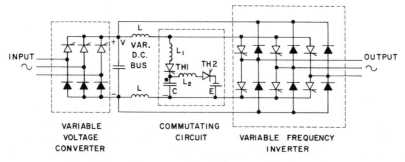

Fig. 3.36. Commutation with an auxiliary supply.

All is now set for the next commutation interval. Two or three of the inverter thyristors will be conducting. At the correct time their gate signals will be reduced to zero, and thyristor *TH*1 fired. Capacitor *C* discharges. The d.c. bus has its polarity momentarily reversed. The inverter thyristors turn-off. Reactive current in the load has a path through the diodes to feed energy back to the d.c. bus and the commutating cycle begins again by *C* charging up with the dot positive.

A compromise for the auxiliary voltage *E* must be made or by-pass circuitry added. Otherwise, at high frequencies, when the d.c. bus voltage is satisfactory for commutation, the capacitor voltage will be too high.

(d) Voltage proportional to frequency

To get the most out of an induction motor means working at the highest reasonable flux density under all conditions of load and speed. This means working at a constant flux density somewhere near the knee of the magnetization curve. To achieve this constant flux density the Equation (3.5) showed that the voltage should be directly proportional to the frequency. The method of keeping the total flux constant when the speed is adjusted can be seen from Faraday's law of induction,

$$e = - \frac{d\Phi}{dt}.$$

Rearranged, this becomes

$$|\Phi| = \int e \, dt. \qquad (3.44)$$

Inspection of the voltage waveform of Fig. 3.37 indicates that the area under the curve, $\int e \, dt$ is the total magnetic flux. The conclusion is that, no matter what the frequency, as long as the area under the fundamental voltage curve can be kept constant, then the induction motor is capable of working at its optimum torque value. That is, the voltage per cycle per second remains constant.

It is an added disadvantage to have to alter two variables separately to get adjustable speed control which is efficient. For small motors or where the speed range is small it is not worthwhile, but for large drives it is imperative that the voltage be altered in accordance with the frequency.

At one time it was rare for frequency to be used as a variable, because it necessitated a variable speed prime mover to drive an alternator to alter the

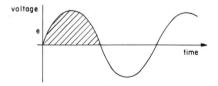

Fig. 3.37. Sinusoidal applied voltage.

frequency. The alternator field was adjusted to provide the correct voltage amplitude. With this bulky equipment and its associated maintenance, it only proved truly feasible for ships' drives. Now, however, the replacement of prime mover and alternator by power semiconductor devices makes this method viable for a much larger range of applications, especially for traction.

There are three different ways of providing a voltage proportional to frequency. The output of the inverter can be fed to a variable ratio transformer whose output is connected to the motor load. The input voltage to the inverter could be the parameter to be controlled. Finally the voltage actually produced at the output of the inverter could have the desired characteristics by adopting pulse modulation.

(i) Variable ratio transformer. Figure 3.38 indicates a conventional and reliable system. The a.c. supply is converted to a constant d.c. voltage by an

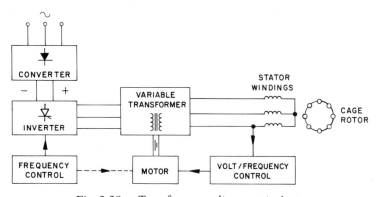

Fig. 3.38.   Transformer voltage control.

uncontrolled rectifier which feeds the inverter. The output is a constant voltage but the frequency is variable, portrayed as open loop control here. However, the variable stepdown transformer has feedback by means of a single closed loop so that a motor can be used to alter the tapping of the transformer in order that voltage and frequency match. The frequency control could provide the signal for the motor.

This is a simple solution. The response is slow because of the electromechanical tap changer and the cost of the transformer as an extra item is high. An advantage with the step down transformer is the capacity for handling high starting currents. The response can be made quicker by replacing the motor by thyristor tap changing facilities as in Fig. 3.6 but this would increase costs even more.

(ii) Variable voltage converter. A more detailed description of the variable voltage converter is more appropriate in the section on d.c. motor control. Briefly, Fig. 3.39 indicates the general form of control. Using a controlled rectifier converter with phase control the d.c. output voltage can be made

proportional to frequency and this automatically allows the induction motor to have its voltage proportional to frequency.

The use of thyristors instead of diodes in the converter increases its cost but the main disadvantage with this method is that it is a difficult problem to provide reliable inverter commutation over a wide range of input voltages. At low voltages the capacitors must be large to store enough energy for commutation unless auxiliary voltage supplies are made available to charge the capacitors.[10]

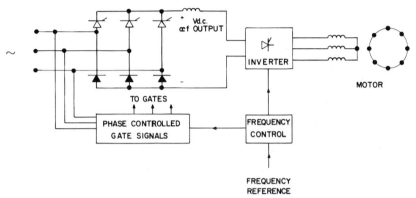

Fig. 3.39.   Converter voltage control.

(iii) Inverter voltage control. A conventional uncontrolled rectifier may be used to provide a constant d.c. voltage input to the inverter. No variable voltage transformer is needed between the inverter output and the motor. An inverter output voltage proportional to frequency can be achieved by the gate control switching circuits. It would be more exact to say that the Vs or the $V c^{-1} s^{-1}$ remains constant no matter what the frequency.

It is shown by Equation (3.44) that for constant flux the area under the voltage curve for each half cycle is to be constant. In the simplest case where the inverter produces a square wave from a constant d.c. input, the amplitude would be constant. The main point is that the length of time the output voltage exists during a half cycle is well within the control of the electronic control circuits for thyristor triggering. For there to be constant flux the voltage amplitude and pulse width should be constant. This pulse modulation is shown in Fig. 3.40 for three different frequencies, each having a voltage V for a fixed time in each half cycle to produce constant flux, that is

$$\int_0^{T/a} V dt = VT = \phi = \text{constant.} \tag{3.45}$$

The highest frequency possible is when the frequency is

$$f = \frac{1}{\tau} = \frac{1}{2T} \tag{3.46}$$

where T is the length of the pulse. This is shown in Fig. 3.40(c).

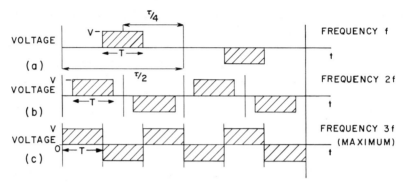

Fig. 3.40.   Constant flux by pulse modulation.

Two questions need to be answered. First, what is the harmonic content of such a waveform and second, how is it possible to produce such a wave from the inverter?

There will be an adjustable frequency oscillator to act as the reference for triggering the thyristors at the correct sequential frequency. This same oscillator can be used as the signal to allow the length of the V waveform to be constant and symmetrically disposed as in Fig. 3.40(a). Figure 3.41 shows a flow diagram. The triangular waves have a peak value at the midpoint of the voltage half cycle. The d.c. level allows the voltage to be at a constant level at a particular time either side of the peak so that a schmitt trigger will turn on and off at the same value to give a fixed length pulse of variable frequency. Pulses from A and B turn-on and turn-off that same thyristor to give a pulse of fixed duration at any frequency.

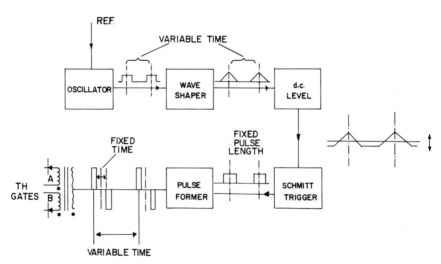

Fig. 3.41.   A general arrangement of thyristor triggering to get fixed time, variable frequency voltage.

If the abscissa axes of Fig. 3.40 were in radians, Fig. 3.42 shows the general pulse waveform which would be produced. This rectangular waveform can be analysed by the Fourier series to give

$$v(\omega t) = \frac{a_0}{2} + a_1 \cos \omega t + a_2 \cos 2\omega t + a_3 \cos 3\omega t + \cdots + a_n \cos n\omega t + \cdots$$

$$+ b_1 \sin \omega t + b_2 \sin 2\omega t + b_3 \sin 3\omega t + \cdots + b_n \sin n\omega t + \cdots \quad (3.47)$$

where the coefficients are

$$a_n = \frac{1}{\pi} \int_{-\pi}^{\pi} v(\omega t) \cos n\omega t \, \mathrm{d}(\omega t) \quad (3.48)$$

and

$$b_n = \frac{1}{\pi} \int_{-\pi}^{\pi} v(\omega t) \sin n\omega t \, \mathrm{d}(\omega t) \quad (3.49)$$

where $n = 1, 2, 3, 4, 5, \ldots$, representing the harmonics.

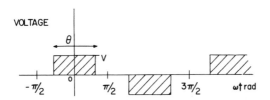

$$-\pi/2 \leq \theta \leq \pi/2 \text{ rad}$$

Fig. 3.42. Inverter output waveform.

The waveshape in Fig. 3.42 is an even function so

$$b_n = 0, \quad (3.50)$$

the waveform is symmetrical about the abscissa so there is no d.c. level, that is

$$a_0 = 0 \quad (3.51)$$

and the waveform has symmetry about each half cycle so there are no even harmonics, that is

$$a_2 = a_4 = a_6 = \cdots = 0. \quad (3.52)$$

Further there are the relations

$$v(\omega t) = V \qquad \text{for } -\frac{\theta}{2} \leq \omega t \leq \frac{\theta}{2} \quad (3.53)$$

and

$$v(\omega t) = 0 \qquad \text{for } \frac{\theta}{2} \leqslant \omega t \leqslant \left(\pi - \frac{\theta}{2}\right). \tag{3.54}$$

Therefore

$$a_n = \frac{4V}{\pi} \int_0^{\theta/2} \cos n\omega t \, d(\omega t) \tag{3.55}$$

and so

$$v(\omega t) = \sum_{n=1}^{n} \frac{4V}{n\pi} \left(\sin \frac{n\theta}{2}\right) (\cos n\omega t) \tag{3.56}$$

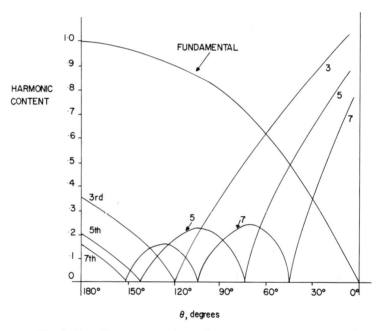

Fig. 3.43. Harmonic content of the rectangular waveform.

Letting $4V/\pi$ be the base voltage for a per unit system, then Fig. 3.43 shows the harmonic variation as a ratio of the fundamental component at the same value of θ. This gives the relative importance of the harmonics with varying θ.

Although the principle of constant flux is simple there is certainly a need to look into the ways of eliminating those harmonics especially at lower powers. One system will be used in preference to another if it is cheaper to buy, cheaper to run and more reliable. A large harmonic content does not mean efficient running. There are a number of ways of approaching this problem of trying to eliminate the harmonics and so their losses.

(e) Harmonic elimination

In order to improve the output waveform of an inverter it is necessary to shape it so that the losses in the line and load are minimized. Therefore it is necessary to make the wave as near sinusoidal as possible. A filter between the inverter and the load can accomplish this task. For large powers the filter becomes both bulky and costly and for variable frequency LC filters are limited. Again the simple step wave output from an inverter could be fed to a multitapped transformer using back-to-back thyristors so that a variable voltage stepped wave could be synthesized. The greater the number of steps per cycle the closer is the wave to a sinusoid. Again the equipment is large and costly. Just as with the voltage magnitude, the voltage shape can be modulated to a shape, which, if not quite sinusoidal, does eliminate any required harmonic. The modulation is by control of the thyristor triggering circuits.

Three variations of modulation, known as pulse width modulation are chosen as the most suitable: multiple pulse width,[11] selected harmonic reduction[12] and harmonic neutralization.[13]

(i) Multiple pulse width control. To obtain a multiple of pulses during each half cycle means that a thyristor in the inverter is turned on and off many times before control passes to another load thyristor. This can only be done if the inverter employs class (d) commutation, that is, capacitor turn-off with an auxiliary thyristor, or complementary turn-off if the arms of the bridge are quite independent.

The single pulse of voltage shown in Fig. 3.42 has a third harmonic, which is particularly high at low powers. By increasing the number of pulses to two per half cycle, as in Fig. 3.44(a) the third harmonic is eliminated. Fourier analysis for varying θ (constant time but variable fraction of cycle depending on frequency) produces low harmonics as in Fig. 3.44(b). Other harmonics can be eliminated by increasing the number of pulses.

A method of obtaining multiple pulses is to supply the pulse forming circuit for triggering the thyristor on and off with a mixed saw tooth wave with a sine wave reference, as in Fig. 3.45. More sophisticated is the double sine wave reference with variable phase shift which is self-explanatory (Fig. 3.46). In all cases the total area of the pulses per half cycle ($\int v(t) dt$) remains constant.

(ii) Selected harmonic reduction. With a much simpler trigger circuit than in the previous section and with the possibility of using either class (c) or class (d) commutation (the former means less thyristors) a pulse form with three positive and two negative pulses in the positive half cycle can be achieved as in Fig. 3.47. There can be less commutations per cycle compared with multiple pulse width control.

In the single-phase inverter the third and fifth harmonics can be eliminated

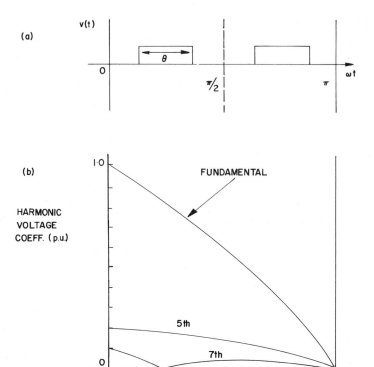

Fig. 3.44.   Double pulse waveform.

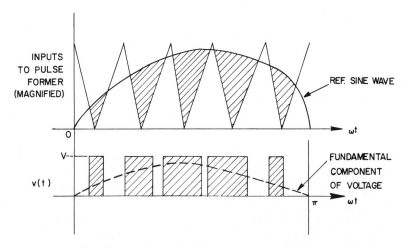

Fig. 3.45.   Multiple pulses by mixing signals.

94

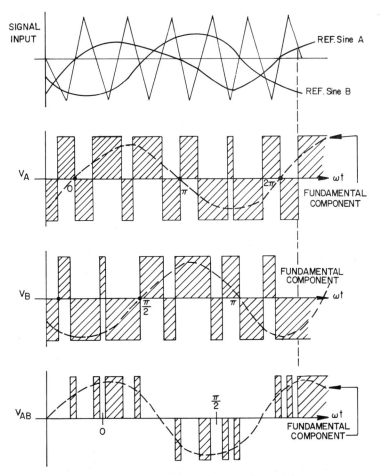

Fig. 3.46. Multiple pulses by complex mixing.

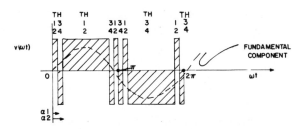

Fig. 3.47. Selected harmonic reduction.

95

while in a three-phase inverter with the same technique the first harmonic in the line voltage is the eleventh. This is accomplished over the whole range by altering the fundamental voltage from zero to full value or, in other words, by keeping the $V \, c^{-1} \, s^{-1}$ constant.

Just as in the single rectangular wave of Fig. 3.42 where the harmonic voltage is

$$v(n\omega t) = \frac{4V}{n\pi} \left(\sin n \frac{\theta}{2} \right) (\cos n \, \omega t) \tag{3.57}$$

so by similar analysis the harmonic voltage for the wave of Fig. 3.47 is

$$v(n\omega t) = \frac{4V}{n\pi} (1 - 2 \cos n\alpha_1 + 2 \cos n\alpha_2) \left(\cos n \frac{\theta}{2} \right) (\sin n\omega t) \tag{3.58}$$

by this time the angle θ is a phase shift between the axes of trigger pulses to obtain a fundamental voltage proportional to frequency and retain the elimination of the third and fifth harmonics.

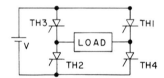

Fig. 3.48.   Single-phase bridge inverter.

If there were no phase shift between $TH1$, 2 and $TH3$, 4 in the single-phase inverter of Fig. 3.48, then the thyristor triggering would be as in Fig. 3.47 representing the maximum voltage at maximum frequency. From Equation (3.58) with θ zero, the term involving α_1 and α_2 shows that any two harmonics may be eliminated and α_1 and α_2 found from solving the two simultaneous equations

$$v(n_1 \omega t) = 0 = 1 - 2 \cos n_1 \alpha_1 + 2 \cos n_1 \alpha_2 \tag{3.59}$$

and

$$v(n_2 \omega t) = 0 = 1 - 2 \cos n_2 \alpha_1 + 2 \cos n_2 \alpha_2, \tag{3.60}$$

where n_1 and n_2 are the two harmonics to be zero. For the third and fifth harmonics ($n_1 = 3$ and $n_2 = 5$) to be zero

$$\alpha_1 = 23.6° \tag{3.61}$$

and

$$\alpha_2 = 33.3° \tag{3.62}$$

For the firing arrangement of Fig. 3.47 it is incompatible to have a variable voltage and keep α_1 and α_2 constant to eliminate the same harmonics. The

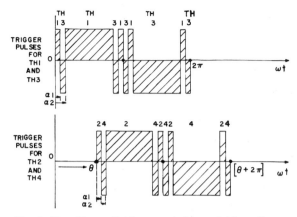

Fig. 3.49. Phase displacement for variable voltage.

requirement is to keep the two chosen harmonics zero and have voltage proportional to frequency by the phase shifting arrangement of Fig. 3.49. In this way α_1 and α_2 always remain the same but the fundamental voltage is variable from a maximum at $\theta = 0$, where the trigger pulses coincide, to zero at $\theta = 180°$, where at no time is there current through the load. Naturally, logic circuitry will prevent either $TH1$, 4 or $TH3$, 2 turning on together or being on together to short-circuit the supply voltage. Also it has been assumed that a thyristor has been turned off before its opposite has been turned on. Only with Fig. 3.34 will there be no short-circuit if $TH2$ follows $TH1$. With the phase displacement θ, there is no voltage across the load whatsoever unless $TH1$ and 2 or $TH3$ and 4 have their gate signals on at the same time and, as soon as one gate signal is removed from a pair, the two thyristors are turned off automatically.

Equation (3.58) gives the coefficients of all harmonic voltages for any phase displacement θ when the third and fifth harmonics have been eliminated by α_1 and α_2 which have values given in Equations (3.61) and (3.62). This is shown in Fig. 3.50. These are theoretical curves and do not take into account

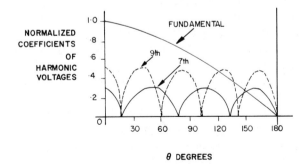

Fig. 3.50. Harmonic content for varying phase shift.

the finite time of turn-on and, more important, turn-off, but the differences will not be great. The normalization of per unit quantities is calculated using a base voltage $4V/\pi$ × 0.839 obtained from the fundamental voltage coefficient at zero phase angle ($\theta = 0$).

(iii) Harmonic neutralization by wave synthesis. Wave synthesis is an attractive means of eliminating the lower harmonics but, because so many thryistors are required, it is only economic above about 20 kVA. The principle is that a number of single-phase inverters, coupled together, are turned on and off sequentially so that the sum of the outputs results in a stepped wave approaching a sinusoid. The greater the number of inverter units the greater the number of steps in the output wave and the greater the number of harmonics are eliminated. Each single phase could be a bridge inverter, as in Fig. 3.48. The load would be the primary of a transformer. A great advantage is that, if a thyristor or a single unit should fail, there is still an output voltage which is provided by the other units although the harmonic distortion would be increased. This is better than a three-phase bridge inverter having one thyristor fail, because then there would be no output.

An example of six stages is chosen to show that the first uncancelled harmonic is the eleventh and is obtained from the formula

$$H = 2kN \pm 1 \qquad\qquad (3.63)$$

where

H is the harmonic present in the wave,
N is the number of inverter stages, and
k = 1, 2, 3, 4 . . . .

Because an induction motor will not respond to the mmf harmonic as high as the eleventh it seems unnecessary to have more stages than six. During the initial description maximum frequency and voltage are considered. The total three-phase capacity is six times the kVA rating of a single stage.

Figure 3.51 illustrates the inverter diagramatically. A controlled oscillator, operating at twelve times the required output frequency, feeds signals into a six bistable ring counter. For example the first signal will turn on the bistable 1, switching stage 1 on at the reference $0°$. Stage 1 remains on until bistable 1 receives the next pulse to reverse it and this is not until six oscillator pulses later. The second oscillator pulse finds bistable 1 on and so turns on the next which turns on stage 2 at the reference period $30°$. Each signal successively turns on a stage until they are all on and half a cycle is complete and the next six signals sequentially reverse them to complete a whole cycle.

On the primary, P, of each transformer there is a voltage as shown in Fig. 3.52(a). The voltages are of equal magnitude but phase displaced in time by $30°$. If these voltages were summed in series then the resultant would be a single-phase multi-stepped voltage with a low harmonic content. This is shown

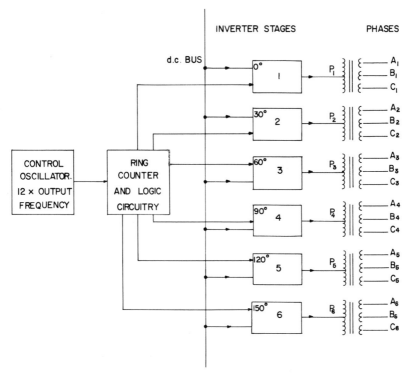

Fig. 3.51.   General arrangement of a wave synthesizer.

in Fig. 3.53. Of course, the primaries themselves could not be summed. It
would have to be the secondaries.

However the requirement is for a three-phase balanced voltage of the form
of Fig. 3.53. The three-phase voltage is synthesized by having a number of
secondary windings on each transformer. Fig. 3.51 shows three with the
voltage ratios P/A, P/B and P/C not necessarily the same. Three series
arrangements to give a balanced three-phase star-connected voltage supply are
illustrated in Fig. 3.54. These phases do not necessarily correspond with the
secondaries of Fig. 3.51, because there is more than one way to synthesize the
voltages to achieve the same end. The transformer turns ratios here are

$$P/A = 1 \qquad\qquad (3.64)$$

$$P/B = \frac{3}{\sqrt{3}} \qquad\qquad (3.65)$$

and

$$P/C = \frac{3}{2\sqrt{3}} \qquad\qquad (3.66)$$

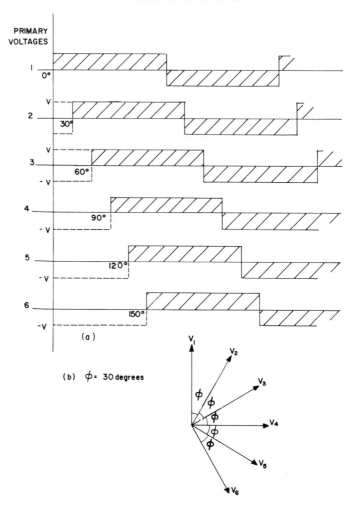

Fig. 3.52. Inverter phase voltages. (a) Voltage phasing of inverter stages; (b) voltage phasor diagram concerning the primary windings.

to give the required harmonic neutralization. Accordingly there would be two A_1 windings with one reversed and no B_1 or C_1 on the secondary side of transformer one in this case.

The output voltage waveform of the phase R of Fig. 3.54 is the sum of the instantaneous values of the voltages B_2, A_1 $-C_6$, $-A_5$ and $-B_4$. This is shown in Fig. 3.55. The other phases B and Y are similar but displaced by plus and minus 120°.

It is necessary to check the harmonic content of this waveform. This can be done by summing the Fourier series of each rectangular waveform of Fig. 3.55(a) since this series has already been calculated. However it is better to

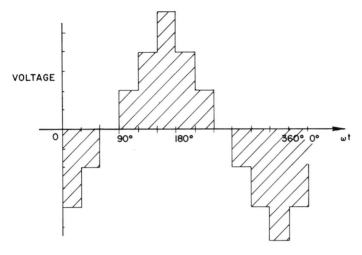

Fig. 3.53.   Inverter voltage if primary voltages were summed.

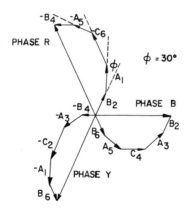

Fig. 3.54.   Synthesis of a balanced three-phase supply.

generalize for voltages of all frequencies and this depends on how the voltage is varied. One possibility is to have two inverters whose voltages are summed in series but those voltages can be phase displaced. Two such voltages as in Fig. 3.55(b), phase displaced by 180°, would be zero while, at the other extreme, zero phase shift would result in a maximum voltage. Whatever the phase difference of the two, the harmonics of the sum are the same as the harmonics of the individual waves. The same method of phase displacing to obtain constant volts per cycle per second can be accomplished by the single inverter triggering circuits, just as in Fig. 3.49. Otherwise, the voltage triggering is such as to maintain a constant pulse length as in Fig. 3.40.

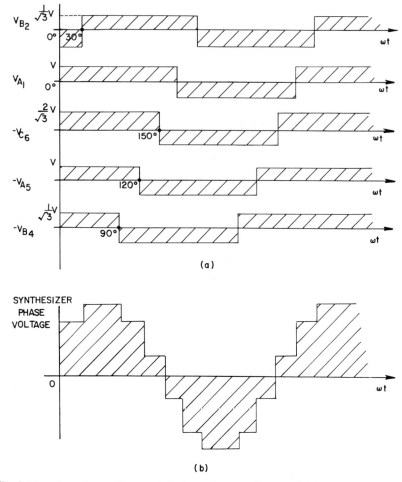

(a)

(b)

Fig. 3.55. Inverter voltages. (a) Secondary voltages which are summed to form; (b) one of the phase voltages applied to a motor.

Using the latter for analysis an individual inverter unit voltage then has the form of Fig. 3.56, which is a greater generalization of Fig. 3.42. If the phase displacement Ψ is taken into account, Equation (3.56) becomes

$$v(\omega t) = \sum_{n=1}^{n} \frac{4V}{n\pi} \left(\sin n\frac{\theta}{2} \right) [\sin n(\omega t + \Psi)] \qquad (3.67)$$

where $n = 1, 3, 5 \ldots$.

For phase R there is the sum of five terms of the form of Equation (3.67) for the resultant, that is

$$v(\omega t) = v_{B_2}(\omega t) + v_{A_1}(\omega t) - v_{C_6}(\omega t) - v_{A_5}(\omega t) - v_{B_4}(\omega t) \qquad (3.68)$$

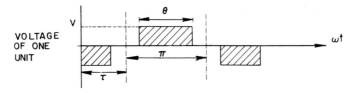

Fig. 3.56.   Simple pulse width modulation for voltage control.

where

$$v_{B_2}(\omega t) = \sum_{n=1}^{n} \frac{4V}{n\pi} \cdot \frac{1}{\sqrt{3}} \left(\sin n\frac{\theta}{2} \right) [\sin n(\omega t + 30°)] \qquad (3.69)$$

$$v_{A_1}(\omega t) = \sum_{n=1}^{n} \frac{4V}{n\pi} \left(\sin n\frac{\theta}{2} \right) [\sin n\omega t] \qquad (3.70)$$

$$v_{C_6}(\omega t) = \sum_{n=1}^{n} \frac{4V}{n\pi} \cdot \frac{2}{\sqrt{3}} \left(\sin n\frac{\theta}{2} \right) [\sin n(\omega t + 150°)] \qquad (3.71)$$

$$v_{A_5}(\omega t) = \sum_{n=1}^{n} \frac{4V}{n\pi} \left(\sin n\frac{\theta}{2} \right) [\sin n (\omega t + 120°)] \qquad (3.72)$$

and

$$v_{B_4}(\omega t) = \sum_{n=1}^{n} \frac{4V}{n\pi} \cdot \frac{1}{\sqrt{3}} \left(\sin n\frac{\theta}{2} \right) [\sin n (\omega t + 90°)] \qquad (3.73)$$

From Equations (3.69) to (3.73) and substituting the fundamental components into Equation (3.68), it follows that

$$v_1(\omega t) = \frac{8\sqrt{3}}{\pi} \sin \frac{\theta}{2} \sin \omega t \qquad (3.74)$$

so that the fundamental phase voltage

$$V_R \propto \sin \frac{\theta}{2} \qquad (3.75)$$

but

$$V_R \propto f \qquad (3.76)$$

the supply frequency, thus

$$f \alpha \sin \frac{\theta}{2}. \tag{3.77}$$

Since the maximum frequency occurs when θ is $180°$ then

$$f = f_{max} \sin \frac{\theta}{2}. \tag{3.78}$$

Summing the 3rd, 5th, 7th and 9th harmonic components in a like manner it is found that they are all zero. Only the harmonics

$$H = 2kN \pm 1, \tag{3.79}$$

which is a repetition of Equation (3.63) exist, and these harmonic voltages are

$$v_n(\omega t) = \frac{8\sqrt{3}}{n\pi} \sin n \frac{\theta}{2} \sin n \, \omega t. \tag{3.80}$$

The definition of total harmonic distortion (THD) is

$$\text{THD} = \sqrt{\left[\sum_{n}^{\infty} (n\text{th harmonic as a per cent of the fundamental})^2 \right]} \tag{3.81}$$

where $n = 2, 3, 4 \ldots$.

The waveform of Fig. 3.55(b) has just over 15 per cent THD whereas the phase voltage of Fig. 3.30 has more than 30 per cent THD.

(f) Appraisal of thyristor three-phase inverters

A brief appraisal is really an attempt to choose an inverter for a particular motor or motors, and this is an attempt to find which is the least costly to construct for a given specification of voltage, current, power, frequency, harmonics and regulating tolerances. Each application has to be considered on its own merits but broad outlines of choice can be made.

These outlines encompass the electronic trigger circuitry, which also involves the logic circuitry of control, and the number of thyristors involved in the system. If one considers that the inverter is a replacement for the commutator of a d.c. machine, then for small powers there must be special reasons for using static equipment. This is because the power electronics is costly in proportion to a commutator or even to an induction motor. The cost of the control circuits does not increase in proportion to the size so that at horsepowers of a few hundred the system can be no more expensive than a d.c. system, such as the Ward-Leonard set, and, perhaps, a little more efficient. It also has the advantages of a brushless machine such as less standing room and less maintenance and it is less hazardous (brush sparking is dangerous in some atmospheres).

The trigger circuits for an inverter with a square wave output would be the simplest, relying on a reference frequency generator and a ring counter. As soon as requirements become more sophisticated so does the logic circuitry controlling the trigger pulses. For example pulse width modulation for voltage/frequency and for harmonic reduction increases the complexity enormously. The simple example of a d.c. position control circuit in the chapter on machine control demonstrates this point.

How many thyristors are used depends entirely on the system chosen. The system which has the minimum number of thyristors (six of them) and which still provides a variable voltage variable frequence output to a motor, would be one where the converter is an uncontrolled rectifier, the inverter is commutated by complementary load thyristors and the voltage is altered by means of a transformer. This is depicted in Fig. 3.35 and Fig. 3.38.

Fast motor response is often specified so that an electromechanical control of transformer tappings cannot be tolerated. As soon as the voltage control is transferred to the converter then three more thyristors are required and for reliable commutation at all times auxiliary turn-off as in Fig. 3.36 means a total of 10 thyristors.

To transfer the voltage amplitude control to the inverter itself can require as little as six thyristors as in Fig. 3.35 because each limb is made quite independent. This is demonstrated by the circuit in Fig. 3.34. If thyristors $TH1$ and $TH4$ are carrying load current, thyristor $TH1$ is commutated by $TH2$ which itself is turned off by the reverse voltage of reactive load power returning to the d.c. bus; thus load current does not have to flow through $TH2$ immediately after $TH1$ has turned off. With auxiliary turn-off the number of thyristors is doubled. When harmonic reduction is an added specification of the inverter, then the number of thyristors must increase, because three single-phase inverters are used for multiple pulse width and selected harmonic reduction of Fig. 3.45 and Fig. 3.47 respectively. This involves a total of 12 thyristors employing complementary turn-off. Harmonic neutralization can have as many single-phase stages as is required to eliminate a particular number of harmonics. The six stages of Fig. 3.51 to eliminate up to the eleventh harmonic, would need 24 thyristors if the inverter is also to maintain constant V c^{-1} s^{-1}. However, in its defence, each stage only handles one-sixth of the total kVA of the load.

In general, it might be said that the more sophisticated the inverter is the more it becomes economical at only the higher power levels.

(g) Inverters in the induction motor rotor circuit

The constant torque Kramer type drive depicted in Fig. 3.57 uses three additional rotating machines to convert the rotor slip power to direct current which is then inverted to the supply frequency. It is also possible to have two way power flow to achieve sub- and super-synchronous speeds. Conversion and inversion suggests thyristor static systems and an outline of the equivalent Kramer system is shown in Fig. 3.58.

Two inverters are shown, although one of them converts alternating current to direct current and the other inverts direct current to the alternating current of the required frequency. Below synchronous speed the inverter *A* converts the slip power to direct current which is inverted by *B* to feed power back into the supply. An autotransformer is added here to provide the voltage with the correct magnitude. The transformer may not be required because the inverter is controlled both for on and off operation by the supply voltage. That is, *B* in this mode, is a phase-controlled, a.c. line voltage commutated

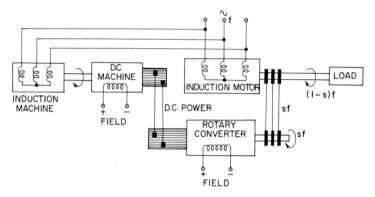

Fig. 3.57.   Kramer system for constant torque.

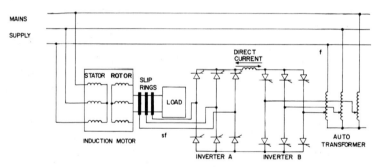

Fig. 3.58.   Outline of thyristor equivalent Kramer system.

inverter[6] and although the d.c. voltage is inherently low, inversion is accomplished by delayed commutation. Delayed commutation does mean there is a high reactive power drawn from the a.c. mains supply and this is not an advantage.

Heumann[14] suggests that the system can be adapted to eliminate this reactive power by including a pulse converter in the d.c. line as in Fig. 3.59 where control is obtained by rapidly turning *TH*1 on and off. This enables the variable rotor voltage to be adapted to the fixed counter voltage of the inverter set for full voltage. The pulse current output would then require buffer capacitors. The operation can be viewed from the energy viewpoint.

When the inverter is off, *TH*1 effectively short-circuits the rotor and as the motor cannot change speed within one cycle of the supply the energy is stored in the inductance of the circuit. Firing the inverter and turning off *TH*1 together, releases that stored energy for transfer to the supply. From another point of view, when the thyristor *TH*1 short-circuits the rotor, the current will rise. By turning off *TH*1 the current decays and causes a high voltage to be induced across the inductance to try to maintain that current. This voltage adds to the rectified rotor voltage such that the sum is greater than the supply so that active power is injected into the supply.

Above synchronous speed the inverter *B* of Fig. 3.58 rectifies to produce direct current at a constant voltage and inverter *A* produces alternating current at the right frequency and voltage to inject into the rotor windings of the induction motor. Inverter *A* cannot be line commutated like inverter *B* because at synchronous speed inverter *B* receives direct current from the bus and injects direct current, but at a different voltage, into the rotor, so that there is no alternating voltage for commutation. Forced commutation using capacitors to store the commutating energy is the only system to provide a full speed range going through synchronism. This also eliminates the use of

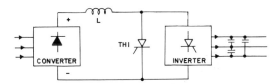

Fig. 3.59.   Pulse-controlled inverter.

phase angle triggering for variable voltage output. A method of pulse width modulation must be used instead. At low voltages, such forms of commutation using capacitors are unreliable because, unless very large values of capacitance are employed, there is not sufficient energy ($\frac{1}{2} CV^2$) stored. Small capacitors can be used if an auxilliary energy source (battery) is added to ensure adequate charging in between commutations. This is not really very satisfactory, and is the reason why inverter *B* does not act as a controlled rectifier to alter the d.c. bus voltage to small values necessary for the rotor circuit. The converter provides a high constant voltage and allows inverter *A* to exercise voltage control.

This is a complicated and expensive system. Why use it at all? It is very efficient and this cannot be said for a variable speed gear box which has to step up the speed. Power flow can be both ways to give speeds both well below and well above synchronism. This cannot be accomplished by control of the stator parameters unless a variable frequency inverter were used. This inverter would be of the same form as inverters *A* and *B* in the rotor injection mode except that it would have to have twice the frequency range. Accordingly there is a choice, a cage motor driven by an inverter whose frequency range is twice the supply or a slip ring motor being controlled by an inverter whose frequency range is up to that of the supply.

A simplified version of Fig. 3.58, achieving only a variable sub-synchronous speed is to make inverter A an uncontrolled rectifier. The phase-controlled a.c. line commutated inverter B is a relatively simple inverter and the pulse converter of Fig. 3.59 could still be used to provide a system with high efficiency.

REFERENCES

1. Hindmarsh, J. (1965), *Electrical Machines,* Pergamon Press, Oxford.
2. *Power thyristors and their applications* (1969), I.E.E. Conference Publication, No. 53, 185 and 168.
3. Shepherd, W. and Stanway, J. (1964), 'The silicon controlled rectifier a.c. switch for the control of one phase series and transformer loads', *I.E.E.E. Int. Con. Rec.* **4**, 155-163.
4. Murphy, R. H. and Nambiar, K. P. P. (1961), 'A design basis for SCR parallel inverters', *Proc. I.E.E.* (B), **108**, 556-562.
5. Mapham, N. W. (1964), 'The classification of SCR inverter circuits, *I.E.E.E. Int. Con. Rec.* **4**, 99.
6. Bedford, B. D. and Hoft, R. G. (1964), *Principles of inverter circuits,* John Wiley, New York, p. 190.
7. McMurray, W. (1964), 'SCR inverter commutated by an auxiliary impulse', *I.E.E.E. Trans. Comm. Elec.* **83**, 824-829.
8. McMurray, W. and Shattuck, D. P. (1961), 'A silicon–controlled rectifier inverter with improved commutation', *I.E.E.E. Trans. Comm. Elec.* **80**, 531-542.
9. Bradley, D. A. *et al.* (1964), 'Adjustable frequency inverters and their application to variable speed drives', *Proc. I.E.E.* **111**, 1833-1846.
10. Bradley, D. *et al.* (1964), 'Adjustable frequency inverters . . . ', *Proc. I.E.E.* **111**, 1833-1846.
11. Molcrytyki, B. (1966), 'Pulse width modulated inverters for a.c. motor drives', *I.E.E.E. Int. Con. Rec.* **8**, 8-23.
12. Turnbull, F. G. (1964), 'Selected harmonic reduction in static d.c. to a.c. inverters', *I.E.E.E. Trans. Comm. and Elec.* **83**, 374-378.
13. Kernick, A. *et al.* (1962), 'Static inverter with neutralization of harmonics', *A.I.E.E. Trans.* (II) **81**, Appl. and Ind. 59-68.
14. Heumann, K. (1964), 'Pulse control of d.c. and a.c. motors by silicon controlled rectifiers', *I.E.E.E. Trans. Comm. and Elec.* **83**, 397.

PROBLEMS

3.1. Prove that the torque/speed characteristics of an induction motor are of the form of Fig. 3.17, when the voltage is altered in direct proportion to the frequency. Discuss how the motor efficiency varies with frequency.

The electromagnetic torque per phase of an induction motor is

$$T = \frac{P_m}{\omega_m} \tag{3.82}$$

where

P_m = the mechanical power output per phase, and

ω_m = the shaft angular speed.

We have the power relations

$$P_1 : P_2 : P_m = 1 : s : (1 - s) \tag{3.83}$$

and the definition of slip

$$s = \frac{\omega/p - \omega_m}{\omega/p} \tag{3.84}$$

where

P_1 = power transferred across the air gap per phase,

P_2 = rotor copper loss (that is the energy dissipated in the rotor due to the winding resistance, "$I^2 r$") per phase,

ω = angular frequency of the supply, and

p = the number of pole pairs.

Accordingly

$$T = \frac{p}{\omega} \frac{P_2}{s} \tag{3.85}$$

$$= \frac{p}{\omega} I_2^2 \frac{r_2}{s} \tag{3.86}$$

where

I_2 = the rotor current per phase,

r_2 = rotor resistance per phase, and if

E_2 = rotor induced emf per phase at standstill, and

x_2 = rotor leakage reactance per phase at standstill, then

$$T = \frac{p}{\omega} \frac{E_2^2 r_2}{(r_2^2 + s^2 x_2^2)} \tag{3.87}$$

Differentiating this torque with respect to slip, s, and equating to zero gives us the relation for maximum torque to be

$$T_{max} = \frac{p}{\omega} \frac{E_2^2}{2x_2} \tag{3.88}$$

at a slip

$$s = \frac{r_2}{x_2} = a \text{ (say)}.$$

(3.89)

If the voltage drop across the stator impedance, $I_1(r_1 + jx_1)$, can be ignored, and this becomes more acceptable the larger the motor, then for constant flux,

$$V \propto E_1 \propto E_2 \propto \omega$$

(3.90)

and as

$$x_2 \propto \omega$$

(3.91)

very nearly, then no matter what the frequency

$$T_{\max} = \text{constant}$$

(3.92)

That is, as long as the applied voltage is proportional to frequency, the maximum available torque at any frequency remains a fixed value. Also, manipulating Equations (3.88), (3.89) and (3.90), the torque at any slip s is

$$T = T_{\max} \frac{2as}{a^2 + s^2}$$

(3.93)

and

$$a \propto \frac{1}{\omega}$$

(3.94)

if r_2 can be assumed to be independent of frequency, and the leakage inductance a constant. At starting the slip is unity so the starting torque, from Equation (3.93) is

$$T_{ST} = T_{\max} \frac{2a}{a^2 + 1}$$

(3.95)

or

$$T_{ST} = \text{constant} \times \frac{\omega}{b^2 + \omega^2}$$

(3.96)

where b is another constant. As the supply frequency is increased, the denominator of Equation (3.96) increases at a greater rate than the numerator to show that the higher the frequency to lower the starting torque.

Equations (3.92) and (3.96) enable the characteristics to be plotted as in Fig. 3.17. It is an advantage in traction applications that the induction motor has a high starting torque for the lower frequencies, especially when the applied voltage is proportionately lower. Other points to notice are that, for the same value of a low working slip, the torque is greater at a high frequency than at a lower frequency and the relation between torque and slip is almost linear. For a particular load torque the horsepower output is directly proportional to the frequency, and as the frequency increases so does the efficiency. This latter point is classified by the following equation for efficiency,

$$\eta = \frac{P_m - (\text{windage and friction losses})}{P_1 + (\text{stator copper losses and core losses})}. \tag{3.97}$$

Without any loss of generality this can be simplified to

$$\eta \simeq \frac{P_m}{P_1} \tag{3.98}$$

so that

$$\eta \simeq (1 - s). \tag{3.99}$$

Using the information portrayed in Fig. 3.17, for a constant load torque, as the supply frequency is increased, the value of the slip, s, decreases. Accordingly the efficiency increases with frequency. It is desirable to start at a low frequency to get a high torque and its associated rapid acceleration, but it is a necessary economic measure to run at the highest possible frequency.

By having the applied voltage vary in direct proportion to the frequency to obtain an almost constant magnetic flux and hence maximum available torque at all speeds, the horsepower output will increase with the speed and so the frequency. This may not be required or always possible. At very low frequencies when the reactance becomes very small the current limitation is produced by the winding resistance. So that a higher voltage at low frequency is desirable if a high torque is to be made available. Often, as in the case of traction, constant power is required above a certain speed, in which case while the frequency is increased the voltage would be held constant. Whatever the application, the voltage/frequency characteristic would be programmed within the framework of the optimum performance.

There have been a number of approximations made in this analysis in which voltage is proportional to frequency and throughout we have assumed sinusoidal quantities. For semiconductor inverters this must be borne in mind. Further, over a limited range of frequency the voltage could be kept constant, but lowering the frequency too much would entail magnetic saturation and its attendant higher losses.

3.2. For the McMurray inverter commutation circuit, (see Example 3.2 and Section 3.131) prove that

$$C = 0.893 \frac{I_L t_0}{E_c} \text{ F,}$$

and

$$L = 0.397 \frac{E_c t_0}{I_L} \text{ H.}$$

3.3. Prove that the first voltage harmonic above the fundamental in the output of the harmonic neutralization inverter of Section 3.1e(iii) is the eleventh.

3.4. Show how an inverter in the rotor circuit of an induction motor is an instrument of speed control.

This is a question of rotor injection voltage control rather than frequency control. The injected voltage at the rotor slip-rings must be of the same frequency as the rotor currents. This is the reason for the use of an inverter.

If the wound rotor of an induction motor has its windings brought out to slip-rings, the phases can be left in open circuit. This would prevent current flowing in the windings so that the torque and hence the speed would be zero. However, if a voltage from an external source were applied to the rotor windings across the slip-rings, there would be an interaction between this voltage and the transformer induced emf of the rotor winding to produce current flow. A constant electromagnetic torque would then be effected to drive the induction motor at some steady state speed, provided that the injection voltage was at the same frequency as the induced emf. Alteration of the magnitude or phase of the injected voltage would alter the current, the current would affect the torque and a new steady-state speed would eventually result.

This is most clearly seen by considering the circuit representation of the induction motor which has an injected voltage at the rotor terminals. The mesh equation of the secondary circuit in phasor form is

$$s\bar{E}_2 \pm \bar{E}_k = \bar{I}_2(r_2 + jsx_2) = \bar{I}_2\bar{Z}_2$$

where Ek = the injected voltage from an external source.

The induction motor is inherently a constant speed machine, or nearly so, therefore the case of no-load simplifies the interpretation of the above equation. At no-load, there is only need for the torque to overcome friction, so that the secondary or rotor current I_2 is almost zero. Hence

$$s\bar{E}_2 \pm \bar{E}_k \simeq 0$$

for no load. Therefore, the slip is

$$s = \mp \left| \frac{E_k}{E_2} \right|$$

$$s = \mp k \text{ (say)}.$$

E_2 is the rotor induced emf per phase measured at standstill, or at supply frequency ($s = 1$) and is therefore a constant. The slip is then directly proportional to the value of the injected voltage, and, what is important, the sign of the slip can be minus, which means that speeds above synchronism can be attained. The no-load speed is

$$n_0 = (1 \pm k)n_s$$

where n_s = synchronous speed which is determined by the supply frequency and number of stator poles.

For induction motors, especially those with a low resistance to reactance ratio, the speed variation between no-load and full load is small, so, for the sake of showing the general trend, the speed at any load is

$$n \simeq n_0 = (1 \pm k)n_s.$$

With an injected voltage allowing sub- and super-synchronous speeds, then it is reasonable to assume that actual synchronous speed can be obtained. At this speed the slip is zero and the rotor currents have zero frequency. Thus the injected voltage is a d.c. one. To make an induction motor run just at synchronous speed is a special case of the injected voltage and becomes the synchronous induction motor. Its operation is as an induction motor during starting then a direct current is injected into the rotor windings and it runs as a synchronous machine at a constant speed.

The ways of employing the injected voltage principle to get adjustable speed are many. The methods vary from the simple but wasteful method of connecting resistance across the slip-rings to the use of commutator machines to draw or return the slip power to the mains supply for maximum efficiency.

The most general way to have the rotor-induced secondary voltage and an actual injected voltage at the same frequency has been to employ a commutator on the rotor shaft to act as a frequency changer. Now the inverter can replace the commutator machine.

3.5. An auxiliary impulse-commutated inverter is depicted in a basic form in Fig. 3.60. Explain its operation, and analyse the commutation circuit to determine the maximum frequency of the inverter.

See Fig. 3.60(b) for an explanation of the operation. This is the same as Fig. 2.26 repeated here for convenience. The capacitor value must be high enough so that the effective load always has a leading power factor. When $TH1$ is turned on at $t = 0$,

$$V = \frac{1}{C} \int_0^t i_c \, dt + L \frac{di_c}{dt}. \tag{3.100}$$

If the initial value of capacitor current is

$$i_c(0+) = I \tag{3.101}$$

and the initial value of the capacitor voltage is zero, the Laplace transform of Equation (3.100) is

$$\frac{V}{s} = \frac{1}{sC} i_c(s) + Lsi_c(s) - LI,$$ (3.102)

so that

$$i_c(s) = \frac{v/L + sI}{s^2 + 1/LC}.$$ (3.103)

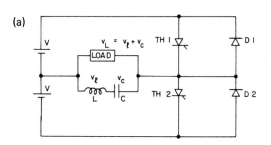

(a)

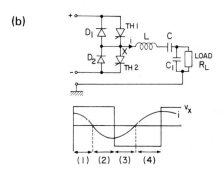

(b)

Fig. 3.60.   (a), (b) Auxiliary impuse-commutated inverter.

Therefore the inverse transform provides

$$i_c(t) = \frac{v}{s} \sin \omega t + I \cos \omega t$$ (3.104)

where

$$x = \sqrt{\frac{L}{C}}$$

and

$$\omega = \sqrt{\frac{1}{LC}}.$$

Similarly

$$v_c = V + xI \sin \omega t - V \cos \omega t. \tag{3.105}$$

The period T of the square-wave voltage across the load is the time of a complete cycle, $TH1$ on, $D1$ on and $TH1$ off, $TH2$ on, and $D2$ on and $TH2$ off. This is the same as the period of v_c. Let

$$T = \frac{2\pi + \theta}{\omega}. \tag{3.106}$$

The peak commutation current occurs when

$$\omega t = \frac{\theta}{4}$$

in Equation (3.104) so that

$$\hat{I}_c = \frac{v}{x} \sin \frac{\theta}{4} + I \cos \frac{\theta}{4}. \tag{3.107}$$

The value of I is obtained from Equation (3.104) by finding i_c at the end of a half cycle which is when

$$\omega t = \frac{\omega T}{2} = \pi + \frac{\theta}{2}.$$

Therefore

$$I = \frac{v}{x} \cot \frac{\theta}{4}. \tag{3.108}$$

The peak voltage $\hat{v}_c$ across the capacitor occurs when

$$\omega t = \frac{\pi}{2} + \frac{\theta}{4}$$

and is

$$\hat{v}_c = V + xI \cos \frac{\theta}{4} + V \sin \frac{\theta}{4}. \tag{3.109}$$

Substitution for I in this equation gives

$$\hat{v}_c = V \left(1 + \operatorname{cosec} \frac{\theta}{4}\right). \tag{3.110}$$

The two products

$$\frac{C\hat{v}_c^2}{TIV} = \frac{(1 + \operatorname{cosec} \theta/4)^2}{(2\pi + \theta) \cot \theta/4} \tag{3.111}$$

and

$$\frac{L\hat{i}_c^2}{TIV} = \frac{\sec^2(\theta/4) \cot(\theta/4)}{2\pi + \theta} \tag{3.112}$$

are proportional to the energy storage ratings or the capacitor and the inductor respectively. The sum is a minimum when $\theta/4$ is nearly $45°$, which is the optimum choice of $\theta/4$. The time t_{off} available for turn-off is the time that a diode conducts before the next thyristor is turned on, so that

$$t_{off} = \frac{(\theta/2)}{\omega} = \frac{(\theta/4)T}{\pi + (\theta/2)} \tag{3.113}$$

when

$$\frac{\theta}{4} \simeq \frac{\pi}{4}$$

then

$$t_{off} = \frac{T}{6}. \tag{3.114}$$

This last equation determines the maximum frequency at which the inverter can operate.

NOTE
    Additional problems on page 212

4 Direct current motor control

The direct current machine was manufactured before the beginning of this century when the available power supply was direct current. Great numbers of d.c. motors are still made today because their characteristics are so well suited to many variable-speed drives.

There are many disadvantages associated with d.c. motors. Special d.c. power supplies must be provided. For the same power, d.c. machines are larger in size and cost more than induction motors. The d.c. motor requires special measures for starting, except for the smallest motors, to limit the inrush current. There is also the need for more maintenance than for the induction motor because of the commutator. Commutators offer other limitations. Current transport from stationary to rotating conductors involves sliding contacts, which make and break current in the winding coils. The result represents frequency changing. There is brush wear from friction and arcing and sparking. The maximum voltage between the segments of a commutator is about 20 V for successful commutation. Therefore, d.c. machines cannot be rated much above 600 V. Induction motors can have kV across their terminals.

There are a few advantages associated with d.c. motors. Their inherent characteristics lend themselves to high starting torques, which are required for traction drives. Their speed range is large both above and below the rated values. Finally the methods of control are in most cases simpler and less costly than the methods of control of a.c. motors to obtain the same performance. These few advantages are enough to make the disadvantages insignificant provided that the application is not for a constant speed drive.

4.2. STARTING DIRECT CURRENT MOTORS

All but the smallest motors must be controlled during the starting operation in order to prevent the input current to the machine rising to a dangerous level where the heating would damage the insulation.

The principles of starting do not change but the techniques to limit the current to acceptable values do in order to suit environmental and economic factors. When resistors are switched out of the circuit mechanically, by either a sliding contact or contactors, there is arcing and sparking and hence wear at the contacts. Strict maintenance is required. However, these conventional methods are cheap.

The use of power electronics can eliminate all moving parts in a resistance starter, or thyristors can be used to replace the conventional starter altogether, especially if the thyristors are also used for subsequent speed control.

4.2.1. Thyristors and the resistance starter

Figure 4.1 illustrates one arrangement whereby thyristors do the work of contactors in an automatic starter and thus eliminate the moving parts. When the low-power starting switch S_1 is closed, thyristor $TH1$ is turned on and

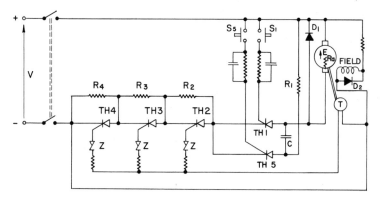

Fig. 4.1.   A resistance starter with no moving parts.

armature current flows. The current is limited by the resistances R_2, R_3 and R_4. This starting switch, S_1, handles mW of power or at the most a few watts whereas the conventional contactor may have to handle power thousands of times greater. Full field current flows as soon as the main switch is closed.

The starting procedure is now automatic. The commutating capacitor C charges up as soon as armature current flows. The armature current and field current produce an electromagnetic torque to accelerate the armature and load: the armature back emf E increases as the speed increases; the armature current drops; the voltage of the tacho-generator increases as the speed increases until the zenor diode, Z_2 breaks down and $TH2$ is triggered into the conduction state; resistance R_2 is short-circuited by $TH2$; the armature current increases once more; the torque increases; the speed increases and the cycle is repeated until all the resistance elements are short-circuited and the motor is running at its rated speed. The Zener diodes Z_2, Z_3 and Z_4 can be rated for, $\frac{1}{3}, \frac{1}{2}$ and $\frac{3}{4}$ full speed, respectively, and the resistances are graded to limit the current surges to acceptable values.

To stop the motor, *TH5* is turned on by closing S_5. The discharge of *C* reverse biases *TH1* and turns it off. All current to the motor armature ceases so that *TH2*, *TH3* and *TH4* will block.

4.2.2. Thyristor starting without resistance

To eliminate resistances altogether involves the principle termed 'voltage chopping'. The supply is switched on and off rapidly to give a variable ratio of the time the voltage is on to the time off. This ratio is sometimes called the mark-space ratio and varying it alters the average voltage and hence the average current of the armature. A low average voltage is needed to limit the current while the motor is being started and gradually the mark-space ratio is

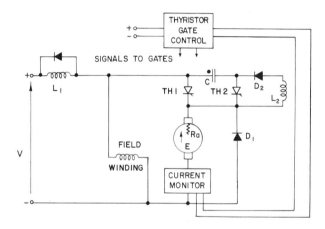

Fig. 4.2.   A motor starter without resistance.

increased to reach a maximum at rated speed. The thyristor circuit which accomplishes this is called a 'chopper'.

Without resistance the system is more efficient and, what might be of greater advantage, this method can be made to be automatic and the starting time can be optimized.

Only a brief outline will be given here as choppers in general are treated in detail in the section on d.c. motor speed control. Figure 4.2 depicts a basic chopper circuit without including all the thyristor protection. This chopper is of the resonating or oscillating *LC* turn-off type incorporating an auxiliary thyristor for controlled commutation.

Thyristor, *TH1*, is switched on for a particular interval. The armature current rises to a value determined by this interval and the value of the circuit resistance. The rate of rise of the current is limited by the armature inductance and an added smoothing choke L_1 which protects the thyristor also. *TH1* is then switched off for a particular interval, during which time the armature current decays through the diode, *D1*. The source supplies no current during this latter period. Repetition of this cycle is continued until rated speed is reached.

One way to accomplish the best mark-space ratio, that is, to get the motor up to speed as quickly as possible, is to include a current monitoring device in series with the armature. When the current rises to a predetermined value, as in Fig. 4.3, a signal from the monitor is used to turn off the main thyristor and when the current falls to a particular value another signal from that monitor allows the thyristor to be switched on again.

Turn-on is accomplished by applying a signal to $TH1$ gate, but turn-off requires a second thyristor $TH2$. The resonating circuit comprises $TH2$, the capacitor, C, the diode $D2$ and the inductor L_2. The sequence of operation requires that $TH2$ should receive a gate signal first. This turns it on and allows

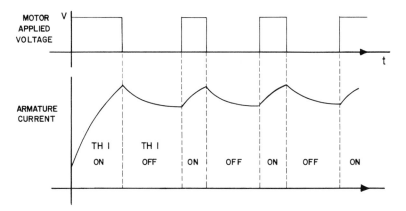

Fig. 4.3.   Armature current controlled by the mark-space ratio.

C to charge up positively at the dot. As soon as C is charged up, $TH2$ turns-off naturally because the voltage across it reduces to zero.

A gate signal can now be applied to $TH1$ which allows current to flow in the armature of the motor. At the same time, C discharges through $TH1$, the circuit being completed by L_2 and $D2$. Due to the oscillating nature of this circuit, introduced by L_2, C not only discharges but recharges with reversed polarity and $D2$ enables this charge to be held. The voltage is now $+V$ at the dot shown in the figure and nearly $+2V$ at the other plate. When the armature current has risen to the allowable maximum, a signal is again applied to the gate of $TH2$ to turn it on. The discharge of C through $TH2$ reverse biases $TH1$ which is then switched off. The cycle is not repeated again until the armature current falls to a value to allow the monitor indirectly to switch on $TH1$ again.

The whole concept of this circuit makes it more versatile than for starting. In addition, speed may be adjusted by altering the average voltage and large on-off servomotors can also embrace this form of control.

4.3. SPEED CONTROL OF DIRECT CURRENT MOTORS

Intimately concerned with adjustable speed control is the reversal and regenerative or dynamic braking of the machine.

For speed adjustment the controlling parameters can be seen from an examination of the main steady state equations

$$E = \frac{p}{a} \phi n Z \qquad (4.1)$$

$$V = E - IR_a \qquad (4.2)$$

and

$$\phi = K_1 I_f, \qquad (4.3)$$

where

E = armature induced emf (V)
p = pole pairs
a = pairs of parallel armature coil paths
ϕ = maximum flux per pole (Wb)
n = armature speed (rps)
Z = total number of armature conductors in series
V = supply voltage or terminal voltage (V)
I = armature current (A)
R_a = total armature resinstance (Ω)
K_1 = a constant over much of the magnetizing curve and
I_f = field winding current (A).

Thus the speed equation is

$$n = \frac{V - IR_a}{K I_f}. \qquad (4.4)$$

The armature current is an extensive quantity depending on the load. The intensive quantities are V, R_a and I_f. It is the latter three parameters which provide the speed control. Speed is proportional to applied voltage if the armature voltage drop is small. A reduction of speed results from an increase in the equivalent armature resistance, or just by resistance added to the line. A speed increase is caused by a decrease in field current. Each individual method has limits but a combination of the methods enables any speed control application to be accommodated, whether it be speed adjustment with constant torque, constant horsepower or both variable. In terms of the extensive variables the speed is directly proportional to the induced or back emf E and inversely proportional to the main field flux.

There are three types of d.c. motors, shunt, compound and series field types. All have different relationships between the variables voltage, current and flux. Accordingly the inherent torque-speed characteristics differ. It is the number of control variables and the number of different characteristics that make the d.c. motor such a versatile machine.

4.3.1. Thyristor speed control

The general principles of speed control have been established. Thyristors can be used in various combinations but whatever the choice, the overall problem is either the voltage adjustment of the supply to the armature or the supply to the field winding. Of course, it could be both.

The type of supply can be either alternating or direct current. A matching thyristor unit can be placed between the supply and the d.c. motor to effect speed control. There are two main types of thyristor unit. One is a thyristor converter for a.c. supplies and the other is a chopper for d.c. supplies. In place of the former type it is possible to use an uncontrolled converter, which provides a constant d.c. voltage, followed by a thyristor chopper to give an adjustable average d.c. voltage output.

There are many variations of every basic thyristor circuit and different forms of control to give reliable operation and degrees of speed regulation. Only a few examples can be given to suggest methods of building specific systems from generalities. The bibliography at the end of this chapter gives a broad range of specific examples of d.c. motor speed control.

4.3.2. Thyristor controlled rectifier converters

The converter[1] is used when the supply is alternating and the motor to be controlled is a d.c. machine. Besides the individual motor control, converters are used for the generator field control for the Ward Leonard set or they may replace the motor generator set or mercury arc rectifier set altogether. Although in most cases the thyristor converter is slightly more expensive, it is more efficient over the whole of the speed and load ranges and installation costs are less.

There are disadvantages when using thyristors to replace a Ward Leonard set. Unlike a generator, which can motor inherently on regenerative braking, the direction of current flow in the converter cannot be reversed. To overcome this problem where regeneration is required the converter must be capable of inverting so that the arms of the bridge must be controlled. For inversion, motor field reversal can be used where slow response is satisfactory. For rapid response or accurate position control, two banks of thyristor converters in back-to-back opposition must be used.

The converter type depends on the power to be handled and how much voltage ripple will be tolerated. For low powers, below 20 kW, single-phase circuits are adequate but they themselves can take different forms. Fig. 4.4 shows the possible configurations for single-phase uncontrolled rectifiers. For the half wave case of Fig. 4.4(a), when the a.c. supply is positive at the dot in the figure, the diode D has virtually zero impedance and the full supply voltage appears as a varying d.c. voltage across the load, R_{load}. When the dot becomes negative over the second half cycle the diode blocks current and appears as infinite impedance, so that all the voltage of the supply appears across the diode and there is zero applied voltage across the load. For the other cases shown, the diodes have the same action but are arranged to make

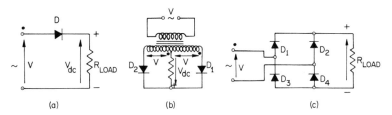

Fig. 4.4. Single-phase uncontrolled rectifiers: (a) half wave circuit; (b) full wave centre-tap supply circuit; (c) full wave bridge circuit.

better use of the available voltage. When the dot is positive, $D1$ conducts and when negative over the other half cycle, $D2$ conducts. The waveforms of the voltage are those in Fig. 4.5.

For higher powers the bridge arrangements can be extended to a three-phase supply or a multiphase centre-tap. Voltage ripple is also much reduced in magnitude and increased in frequency. The circuit may be half wave, full wave bridge, centre-tap or even double star as in Fig. 4.6 with the

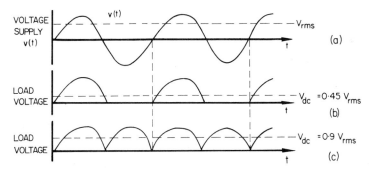

Fig. 4.5. Rectifier voltage waveforms: (a) supply voltage; (b) half wave output voltage; (c) centre-tap and full-wave bridge output voltage.

waveforms as in Fig. 4.7. All these uncontrolled rectifiers give an output d.c. voltage which has a constant average value. It is the replacement of some or all of the diodes by thyristors that enables the output voltage to be adjusted. The method of adjustment is phase control and the method of thyristor commutation is natural, or phase, commutation. Each thyristor experiences an alternating voltage from the supply so that it is reverse biased every half cycle and turns off. The basic circuits with some of the waveforms are shown in Fig. 4.8. No transformers, filters, protection or gating circuits are shown.

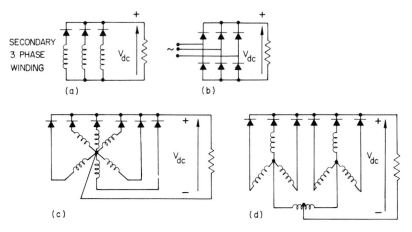

Fig. 4.6. Three-phase rectifier circuits: (a) half wave; (b) full-wave bridge; (c) centre-tap; (d) double star.

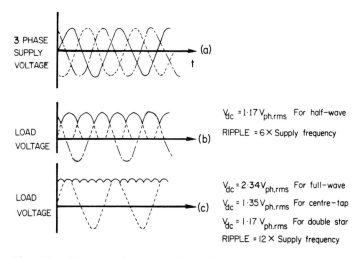

Fig. 4.7. Output voltage waveforms from a three-phase supply.

(a) Single-phase, half wave converter

Because only half the available power can be utilized the circuit of Fig. 4.8(a) is limited to fractional horsepower machines. Not shown is an isolation transformer which would be used and besides isolation, voltage matching is

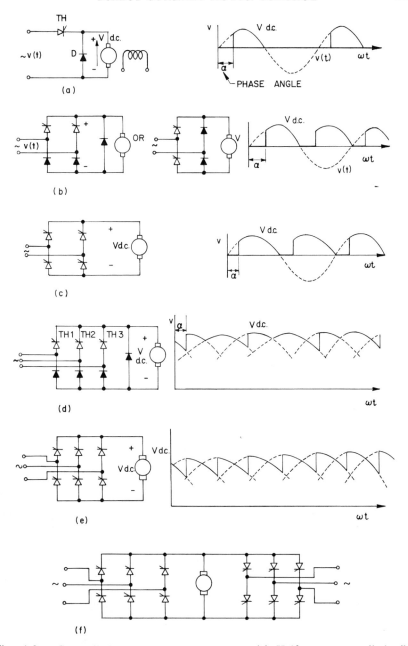

Fig. 4.8. Controlled converter arrangements. (a) Half-wave controlled; (b) full-wave, half-controlled single-phase bridge; (c) full-wave, fully controlled single-phase bridge; (d) full-wave, half-controlled, three-phase bridge; (e) full-wave, fully controlled, three-phase bridge; (f) full-wave, fully controlled, double bridge.

achieved. Also, the inductance aids converter commutation, and improves the
d.c. waveform which aids motor commutation.

The freewheeling diode is needed to dissipate the stored energy in the
inductive load when the thyristor blocks. Without it, the thyristor would have
to provide the current path and this is damaging.

Of all the converter circuits, the form factor, given by

$$\text{form factor} = \frac{\text{rms } V(\text{or } I)}{\text{average } V(\text{or } I)},\tag{4.5}$$

for this circuit is the highest and hence poorest. This indicates a relatively low
average value and for a d.c. machine the average value is the useful value. It
further indicates a relatively high effective value of current with its inherently
high ripple which causes both heating and motor commutation problems.

The angle α in Fig. 4.8 is the gating or phase angle or the instantaneous
point in the a.c. cycle at which the thyristor is turned on. As α is increased,

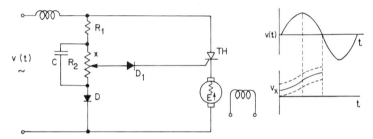

Fig. 4.9.   Half wave converter with 180° firing angle control.

the output voltage is decreased and so the motor speed would be reduced. A
circuit to give almost 180° firing range is shown in Fig. 4.9. The phase
shifting network R_1, R_2, C and D enables a voltage at x to be lagging nearly
90° behind the supply voltage and the potential divider provides an adjustable
d.c. level. It is the ramp shape of v_x which is so useful. A particular d.c. bias
of v_x sets the desired speed because at a particular value of v_x the thyristor
will be turned on and the armature will have current flowing through it. An
increase of the effective d.c. level of the ramp means that the thyristor fires
earlier in the cycle. This produces a higher average load voltage and a higher
speed.

Although far from perfect, the motor armature in the circuit provides
simple feedback to give lower speed regulation than if the motor were in the
anode circuit. If an increased load is applied to the motor, the speed will tend
to drop and the induced emf, E, will also tend to drop. As the voltage v_x,
which triggers the thyristor is equal to the voltage drops across the diode, the
armature resistance drop, the gate to cathode voltage drop plus the back emf,
E, then the thyristor will fire earlier in the cycle. A smaller α means more

power and an increased speed until, ideally, the emf is back to the same E and hence the motor is back to the same speed as before.

(b) Single-phase full-wave converter

The bridge has the advantage over the centre-tapped supply circuit, because, for the same d.c. voltage output the centre-tapped converter has twice the a.c. voltage to block. Compared with the previous half-wave circuit, this one, shown in Fig. 4.8(b) and (c) has a much improved form factor. Therefore, less derating of the motor is required. The motor drives controlled in this manner vary from 1 to 20 kW. In the half-controlled circuit of Fig. 4.8(b), where no inversion can take place, the first circuit has a freewheeling diode added whereas the second circuit has inherent freewheeling. In the fully controlled bridge of Fig. 4.8(c) inversion, and so regenerative braking, is possible, but if the bridge is not to be doubled then the polarity of the motor field winding must be reversed. Where regeneration is not required, only the half-controlled circuits would be used.

Worked example 4.1. Analyse one of the full wave, half controlled converters of Fig. 4.8(b).

A practical circuit is shown in Fig. 4.10. The phase angle for conduction adjustment is controlled by the resistances R in the gate circuit. Only a 90° range of α is provided in this specific example although 180° can easily be obtained. Figure 4.11 shows the form of the applied voltage and current to the motor.

At a phase angle α equal to θ_1 in Fig. 4.11 the resistance R has been set so that one of the thyristors fires at every half cycle. For the case of steady motoring conditions and hence a constant motor induced emf E, the current $i(t)$ from the supply rises slowly because of armature and line inductance. This inductance prolongs conduction after the voltage across the terminals becomes

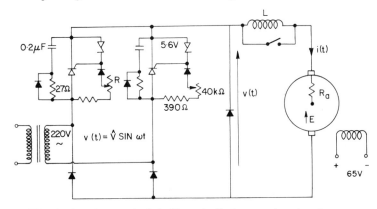

Fig. 4.10. A practical, half controlled converter circuit.

negative, until the current becomes zero and the terminal voltage becomes equal to E.

Because of the back emf E, current will only flow from the supply while the thyristors are fired between α_1 and α_2 in Fig. 4.11. The remaining conduction, between α_2 and θ_2 is due to the stored energy, $\frac{1}{2}Li^2$. A path for this current is provided by the freewheeling diode.

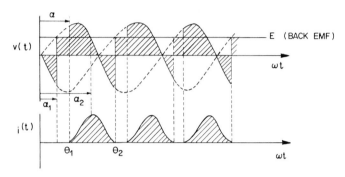

Fig. 4.11.   Applied voltage and current to the motor of Fig. 4.10.

The solution of the transient circuit equation

$$L \frac{di}{dt} + R_a i = \hat{V} \sin \omega t - E \tag{4.6}$$

is

$$i(t) = A\, e^{-R_a t/L} + \frac{\hat{V}}{\sqrt{R_a^2 + \omega^2 L^2}} \sin (\omega t - \phi) - \frac{E}{R_a}, \tag{4.7}$$

where A is a constant and

$$\phi = \tan^{-1} \frac{\omega L}{R_a}. \tag{4.8}$$

The constant A is found from the conditions that at

$$\omega t = \theta_1 \tag{4.9}$$

then

$$i(t) = 0. \tag{4.10}$$

There are two conditions to consider.

First, when the current is discontinuous,

$$\theta_1 > \theta_2 - \pi \tag{4.11}$$

and

$$i(t) = \frac{\hat{V}}{R_a} \left\{ \cos \phi \sin (\omega t - \phi) - \frac{E}{\hat{V}} + \left[\frac{E}{\hat{V}} - \cos \phi \sin (\theta_1 - \theta) \right] e^{-(R_a/\omega L)(\omega t - \theta_1)} \right\}$$

$$\tag{4.12}$$

over the range

$$\theta_1 \leqslant \omega t \leqslant \theta_2. \tag{4.13}$$

Second, when the current is continuous

$$\theta_2 - \theta_1 > \pi$$

and

$$i(t) = \frac{\hat{V}}{R_a} \left\{ \cos\phi \sin(\omega t - \phi) - \frac{E}{\hat{V}} - \frac{2\cos\phi \sin(\theta_1 - \phi) \cdot e^{-(R_a/\omega L)(\omega t - \theta_1)}}{(1 - e^{-(\pi R_a/\omega L)})} \right\} \tag{4.14}$$

using the range

$$\omega t = \theta_1 \tag{4.15}$$

and

$$\omega t = \theta_2 = \theta_1 + \pi. \tag{4.16}$$

The torque is

$$T = \frac{E I_{av}}{2\pi n} = \frac{(v - I_{av}R_a)}{2\pi n} \cdot I_{av}. \tag{4.17}$$

For limited conduction

$$T = \frac{\theta_2 - \theta_1}{\pi} \cdot \frac{(v - I_{av}R_a)}{2\pi n} \cdot I_{av} \tag{4.18}$$

but

$$I_{av} = \frac{1}{\pi} \int_{\theta_1}^{\theta_2} \frac{\hat{V}\sin\omega t - E}{R_a} \, d(\omega t) \tag{4.19}$$

so that, for limited conduction

$$I_{av} = \frac{\hat{V}}{\pi R_a} \left[\cos\theta_1 - \cos\theta_2 - \frac{E}{\hat{V}}(\theta_2 - \theta_1) \right] \tag{4.20}$$

and for continuous conduction

$$I_{av} = \frac{\hat{V}}{\pi R_a} \left(2\cos\theta_1 - \frac{E}{\hat{V}}\pi \right). \tag{4.21}$$

Regulation of speed would then be expected to be greater for the discontinuous range than for the continuous range. Practical results are shown in Fig. 4.12.

For the speed to become independent of the load, velocity feedback must be used. As the induced emf is proportional to the speed a signal proportional to this voltage could be used for feedback. To measure this actual voltage is impossible. The next best thing is to take the applied voltage and subtract from it a voltage equal to the 'IR_a' drop and this is possible because a voltage across any resistance in the line is proportional to the armature 'resistance' drop. The non-steady state circuit operation with phase control does add to the difficulties.

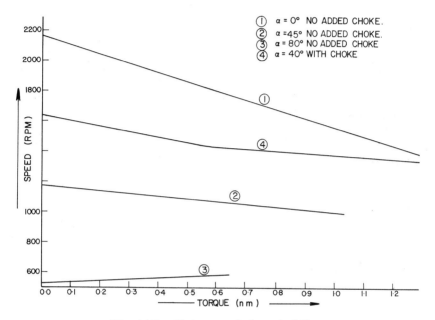

Fig. 4.12.   Motor speed characteristics.

(c) Three-phase controlled converters

Figure 4.8(d), (e) and (f) show some but not all of the arrangements which are used from a few kW up the hundreds of kW for (d) and (e), and up to the 2000 kW mark for (f). It is this arrangement which competes with the Ward Leonard set, replacing the a.c. driving motor and the d.c. generator and eliminating all the moving parts except the final motor drive.

Figure 4.8(f) allows reversal of rotation and regeneration. For the fastest response both bridges are fired at once but this does require the addition of inductors to limit the bridge circulating current. This condition is armature current forcing which is more rapid than field current forcing because of the difference in circuit inductance.

For high voltage (600 V is a high voltage for a d.c. machine) two bridges can be used in series for sharing. Where inversion is not required then one of those bridges can be uncontrolled. With a free firing diode bridge the equipment operates at reduced kVAr. Further, all the bridge arrangements shown in Fig. 4.13 are to be seen to be high voltage versions of Fig. 4.8(d), (e) and (f). The two secondaries are phase displaced by 30°. This results in a higher power factor and a lower harmonic distortion of the current drawn from the supply. The boxed rectifiers in the figure represent three-phase converters.

(d) Armature and field control

The Figs.4.8 and 4.13 both have the motor armature as the converter load. In this case the increase in phase angle α produces a speed reduction below a rated value. With a fully controlled converter, inversion can take place but reversal is only possible if there is a double, back-to-back, fully controlled converter.

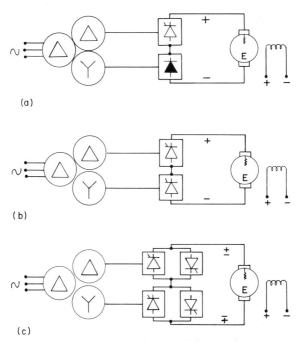

(a)

(b)

(c)

Fig. 4.13. High voltage converters. (a) Series bridges, half-controlled; (b) series bridges, fully controlled; (c) series, double bridges, fully controlled.

The double converter can be fired separately for each direction of rotation or regenerative braking or both can be fired together for a faster response. The choice of converter depends on the power involved and how smooth the current is required to be without filtering.

Such armature control is the static version of the Ward Leonard set. The only advantage of the latter seems to be its inherent capability of regenerative braking. The thyristor converter, however, needs similar control circuits for voltage and current protection and for feedback loops, and, if a double converter is used separately, then current detection is imperative so that changeover does not occur while armature current flows.

Nothing has been written about the thyristor firing circuits of the converters. Very little new could be added that has not been treated generally in the previous two chapters. The sequence of firing the thyristors remains the same as for the inverters, and the type of firing circuits for phase control really is the choice of the designer. The general form, already described, is the use of the supply voltage as a reference signal for the phase. However, the sine wave is usually converted to a sawtooth wave whose d.c. level can be controlled, and then follows a schmitt trigger and a bistable and a differentiating amplifier and a gating output and a pulse amplifier. Finally the signal might reach the thyristor gate by means of an isolation transformer. The following worked example describes the thyristor firing circuits accommodated in the logic network.

The foregoing explanation of armature control by converters can equally apply to field control except that an increase in phase angle produces an

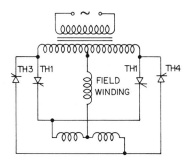

Fig. 4.14.   Thyristor amplifier for field control.

increased speed. Here the powers involved are never more than a few kW, so it is possible to use a field amplifier of the form shown in Fig. 4.4(b) is which the diodes must be replaced by thyristors. The term amplifier is used because the controlling signals are those to the gate triggering circuits whose power requirements are so small compared with the thyristor output to the field winding. A basic circuit which has been used for continental traction is shown in Fig. 4.14. In this way the traction motor field becomes separately excited, by voltage phase control, to permit reversal and braking without mechanical contractors. It will be appreciated that the operation of this centre-tapped supply converter is the reverse of the $C1$ inverter described in the previous chapter. No capacitor is needed because of the a.c. line commutation and the feedback diodes are replaced by thyristors $TH3$ and $TH4$ for inversion and reversal.

Even when field forcing is used the response cannot compare with that of armature control.

Worked example 4.2. The field coil of a large d.c. motor has an inductance of 1 H and a resistance of 1 Ω. Its rated current is 30 A. It is required that the rated current should be regulated to within 0.1 per cent and that the current be reversed in the shortest possible time. Design a thyristor converter with these specifications.

This is an example of a bidirectional converter to be used to regulate and reverse the current in a field excitation system. A brief outline of the design requirements are suggested here. More exact details of the component values and logic circuitry are described in Appendix II.

An excitation coil has a high inductance which prevents a rapid change of current and which stores magnetic energy. These characteristics tend to prevent current reversal occuring in a short time. For example, since the coil has an inductance of 1 H and a resistance of 1 Ω, its time constant is 1 s. A little more than 8 s is needed to reverse the current by natural decay and rise. The time can be speeded up. From the instant a voltage is applied to a coil,

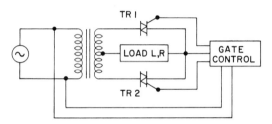

Fig. 4.15.   Power circuit.

the rise time of the current to reach its final steady value can be decreased by field forcing. That is, a higher voltage is applied initially, the current rises more quickly and the voltage is reduced when the current reaches its desired value.

Instead of removing the supply voltage and allowing the current to flow through a freewheeling diode to decay to zero, the converter can be used as an inverter to pump the stored energy back into the supply. When the current is zero the voltage applied to the coil can be reversed and field forcing used again.

To regulate the direct current in the excitation coil, to field force, to return the energy stored in the magnetic field to the supply and to reverse the direct current requires a phase controlled a.c. supply.

Figure 4.15 shows the power circuit and Fig. 4.16 indicates a typical load voltage waveform. This waveform is ideal. It assumes that transients have died away and that the source has zero impedance. When the voltage across the load becomes zero this is an indication that the current through a rectifying element has become zero and that the element blocks further current flow

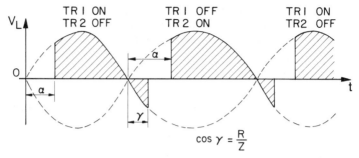

Fig. 4.16.　Load voltage waveform.

until another trigger signal is applied. The rectifying element in Fig. 4.15 is a triac. A pair of back to back thyristors in opposition could be used. The choice depends on the load characteristics and economics. The triac or double thyristor is used so that the load current can be reversed.

If the phase angle α, at which the triac is switched, is altered then the power flow to the load changes. The control of the phase angle is then an important aspect of design. The triggering signal must be both synchronized to the supply and have an adjustable delay. The sinusoidal voltage is not the best waveshape for switching. A good waveshape is given by a rectangular pulse because of the rapid rise time of the signal. The rectangular pulse is obtained from the sinusoid if a pulse shaper circuit is used. Figure 4.17 shows such a

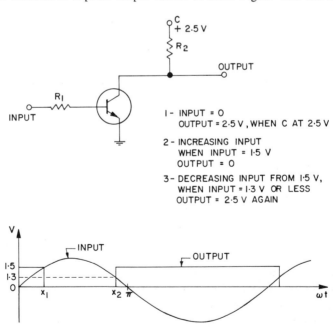

Fig. 4.17.　Pulse shaper.

pulse shaper. It is an integrated circuit and the figure indicates the characteristics. For an input up to 1.3 V the output is 1 (binary form) and for an input greater than 1.5 V the output is 0 (binary form). The backlash is 0.2 V.

In order that the variation of supply voltage should have little effect on the position of switching, x_1 and x_2 in Fig. 4.17, it is desirable that the

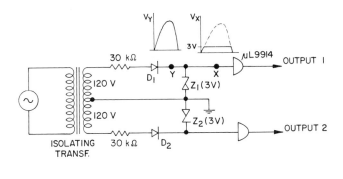

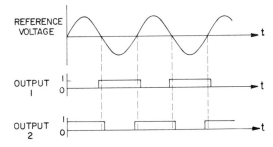

Fig. 4.18. Reference voltage circuit and output voltages to the triac trigger control circuit.

magnitude of the input sinusoid be large. For a sinusoidal voltage, whose regulation is ± 10 per cent, and whose rms value is 2.5 V

$$22°45' \leqslant x_1 \leqslant 28°12';$$

whereas if its rms value is 120 V

$$28' \leqslant x \leqslant 33'.$$

Although the high voltage is convenient, it becomes necessary to protect the pulse shaper. Zener diodes can provide the protection so that the reference square waves can be obtained from such a circuit as that illustrated in Fig. 4.18. The pulse shaper is part of an *IC* logic *NOR* gate and used here because the output, when switched, has a very short rise time. Each micro logic unit consists of two *NOR* elements. If only one input is used each element is a *NOT* element.

One of the requirements is that the current in the excitation coil should be regulated. A simple feedback loop, whereby a signal proportional to the difference between a reference and the actual current either increases or decreases the phase angle, is needed. While there is no difference between the reference and actual currents the phase angle is constant. A delay circuit using logic elements is shown in Fig. 4.19 where the input at A is the inverse of the

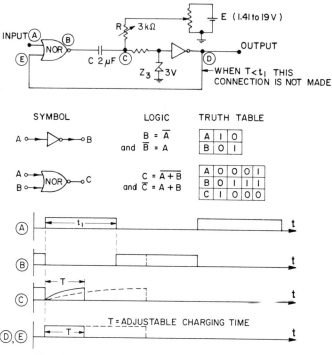

Fig. 4.19. Delay circuit for the phase angle α.

pulse shaper output of Fig. 4.18. The circuit is a one-shot multivibrator with a single dual gate, the length of the pulse in seconds being given by

$$T = \frac{KRC}{E}$$

K = constant = 1.85

The circuit can be understood by the accompanying explanation of the logic symbols and the signal diagram with an without inputs. An application of an input signal will initiate an output signal for an adjustable length of time T.

The outputs of the pulse shaper in Fig. 4.18 overlap for part of the cycle. This is inadvisable because the application of a signal to each triac simultaneously could result in the power transformer of Fig. 4.15 being short-circuited. The signal overlap is eliminated if a *NOR* element is added in series with the pulse shaper outputs.

The output of the multivibrator cannot be used to trigger the triac because the signal is initiated at the same point in the cycle every cycle. The added logic circuitry to alter the time of rise of a signal with respect to the reference, that is to alter the phase angle α, is shown in Fig. 4.20. The double *NOR* gate makes the signal more 'square'. In essence, by reducing the time T

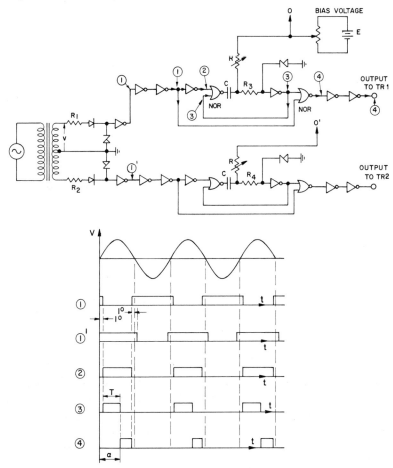

Fig. 4.20.   Phase angle control circuits for current regulation and a single time chart.

of the multivibrator of Fig. 4.19 the phase angle α, as shown in the signal time chart of Fig. 4.20, is reduced. A decreased α means an increased current in the load.

Operation of the converter would be controlled by units shown in block form in Fig. 4.21. When starting, field forcing is obtained by making the phase angle zero. Full voltage is applied to the converter so that the rate of rise of current is a maximum. There is a step change of α from zero to about

70° when 30 A has been reached. The current is regulated at this value. In order to reverse the current in a minimum time the current is brought to zero by inversion. The phase angle is step-changed to about 177° so that the field coil acts as a generator and the magnetic stored energy is returned to the supply. At zero current field forcing occurs again to drive the current rapidly in the opposite direction.

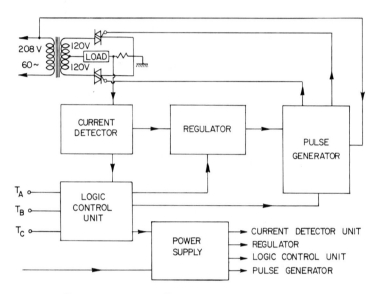

Fig. 4.21.   Block diagram of the control circuit.

(e) Converter voltage ripple

The problem of motor commutation is increased when converters replace the d.c. generators and becomes even more critical when phase control is introduced. Voltage ripple creates a problem because of the larger value of the voltage of self-induction $[L(\mathrm{d}i/\mathrm{d}t)]$ due to the current rate of change.

The effect of voltage ripple on the motor commutation is seen by inspection of the voltage equation

$$v(t) = L\frac{\mathrm{d}i}{\mathrm{d}t} + E + iR_a \qquad (4.22)$$

where

$v(t)$ = instantaneous terminal voltage
L = armature inductance
i = instantaneous armature current
E = motor back emf, assumed constant and
R_a = equivalent resistance between motor terminals.

Had the supply voltage been ripple free then

$$V_D = E + IR_a \qquad (4.23)$$

would have been the equation of steady state. If the small armature resistance drop is neglected, then $L(di/dt)$ makes up for the instantaneous difference of voltage existing between the terminal voltage, $v(t)$, and induced emf, E. This is shown in Fig. 4.22 for a three-phase converter. Because V_D and E remain substantially constant for constant load and speed, then $L(di/dt)$ must change drastically with its adverse effect on motor commutation. Further, $L(di/dt)$ increases with increase of phase angle α.

Added to commutation difficulties are the heating effects of the current ripple which can produce no useful work. The armature loss, or copper loss, is proportional to the square of the armature current so any ripple results in higher copper loss. Ripple current also increases the iron losses in the armature core and non-laminated parts of any interpole because of the cross magnetizing component of armature reaction.

This is enough to see the importance of having filters in the line to eliminate harmonics on the a.c. side and to smooth the d.c. side.

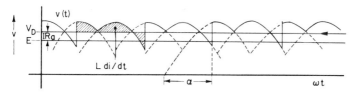

Fig. 4.22.   Voltage ripple.

4.3.3. Thyristor voltage choppers

Control of a motor's speed by a thyristor voltage chopper is expected where the supply is direct current or where an uncontrolled converter has already rectified the a.c. supply. It is the case that a d.c. supply is most needed for traction purposes, whether because of the necessity of storage in batteries or whether because of the superior torque-speed characteristics of the d.c. machine, so voltage choppers find most application in this field.

As the name chopper implies, a d.c. voltage can be switched on and off by a thyristor in a form shown in Fig. 4.23. This means that, although the input voltage is constant, the average or d.c. voltage can be adjusted. There are three ways of obtaining the variable mark-space ratio or time on to time off (time ratio control, TRC) for voltage control,

(1) t_{on} constant and T (or frequency) adjustable
(2) T constant and t_{on} adjustable or
(3) t_{on} and T both adjustable, and for all three

$$V_0 = V t_{on}/T. \qquad (4.24)$$

The frequency of switching is made high so that filtering is minimal and the response is high compared with the power frequency phase controlled methods of voltage adjustment. Frequencies between 500 and 2000 Hz are common. At higher frequencies the commutating capacitors do not have sufficient time to charge up.

Three chopper circuits are described, the Morgan, Jones and oscillation circuits, but only the latter is analysed in any detail.

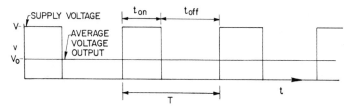

Fig. 4.23.   Voltage chopping.

(a) The Morgan chopper

This circuit, as shown in Fig. 4.24, is characterized by class (b) commutation, that is self-commutation by a resonating circuit aided by a saturable reactor, and its major advantage is that it uses only one thyristor. Hence the time on, t_{on}, is fixed by the LC parameters and the average voltage across the motor is altered by adjusting T. That is, the gating oscillator generates a variable frequency.

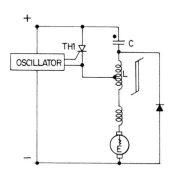

Fig. 4.24.   The Morgan chopper.

When thyristor $TH1$ is fired, the capacitor, positive at the dot in the figure, discharges around the C, $TH1$ and L circuit to acquire a reverse polarity. As the current again reverses the voltage across L is held for a certain time and then saturation occurs so that the whole of the capacitor voltage appears across the thyristor. The thyristor is reverse biased and, if the discharge current is greater than the thyristor load current, the thyristor turns off. The capacitor continues to carry load current until it charges up fully with the dot positive again. The freewheeling diode will provide a path to dissipate further stored energy ($\frac{1}{2}Li^2$) and if that is dissipated before the thyristor is turned on again the motor will coast.

It is possible, among a number of variations, to add a reverse diode across the thyristor to provide impulse commutation, as described in the section on inverters.

Although the frequency of switching is under the precise control of the oscillator, the time $TH1$ is on can be affected by fluctuations of the load.

(b) The Jones chopper

This circuit, shown basically in Fig. 4.25 is characterized by class (d) commutation, that is, a charged capacitor switched by an auxiliary thyristor, $TH2$, and the autotransformer, T. Because of $TH2$, both the on time, t_{on} and the off time t_{off} can be varied, but as shown in the figure the off time, t_{off}

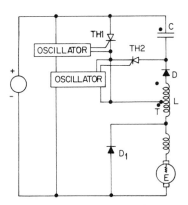

Fig. 4.25. The Jones chopper.

or period T is the controlled parameter governed by means of the $TH1$ oscillator, whereas the $TH2$ oscillator is made constant so that t_{on} is fixed.

This circuit is more stable than the basic Morgan circuit and the autotransformer provides a more reliable commutation of the load thyristor.

As with the Morgan chopper, when the thyristor $TH1$ of the Jones chopper is fired, the capacitor, charged positively at the dot, discharges around the C, $TH1, L$ and D circuit and reverses polarity. The diode D, however, prevents further oscillation of the resonating LC circuit. Therefore, the capacitor retains its charge until thyristor $TH2$ is fired. Then the discharge reverse biases $TH1$ and turns it off, the capacitor charges up with the dot positive again and $TH2$ turns off, because the current through it falls below the holding value when C is recharged. The cycle repeats itself when $TH1$ is fired again.

If the capacitor had not charged up sufficiently by the time $TH1$ was fired again, it would not matter, because the load current ensures that the autotransformer induced emf in L gives the capacitor sufficient commutating energy. The thyristors have to be rated at a higher voltage as a result of this.

(c) The oscillation chopper

The oscillation chopper differs from the two previous choppers in that there is no saturable reactor or autotransformer in the load circuit. The name is given because of the resonating or oscillating nature of the class (d) commutation. Although the switching mode is similar to the Jones chopper, it has a higher characteristic frequency of switching.

The order of operation is that *TH2* of Fig. 4.26 must be triggered first so that *C* may charge up with the dot positive. Otherwise, *TH2* commutation is

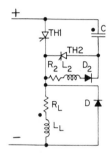

Fig. 4.26.   The oscillation chopper.

not possible. Then when *TH1* is fired, so that load current can flow, *C* reverses polarity through the resonating circuit *C*, *TH1*, R_2, L_2 and *D2* and remains in that state of charge because of *D2* until *TH2* is fired. This discharges *C*, reverse biases *TH1* and turns it off.

With any resonating circuit the capacitor cannot hold its reverse polarity charge indefinitely. The components are not ideal and so *C* would discharge slowly by leakage through both *TH2* and *D2*. However, assuming ideal conditions except that the commutating circuit does have a resistance, R_2 in the figure, then the analysis of the commutating circuit is as follows.

(i) Charging analysis. The initial conditions are that the thyristor *TH1* is fired at zero time when the capacitor is charged to *V* at the dot as in Fig. 4.27.

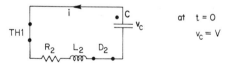

Fig. 4.27.   Equivalent commutating circuit.

The circuit can only be analysed while the current is flowing in an anticlockwise direction. The transient equations are

$$L_2 \frac{di}{dt} + R_2 i + \frac{1}{C} \int_{-\infty}^{t} i \, dt = 0 \qquad (4.25)$$

and

$$v_c = -\frac{1}{C} \int_{-\infty}^{t} i \, dt \qquad (4.26)$$

and the Laplace equations are

$$i(s) = \frac{V}{L_2(s^2 + 2\xi\omega s + \omega^2)} \quad (4.27)$$

and

$$v_c(s) = \frac{V}{s} - \frac{V}{L_2 Cs(s^2 + 2\xi\omega s + \omega^2)}, \quad (4.28)$$

where the damping factor ξ is

$$\xi = \frac{R_2}{2}\sqrt{\frac{C}{L_2}} \quad (4.29)$$

and the natural frequency of oscillation of the circuit, ω, is

$$\omega = \sqrt{\frac{1}{L_2 C}} \text{ rad s}^{-1}. \quad (4.30)$$

The solutions of Equations (4.25) and (4.26) are

$$i(t) = \frac{V}{L_2\omega\sqrt{1-\xi^2}} e^{-\xi\omega t} \sin(\omega t\sqrt{1-\xi^2}) \quad (4.31)$$

and

$$v_c(t) = V e^{-\xi\omega t}\left[\cos(\omega t\sqrt{1-\xi^2}) + \frac{\xi}{\sqrt{1-\xi^2}}\sin(\omega t\sqrt{1-\xi^2})\right]. \quad (4.32)$$

The capacitor will eventually charge up until current ceases to flow in the anticlockwise direction. Current cannot flow in the clockwise direction because of the diode and in any case the above equations would not hold. The limit occurs when the capacitor has charged and

$$i(t) = 0 \quad (4.33)$$

and so Equation (4.31) provides the time taken to charge; t_c is

$$t_c = \frac{\pi}{\omega\sqrt{1-\xi^2}} = \sqrt{L_2 C}, \quad (4.34)$$

when the voltage across the capacitor, v_C is

$$v_c = V e^{-\xi\pi/\sqrt{1-\xi^2}} \simeq V e^{-(\pi R_2/2)\sqrt{(C/L_2)}}, \quad (4.35)$$

obtained from Equation (4.32). It will be noted that the voltage, negative at the dot with respect to the other plate, is less than V because of energy loss due to R_2.

(ii) Commutation analysis. When the thyristor, TH2 is fired the capacitor discharges and reverse biases TH1. TH1 stops conducting but current still

flows in the load and the path to complete the circuit is given by the capacitor as shown in Fig. 4.28. This again can only be analysed for half of the cycle of the natural resonating circuit of C and L_L. When current reverses the circuital path changes to C, V, D, R_2, L_2 and $D2$. It is assumed that $TH1$

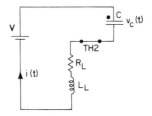

Fig. 4.28.   Commutation and first discharge circuit.

turns off as soon as $TH2$ turns on, but, of course, it does not recover its blocking state immediately. The transient equations are

$$L_L \frac{di}{dt} + R_L i + \frac{1}{C} \int_{-\infty}^{t} i \, dt = V \tag{4.36}$$

and

$$v_c(t) = \frac{1}{C} \int_{-\infty}^{t} i \, dt. \tag{4.37}$$

The initial conditions provide

$$t = 0$$

$$i = I_L \tag{4.38}$$

$$v_c(0) = -V_c$$

so that the Laplace transform yields

$$i(s) = \left[\frac{(V + V_c)}{L_L} + I_L s \right] \Big/ (s^2 + 2\xi_c \omega_c s + \omega_c^2) \tag{4.39}$$

and

$$v_c(s) = \left\{ \left[\frac{(V + V_c)}{L_L C s} + \frac{I_L}{C} \right] \Big/ (s^2 + 2\xi_c \omega_c s + \omega_c^2) \right\} - \frac{V_c}{s} \tag{4.40}$$

where

$$\omega_c = \frac{1}{\sqrt{L_L C}} \tag{4.41}$$

and

$$\xi_c = \frac{R_L}{2} \sqrt{\frac{C}{L_L}}. \tag{4.42}$$

There are three solutions to these equations depending upon whether the system is underdamped ($\xi_c < 1$), critically damped ($\xi_c = 1$) or overdamped ($\xi_c > 1$) and this is load dependent. What information are the solutions to give? Design information is required to enable a choice to be made for L_2 and C which will enable $TH1$ to be reverse biased long enough to regain its blocking state. Now, as C proceeds to discharge during the commutation interval, the thyristor, $TH1$, starts to become forward biased after the voltage across the capacitor becomes zero. The time taken for that voltage to become zero must be greater than the recovery time of the load thyristor.

When the circuit is underdamped and

$$\xi_c < 1 \tag{4.43}$$

the solution of Equation (4.40) is

$$v_c(t) = V - [(V + V_c)e^{-\xi_c \omega_c t}]\frac{\cos(\omega_c t\sqrt{1 - \xi_c^2} - \phi)}{\cos \phi} \tag{4.44}$$

where

$$\phi = \tan^{-1}\left[\xi_c - \frac{I_L}{\omega_c C(V + V_c)}\right]\bigg/\sqrt{1 - \xi_c^2}. \tag{4.45}$$

Equation (4.44) holds until

and

$$\left.\begin{array}{c} \dfrac{di}{dt} < 0 \\[2em] v_c(t) = V \end{array}\right\} \tag{4.46}$$

Putting

$$v_c(t) = 0$$

in Equation (4.44) to give the maximum thyristor turn-off time, t_{off}, yields for

$$\phi > 0 \tag{4.47}$$

$$t_{off} = \frac{\xi_c}{\omega_c}\ln\left(\frac{V + V_c}{V}\right) + \frac{2\sqrt{1 - \xi_c^2}}{\omega_c}\phi \tag{4.48}$$

and for

$$\phi \leqslant 0 \tag{4.49}$$

$$t_{off} = \frac{\xi_c}{\omega_c}\ln\left(\frac{V + V_c}{V}\right) = \frac{R_L C}{2}\ln\left(1 + \frac{V_c}{V}\right). \tag{4.50}$$

When the circuit is critically damped or overdamped,

$$\xi_c \geqslant 1, \tag{4.51}$$

it is found that

$$t_{off} \simeq \frac{CV_c}{I_L} \tag{4.52}$$

Equation (4.50) gives the shortest time because the circuit is underdamped, that is highly oscillatory, but Equation (4.52) can be important. As well as reverse biasing *TH*1 for the turn-off time of the thyristor it is necessary for *C* to charge up again in a time short enough for

$$v_c(t) = V \tag{4.53}$$

with the dot positive before *TH*1 is turned on again. Otherwise commutation will not be successful. The conduction period of *TH*2 could be shortened by adding in parallel with *TH*1 a diode in series with an inductance. The inductance is added to prevent the capacitor being short-circuited during commutation. Another improvement is to replace *D*2 with a thyristor so that, during commutation, it would block reverse current in the second half cycle

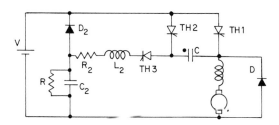

Fig. 4.29.   An alternative oscillation chopper.

of oscillation and allow a higher positive voltage at the dot of the capacitor. This is certainly necessary when the load is an armature and the back emf tends to limit the amount of charging in the positive direction (i.e., the dot).

Another oscillating chopper circuit, which overcomes the difficulty of charging the capacitor due to the motor back emf and eliminates the need to fire the auxiliary thyristor first, is shown in Fig. 4.29.

If *TH*2 is fired first, then the capacitor *C* will charge up positively at the dot and then *TH*2 turns off. Thyristor *TH*1 is fired to enable load current to flow but *TH*3 is always fired simultaneously. There is now a unilateral oscillating circuit, *C*, *TH*3, L_2, *D*2 and *TH*1 for *C* to reverse polarity and remain at that polarity until *TH*2 is fired once more so that *TH*1 becomes biased and turns off.

If *TH*1 and *TH*3 are fired first, the capacitor still charges up with the dot negative, all ready for commutation of the load thyristor. The charging circuit is *TH*1, *C*, *TH*3, L_2, R_2 and C_2 and this is independent of the load circuit so that *C* charges up to the same voltage no matter what the motor back emf is.

4.4. POSITION CONTROL BY DIRECT CURRENT MOTORS

Two methods of position control entail hoisting a load onto a platform, and aiming a trajectile onto a target. The two require different approaches, the former being an open loop manual operation and the latter requiring closed loop automatic operation. Both utilize electric motors to provide the motion.

'Inching' is the name usually given to manual position control where the motor is allowed to rotate through small distances at low speeds and in discrete steps.

This control is arranged by having a resistance in series with the armature, just as for starting the motor. A contactor enables the supply to be switched on and off at the will of the operator. Accordingly the principle is that, when the supply is switched on, the added resistance limits the armature current to such a level that the initial electromagnetic torque is not much greater than the load torque. Consequently, the starting acceleration is low and the final speed is low. Starting and stopping in rapid succession leads to load movements of fractions of an inch at a time, if necessary; hence the term 'inching'. Accomplishment of 'inching' is, in practice, the same as motor starting except that only a single resistance need be used and it is not switched out of the armature circuit. Therefore all the systems described for starting can be used. This includes the thyristor chopper circuits of Figs. 4.24, 4.25 and 4.26, which eliminate the use of resistance and, instead, have a constant low mark-space ratio to maintain a low average voltage across the armature with its associated low current, low torque and hence low speed.

If the load to be positioned is a light one, then the motor to control it can be a small one and the armature can be supplied with substantially constant current. The torque would rely on only one adjustable parameter and that is the field excitation, which can be high initially (field forcing) to accelerate the load to its required position and zero when it actually reaches that position.

Figure 4.30 represents an automatic position control scheme in basic form. Two potential dividers are supplied from a constant voltage source. Divider I

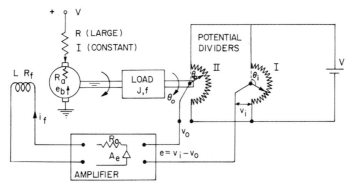

Fig. 4.30.   Automatic position control.

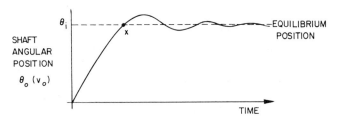

Fig. 4.31.   Shaft motion for position control.

gives the reference voltage, v_i, which is the analogue of the required angular position of the shaft, while the wiper of divider II is attached to the shaft to enable the output voltage, v_0, to be the analogue of the actual position. The error, e, or difference between these two voltages is fed to an amplifier to allow a current, proportional to this difference, to excite the field winding of the motor.

For a particular reference setting, the motor will provide a torque proportional to the field current and hence proportional to the error voltage. The motor will rotate, together with the wiper of divider II, until v_0 equals the voltage v_i. At this point, x in Fig. 4.31, the shaft will have reached the required angular position. The shaft, due to its momentum, will overshoot this position by an amount depending on the damping of the system. However, the error voltage will now reverse the polarity of the exciting current to give a reverse torque, which will bring the shaft back into position again. The likely motion before the shaft reaches its steady state position is shown in Fig. 4.31. It represents a slightly under-damped system.

The block diagram of the automatic position control circuit has the form of Fig. 4.32.

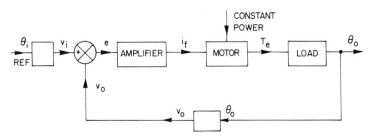

Fig. 4.32.   Block diagram for simple position control.

4.4.1. Thyristor position control

In the automatic position control system of the previous section, the high inductance of the field winding results in relatively slow electrical response. The low armature inductance offers much faster response although higher controlling powers are involved. However, the high gain of the thyristor permits high power motors to have armature control.

Here a quasi-optimized position control through the armature will be analysed in some detail. This will give some insight into the complexity of control circuit design after a basic circuit has been chosen.

(a) Design study of a discontinuous servomechanism for position control using thyristors

Servomechanisms are closed loop systems for controlling position, speed or acceleration of an inertial load. They are operated automatically and actuated by error signals, so that there is continuous comparison between the desired input and the actual output. The difference between the two signals, or the error, is then amplified and the amplified power is used by some drive or controller to correct the output.

The discontinuous servo is an on-off or bang-bang system. That is, the power to the controller is either fully on or completely off. The thyristor, as a switch, is ideally suited to this operation. Why use an on-off system? To a large extent on-off controllers are simpler and cheaper than the continuous controller used in the previous section. With considerable advances in linear feedback systems the continuous controller was the easier to analyse and its performance easier to predict. However, with the increased interest in optimal control, there is renewed interest in on-off controllers.

Much has been written on the general subject of optimal control, of which the minimum time control problem is closely related to that of positional servos. In a positional servo one is generally interested to have the output of the system proceed from some initial value 'a' to a final value 'b' in minimum time. Among a number of workers, Bellman, Feldbaum, La Salle, Pontryagin and Chandhusi have considered the minimum time problem and proved with various rigour and generality that an on-off system is the time optimal system. An on and off system is defined as a system which at all times utilizes maximum power and may be mathematically written as

$$U_{opt} = U_{max} \ (Sgn \ \text{of some function}) \qquad (4.54)$$

where

U_{opt} is the optimum forcing variable
U_{max} is the maximum value of the forcing variable (an example of a forcing variable is the applied voltage to a motor) and
Sgn is a sign function.

An on-off system in non-linear and an essential characteristic of a non-linear system is that the principle of superposition no longer holds. For this reason analysis using Laplace Transform or Frequency Domain methods are no longer applicable. There are a number of methods such as Lyapunov, describing function and phase-plane methods, to analyse non-linear systems. The first two methods are applicable to systems of high order and give information mainly about stability. The phase-plane is applicable to all second order systems or those systems which can be reduced to second order, linear or non-linear, and has the advantage of giving full information on transients. The method is therefore used in the following study.

If the moment of inertia of a d.c. motor and its load is J, the viscous friction factor is B and the motor torque over the range of operating speed is constant at T, then the output torque of the servo system, shown in Fig. 4.33, will depend on the sign of the error, that is

$$T = Sgn(e)T_{\max} \qquad (4.55)$$

where

$$e = \theta_i - \theta_0 \qquad (4.56)$$

with θ_i defined as the input positional reference and θ_0 as the output position. The torque equation of the load and motor is given by

$$J\ddot{\theta}_0 + B\dot{\theta}_0 = \pm T. \qquad (4.57)$$

Assuming a step input to the system, Equation (4.57) becomes

$$\ddot{e} = \mp \frac{T}{J} + \frac{B}{J}\dot{e}. \qquad (4.58)$$

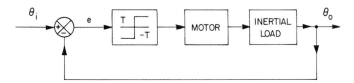

Fig. 4.33.   A minimal on-off positional servo system.

Since

$$\ddot{e} = \dot{e}\frac{d\dot{e}}{de} \qquad (4.59)$$

Equation (4.58) becomes

$$\frac{\dot{e}\,d\dot{e}}{\mp\dfrac{T}{J} + \dfrac{B}{J}\dot{e}} = de \qquad (4.60)$$

and its solution, the phase-plane trajectory of error e plotted against rate of error $\dot{e}$ is

$$\frac{T}{J}e = \frac{T}{B}\dot{e} \pm \frac{T^2}{B^2}\ln\left(1 \pm \frac{B}{T}\dot{e}\right). \qquad (4.61)$$

The system's phase trajectory and its actual output are shown in Fig. 4.34. Theoretically then, a positional servo system with a step input whose output torque has the same sign as the error will result in a lightly damped system.

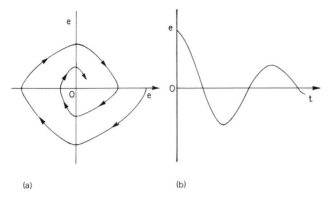

(a)   (b)

Fig. 4.34. Trajectories of an on-off positional servo with a step input. (a) Phase-plane trajectory. (b) Actual output with time.

(i) Power circuit. To achieve the sudden reversal of the torque of a d.c. motor as just described, it is necessary to reverse either the field current or the applied armature voltage. The latter is chosen because it gives faster response, although this method entails the rupture of high currents.

A basic circuit to control the power flow is shown in Fig. 4.35 and is essentially a bridge circuit. The circuit is symmetrical about the load, which is the armature of a separately excited d.c. machine. The components $TH1$, $TH3$, $TH5$, C_1, L_1, $D1$ and R_1 are used to control the power flow through the load in one direction while $TH2$, $TH4$, $TH6$, C_2, L_2, $D2$ and R_2 are used for power flow in the opposite direction. The operation of only one-half of the circuit need be considered.

It is similar to the oscillation chopper circuit of Section 4.3.3. Suppose initially that capacitor C_1 is charged, by firing $TH5$ and $TH3$, so that the potential at Y is V volts above that of X. If $TH1$ and $TH3$ are turned on, current will flow through the load and at the same time point X will rise to potential V causing Y to rise to $2V$. This initiates current flow from Y through L_1 and $D1$. The circuit behaviour may be analysed by using the equivalent ideal circuit of Fig. 4.36.

The current in the circuit of Fig. 4.36, in the Laplace or s-domain is

$$I(s)\left(L_1 s + R_{L1} + \frac{1}{C_1 s}\right) + \frac{V(0+)}{s} = 0, \qquad (4.62)$$

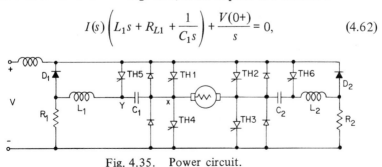

Fig. 4.35. Power circuit.

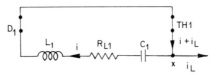

Fig. 4.36.   Equivalent circuit when *TH*1 conducts.

whose solution is

$$i(t) = -\frac{V(0+)}{L_1 b} e^{-at} \sin bt \tag{4.63}$$

where

$$a = \frac{R_{L1}}{2L_1}$$

and

$$b = \sqrt{\frac{1}{L_1 C_1} - \frac{R_{L1}}{4L_1^2}} \quad . \tag{4.64}$$

The capacitor voltage is now found by integrating

$$v_c = \frac{1}{C_1} \int_{-\infty}^{t} i\, dt \tag{4.65}$$

$$v_c = -\frac{V(0+)}{L_1 b} \int_{-\infty}^{t} e^{-at} \sin bt\, dt. \tag{4.66}$$

That is,

$$v_c(t) = \frac{V(0+) e^{-at}}{b} (a \sin bt - b \cos bt). \tag{4.67}$$

Since R_{L1} is the resistance of the inductor L_1

$$b \gg a, \tag{4.68}$$

so that

$$v_c(t) \simeq V(0+)\, e^{-at} \cos bt. \tag{4.69}$$

The form of Equations (4.63) and (4.69) are shown in Fig. 4.37.

With the diode *D*1 in the circuit, then at time t_1, given by

$$t_1 = \frac{\pi}{b}, \tag{4.70}$$

the current attempts to reverse but is blocked so the capacitor is charged in the reverse direction at a potential Y above X,

$$v_c = -v \exp\left(-\pi a/b\right) \tag{4.71}$$

which is just less than V in absolute terms.

Firing *TH5* causes the potential at *Y* to rise to *V* volts, bringing the potential at *X* to *2V* volts. This temporarily reverse biases *TH1* allowing it to regain the forward blocking state. Capacitor C_1 will charge up again with *Y* at *V* above *X*, neglecting the back emf, which should be low or zero at this point, and *TH5* will turn-off because the current through it becomes limited below the holding value by R_1. With the cessation of current through the load, *TH3* also regains its blocking state, or, with the resonating nature of C_1, the armature inductance and the supply, when the load current tends to reverse, *TH3* turns-off. The operation of one cycle is complete and either *TH1* and *TH3* or *TH2* and *TH4* may now be triggered again.

The primary purpose of R_1 is to provide a bleeding path for the leakage current of diode *D1* and thyristor *TH5* to prevent the potential at *Y* rising to that of *X* when thyristors *TH1* and *TH3* are conducting. However R_1 acts as a potential divider with the blocking resistance of *D1* and *TH5* and so the potential at *Y* is clamped at some minimum value. Since it is desirable for

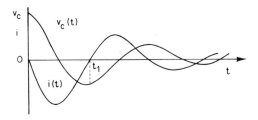

Fig. 4.37. Capacitor voltage and current from circuit of Fig. 4.36.

commutating purposes to have as large a potential difference as possible across the capacitor plates, R_1 should only be large enough to limit the current through *TH5* to less than the holding current. With a small bleeder resistor the time constant R_1C_1 would be small and if the load thyristors *TH1* and *TH3* were not on, the potential at *Y* would fall rapidly to zero. Therefore, to maintain a high potential between *Y* and *X* in this situation, *TH5* should be triggered continually.

The armature does not have a freewheeling diode for the dissipation of inductive energy because rotation is reversible. For small machines with low inductance this can be tolerated. For high powers other circuits must be considered. A diode bridge in parallel with the thyristor bridge is a solution to the problem of returning inductive energy to the supply.

(ii) Control circuit. A logic circuit is required to control the switching operation of the thyristors in the bridge of Fig. 4.35. There are three switching functions:

(1) Switching of thyristors *TH1* and *TH3*
(2) Switching of thyristors *TH2* and *TH4* and
(3) Switching of thyristors *TH5* and *TH6*.

The switching variables are defined here and the final logic functions are stated.* The variables are defined as

(a) T_{13} is the variable to indicate whether thyristors $TH1$ and $TH3$ are on or off

(b) T_{24} is the variable to indicate whether thyristors $TH2$ and $TH4$ are on or off

(c) T_{56} is the variable to indicate whether thyristors $TH5$ and $TH6$ are on or off

(d) P_{13} is the variable to indicate the positional error which can be rectified by firing thyristors $TH1$ and $TH3$

(e) P_{24} is the variable to indicate the positional error which can be rectified by firing thyristors $TH2$ and $TH4$ and

(f) C is the variable to indicate the load current limit.

The switching functions are

$$T_{56} = C + \bar{P}_{13} \cdot \bar{P}_{24} + T_{13} \cdot P_{24} + T_{24} \cdot P_{13} \tag{4.72}$$

$$T_{13} = P_{13} \cdot \bar{P}_{24} \cdot \bar{C} \cdot \bar{T}_{13} \cdot \bar{T}_{24} \cdot \bar{T}_{56} \tag{4.73}$$

$$T_{24} = \bar{P}_{13} \cdot P_{24} \cdot \bar{C} \cdot \bar{T}_{13} \cdot \bar{T}_{24} \cdot \bar{T}_{56}. \tag{4.74}$$

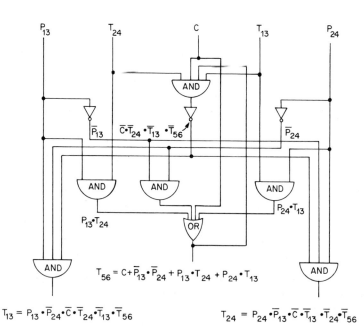

Fig. 4.38. Block diagram of switching functions.

* See Appendix III for the logic function derivation.

Equation (4.72) indicates that thyristors $TH5$ and $TH6$ will be triggered on if the load current has exceeded the maximum allowable (C) OR there is no position error ($P_{13} \cdot P_{24}$) OR one set of load thyristors are on but the positional error is such that the other set should be on ($T_{13} \cdot P_{24} + T_{24} \cdot P_{13}$). Similarly Equation (4.73) indicates that thyristors $TH1$ and $TH3$ receive gate signals to turn them on when the error is such that P_{13} exists but not P_{24}, ($P_{13} \cdot \bar{P}_{14}$) AND the current is below the maximum value ($\bar{C}$) AND all the thyristors are blocking ($\bar{T}_{13} \cdot \bar{T}_{24} \cdot \bar{T}_{56}$).

The switching functions of Equations (4.72), (4.73) and (4.74) can be drawn in the form of a logic block diagram as shown in Fig. 4.38.

The inputs to the logic control circuit must come from detection networks and the outputs must feed the thyristor gate trigger circuits.

Worked Example 4.3. Determine the response of an on-off servo to a step input.

Use is made of Fig. 4.33 and Equation (4.57) to simulate an actual system on an analogue computer simulator (PACTOLUS program). Symbols are illustrated in Fig. 4.39 and the block diagram to simulate simple positional error switching is shown in Fig. 4.40. The values for the moment of inertia and torque are fixed, but several friction factors are used. Figure 4.41 shows typical computer results while Fig. 4.42 indicates experimental results.

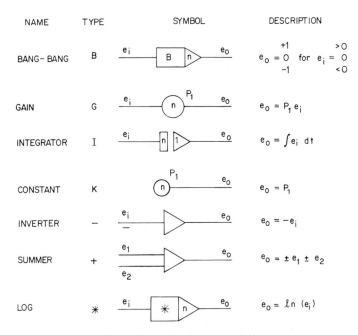

Fig. 4.39. Simulator symbols.

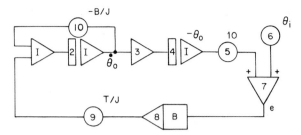

Fig. 4.40. Block diagram to simulate the simple error switching.

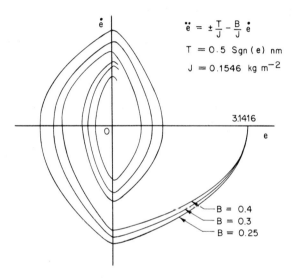

Fig. 4.41. Analogue results of positional servo switching on the sign of the error.

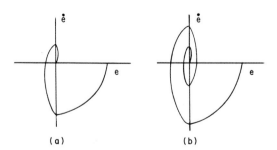

Fig. 4.42. Phase trajectories of an experimental system. (a) Armature current 4.7 A, input step 15 V; (b) armature current 7.0 A, input step 15 V.

The system is shown to be lightly damped and requires improvement to optimize the response. One method of improvement is to include a phase-compensating network between the error signal and the logic circuitry. This would cause the d.c. motor to be switched into reverse before it reaches the required position. It would then brake to rest at the zero error point without overshoot.

4.4.2. Alternative circuits

The bridge circuit used as the example for position control and depicted in Fig. 4.35 is in part the oscillation chopper. It does have disadvantages. Because the capacitor discharges partially through the load, the time of discharge and recharge can be long compared with the actual commutation time. An active load, such as the d.c. motor, can prevent the capacitor storing enough commutation energy because of the back emf. If the motor is small and the speed of rotation is kept low by small position errors then the bridge circuit operates satisfactorily. Figure 4.43 shows one alternative arrangement.

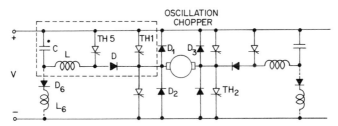

Fig. 4.43.   Alternative bridge circuit for position control.

Load current flows when $TH1$ and $TH2$ are fired. This provides circuit continuity $(C, L, D, TH2)$ for C to charge up to $+V$ at the dot. To commutate the load current, $TH5$ is fired. The oscillation circuit C, $TH5$ and L enables C to reverse polarity so that ideally there is $+V$ at the dot and $+2V$ at the other plate. At the end of the first half cycle of oscillation the current attempts to reverse so that $TH5$ blocks and turns off and C discharges through the load, starving $TH1$ of current. When the capacitor current exceeds the load current the excess current flows through diode $D1$. The thyristor $TH1$ is thus reverse biased and turns-off. When C is charging up with the dot positive again and the point X drops to the potential of the negative rail and is clamped there by diode $D2$, the flow of load current is via $D2$ and $D3$ to return the load inductive energy to the supply. When the load current has reduced to zero, the other pair of bridge thyristors may be fired.

For very light loads or open circuit conditions C would not charge up unless $D6$ and L_6 were added to the circuit. This ensures that C charges under all conditions, but the value of L_6 must be many times the value of L so that during commutation L_6 does not bleed an excessive amount of the discharge current.

Another circuit adapted from Wouk's inverter[2] is a possibility. Although the number of thyristors is great, it serves to show the difficulties involved in picking the best thyristor system for any given application. This circuit is shown in Fig. 4.44.

*TH*1, *TH*2 and *TH*5 are fired at the same time. *TH*1 and *TH*2 allow load current to flow and *TH*5 allows *C* to be charged positively at the dot independent of load conditions.

Firing *TH*6 discharges *C* through the load and at the same time it reverse biases *TH*1 and turns it off. This is not all, because *C* is still discharging and load current is still flowing via *TH*6 and *C*.

*TH*7 is fired as soon as *TH*1 is off. This enables *C* to be discharged much more rapidly via *L*, *TH*7, *TH*6 and *C* then via the load. *TH*7 will turn off again as the current in the *LC* oscillating circuit tries to reverse.

*TH*4 is then fired so that *C* charges up again as quickly as possible, through *TH*6, *C* and *TH*4, with the reverse polarity, ready to commutate when reverse current flows in the load.

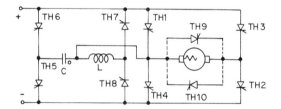

Fig. 4.44.   Another bridge circuit for position control.

This circuit does not allow a reverse freewheeling diode bridge, but the circuit shows back-to-back freewheeling thyristors to provide a path for the 'inductive' current of the load. In this present cycle *TH*10 would be fired at the same time as *TH*6 or *TH*7 or *TH*4. Before *TH*3 and *TH*4 could be fired to reverse the current in the load *TH*10 would have to be in the blocking state again.

The time between firing *TH*6 and *TH*4 need only be about 50 μs.

The cycle of switching for current in the reverse direction would be *TH*3 *TH*4 *TH*6, *TH*5, *TH*9, *TH*8 and finally *TH*1 to complete the cycle.

REFERENCES

1. Pelly, B. R. (1971), 'Thyristor phase. Controlled converters & cyclo-converters', John Wiley, Interscience, New York.
2. Wouk, V. (1967), 'High power thyristor battery drive for high peak low average power pulser', *Proc. I.E.E.E.*, 1456.
3. Mills, J. (1961), 'An output prediction system to improve the performance of on/off and saturating control systems', *Proc. I.E.E.*, **108** (B), 667-671.

BIBLIOGRAPHY

Griffin, A. W. J. and Ramshaw, R. S. (1965), 'The thyristor and its applications', Chapman and Hall, London.

Power applications of controllable semiconductor devices (1965), I.E.E. Conference Publication, No. 17.

Morgan, R. E. (1966), 'Basic magnetic functions in converters and inverters including new soft commutation', *I.E.E.E. Trans.*, IGA-2 (No. 1), 58-65.

Sato, N. (1967), 'Improvement of SCR chopper circuit', *Electrical Engineering in Japan*, **87** (2), 75-83.

'Morgan Chopper Circuit', *I.E.E.E. Communications and Electronics*, **80**, 152; (1961); **83**, 336, (1964); **83**, 198, (1964).

Mapham N. W. and Hey, J. C. (1964), 'Jones chopper circuit', *I.E.E.E. Int. Conf. Rec.* p. 124.

Heumann, K. (1964), 'Oscillation chopper circuit', *I.E.E.E. Communications and Electronics* **83**, 390.

Turnbull, F. (1963), 'D-C to D-C 30 HP motor drive', *A.I.E.E.* **81** (1), 458-62.

Heumann, K. (1964), 'Pulse control of d.c. and a.c. motors by SCRs', *I.E.E.E. Communications and Electronics*, **83**, 390-399.

Engelhart, R. (1963), 'A study of the Morgan D-C to D-C stepdown circuit', *Proc. Intermag. Conf.* 11.5.1-8.

McMurray, W. (1970), 'Analysis of thyristor d.c. chopper power converters including non-linear commutating reactors', *I.E.E.E. Transactions on Magnetics*, **MAG-6** (1).

Dewan, S. B. and Duff, D. L. 'Analysis of energy recovery transformer in d.c. choppers and inverters', *I.E.E.E. transactions on Magnetics*, **MAG-6** (1).

Maresca, T. J. (1970), 'Regulated DC-D-C converter', *I.E.E.E. Transactions on Magnetics*, **MAG-6** (1).

Ramshaw, R. S. and Padiyar, K. R. (1970), 'Digital simulation of a full wave single phase converter system', *Proc. I.E.E.*, **117** (11), 2151-2158.

Sato, N. and Murase, K. (1969), 'A step-up and step-down d.c. voltage converter using thyristor time ratio control', *Electrical Engineering in Japan*, **89** (11).

Kusko, A. (1971), *Solid-state d.c. motor drives*, M.I.T. Press, USA.

PROBLEMS

4.1. The circuit of the form of Fig. 4.29 provides a commutating voltage across the capacitor which is independent of the motor back emf. Analyse the commutation circuits for the two cases (i) when *TH*2 is fired first and charge *C* positively at the dot and (ii) when *TH*1 is fired first.

Case (i): When *TH*2 is fired first and *C* is charged positively at the dot to reach a steady state voltage V_c, then at the instant $t = 0$ Fig. 4.45 represents the final state of charging in preparation for the load thyristor commutation. The discharge resistor R is neglected.

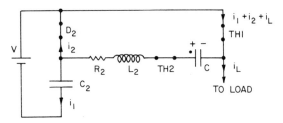

Fig. 4.45.   Final charging of commutating circuit.

The circuit equations can be written down from an inspection of Fig. 4.45 and they are

$$R_2(i_1 + i_2) + L_2 \frac{d(i_1 + i_2)}{dt} - v_c = 0 \tag{4.75}$$

$$R_2(i_1 + i_2) + L_2 \frac{d(i_1 + i_2)}{dt} - v_c + v_{c2} = V \tag{4.76}$$

$$v_c = -\frac{1}{C} \int_{-\infty}^{t} (i_1 + i_2)\, dt \tag{4.77}$$

and

$$v_{c2} = -\frac{1}{C'} \int_{-\infty}^{t} i_1\, dt. \tag{4.78}$$

The initial conditions are

$$\left.\begin{array}{c} t = 0 \\ i_1 = i_2 = 0 \\ v_c = V_c \\ v_{c2} = V_{c2} \end{array}\right\} \tag{4.79}$$

The Laplace transforms of the voltages are

$$v_c(s) = \frac{V_c}{s} - \frac{V_c}{L_2 Cs(s^2 + 2\xi\omega s + \omega^2)} \tag{4.80}$$

and

$$v_{c2}(s) = \frac{V}{s}. \tag{4.81}$$

The voltage $v_c(s)$ is the same as before so that $v_c(t)$ is obtained from Equation (4.32) with V_c replacing V and the final value of the voltage being as Equation (4.35), again with V_c replacing V. The capacitor remains at this voltage because of the diode $D2$ until $TH2$ is fired. The voltage across C_2

jumps from V_{c2} to V at $t = 0+$ and V_{c2} is determined from the blocking period of the chopper and the discharging time constant RC_2.

Case (ii): When $TH1$ is fired first then the diode $D2$ does not conduct. The charging circuit is then as in Fig. 4.46, and the initial charge on C is zero. The governing equations are

$$R_2 i + L_2 \frac{di}{dt} + v_c + v_{c2} = 0, \qquad (4.82)$$

$$v_c = \frac{1}{C} \int_{-\infty}^{t} i \, dt \qquad (4.83)$$

and

$$v_{c2} = \frac{1}{C_2} \int_{-\infty}^{t} i \, dt. \qquad (4.84)$$

The initial conditions are

$$\left.\begin{array}{c} t = 0 \\ i = 0 \\ v_c = 0 \\ v_{c2} = V_{c2} \end{array}\right\}. \qquad (4.85)$$

So that the solutions of Equations 4.82, 4.83 and 4.85 are

$$i(t) = (V - V_{c2}) \, e^{-\xi \omega t} \frac{\sin \omega t \sqrt{1 - \xi^2}}{L_2 \, \omega \sqrt{1 - \xi^2}}, \qquad (4.86)$$

$$v_c(t) = \frac{C_2(V - V_{c2})}{(C + C_2)} \left[1 - e^{-\xi \omega t} \frac{\cos (\omega t \sqrt{1 - \xi^2} - \phi)}{\sqrt{1 - \xi^2}} \right] \qquad (4.87)$$

and

$$v_{c2}(t) = V_{c2} + \frac{C_2(V - V_{c2})}{(C + C_2)} \left[1 - e^{-\xi \omega t} \frac{\cos (\omega t \sqrt{1 - \xi^2} - \phi)}{\sqrt{1 - \xi^2}} \right] \qquad (4.88)$$

where

$$\omega = \sqrt{\frac{C + C_2}{CC_2 L_2}}, \qquad (4.89)$$

$$\xi \frac{R_2}{2} \sqrt{\frac{CC_2}{L_2(C + C_2)}} \qquad (4.90)$$

and

$$\phi = \tan^{-1} \frac{\xi}{\sqrt{1 - \xi^2}}. \qquad (4.91)$$

Figure 4.46 is an oscillating circuit. The capacitors charge up, the current rises to a maximum and falls to zero at which point the differential equations have reached their limit. Beyond this they do not hold because the circuit is unilateral and hence non-linear. However, it is at this limiting point that we require the values of the voltage on the capacitors. The resonating circuit has passed through half of a cycle so that

$$i(t) = 0, \tag{4.92}$$

when

$$\omega\sqrt{1 - \xi}\, t = \pi \tag{4.93}$$

and the reverse voltage across $TH1$ during commutation is obtained from $v_c(t)$ and if

$$\xi \ll 1, \tag{4.94}$$

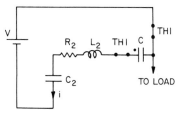

Fig. 4.46.   Charging the commutation circuit.

that is, the circuit is under-damped, then

$$v_c(t)_{i=0} = \frac{2C_2(V - V_{c2})}{(C + C_2)} \tag{4.95}$$

and

$$v_{c2}(t)_{i=0} = V_{c2} + \frac{2C(V - V_{c2})}{(C + C_2)}. \tag{4.96}$$

Since the ω of the case (i) is less than the ω of case (ii), then the charging period is must shorter in the latter case.

The resistor R discharges C_2 during the non-conduction period of $TH1$ to make V_{c2} lower when $TH1$ is turned on.

4.2. Determine suitable component values for the on-off servo power circuit of Section 4.4.1. Add suitable protection for the thyristors and design a trigger circuit to interface the output of the logic circuitry and the thyristors' gates.

The load is assumed to be rated at 2 kW and the d.c. supply is 150 V. Half

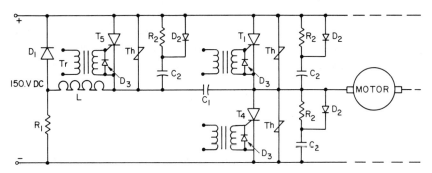

Fig. 4.47. Power circuit.

of the symmetrical power circuit is shown in Fig. 4.47 and the component values are as follows:

Legend	T_1, T_2, T_3, T_4	thyristors GEC38D, 35 A, 400 V
	T_5, T_6	thyristors 20 A, 400 V
	L	200 m
	D1	4JA41D
	D2, D3,	IN55
	C_1	28 μF
	C_2	33 pF
	Th	6RS21VA/5D (thyrector, voltage surge protection)
	R_1	15 K
	R_2	10 Ω
	MOTOR	Mawdsley's generalized machine 4 pole, separately excited.

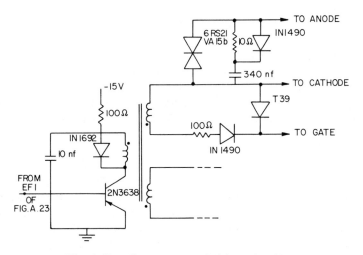

Fig. 4.48. Suppressor and driver circuit.

The unit labelled *PS*1 (oscillator) of the control circuitry (Fig. A.23) of the on-off servo produces an 18 kHz square-wave pulse with an amplitude of 2.2 V peak to peak. A 220 pF capacitor is used to obtain this frequency. The signal is inverted and amplified to supply a driver circuit for the thyristors. As can be seen from Fig. 4.48 each of these driver circuits drives two thyristors. The pulse transformers have a turns ratio 2500 : 1000. Thyristor protection is also shown in the figure.

4.3. The on-off servo of Section 4.4.1 and Appendix III was described in outline. Details of the detection circuits were not supplied. Design suitable detection circuits.

There are six variables, T_{13}, T_{24}, T_{56}, P_{13}, P_{24} and C whose states must be determined for satisfactory logic circuit operation.

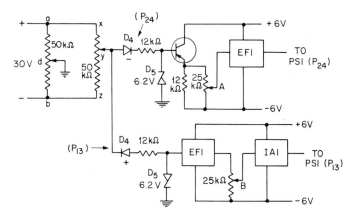

Fig. 4.49.   Positional error detection.

Positional error detection (P_{13} *and* P_{24}). A bridge circuit using two 50 kΩ one-turn potentiometers is used. One potentiometer is the reference input and the other, which is connected to the motor shaft, is the output position. The entire positional detection circuit including modifications to adapt its signal to the control circuitry is shown in Fig. 4.49. Since the potentiometers are equal

$$\frac{ad}{db} = \frac{xz}{zy}$$

and an error voltage will exist between d and z. The error voltage can be either positive or negative since the reference shaft is earthed. The two diodes $D4$ differentiate between the two levels of voltage. In order to protect the control circuitry zener diodes $D5$ are connected to hold the voltage to a maximum of 6.2 V. The 12 kΩ resistor is to limit the current.

To set the 25 kΩ potentiometer for P_{13} (or P_{24}) one must set the output

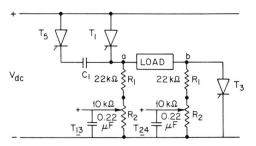

Fig. 4.50.   Thyristor on-off detection.

of the bridge network at negative or zero volts. The 25 kΩ potentiometer is then adjusted so that the output of the pulse shaper (see Fig. A.23) has just switched to zero volts.

Thyristor on-off detection (T_{13}, T_{24}). In the Fig. 4.50 if thyristors *TH*1 and *TH*3 are on and *TH*2 and *TH*4 are off the potential at the point '*a*' would be V volts and point '*b*' would be at ground potential approximately. Therefore, there would be an output signal for T_{13} on and T_{24} off.

During commutation when *TH*5 and *TH*6 are on the potential at '*a*' and '*b*' will be V volts and thus there is a signal that T_{13} and T_{24} are on. Since the potential is positive, the signal cannot be applied directly to the logic unit since it operates on zero to −6 V. The signal can be inverted by inserting the transistor circuit as shown in Fig. 4.51. The values of R_1 and R_2 are 22 kΩ and 10 kΩ, respectively. The resistor is set as follows. Apply the positive line

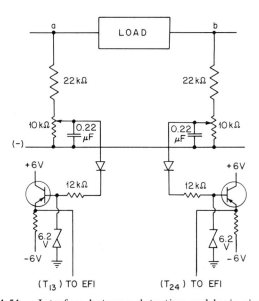

Fig. 4.51.   Interface between detection and logic circuitry.

voltage to point 'a', and then adjust the resistance R_2 so that the output of the pulse shaper (as in Fig. A.23) has just switched to −6 V. The 0.22 μF capacitor is added to filter noise.

Load current detection (C). The resistance R of Fig. 4.52 will measure the instantaneous load current. If the current exceeds the maximum allowable value, the voltage V_L will be sufficiently high to initiate a signal to the

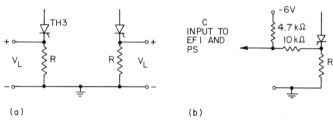

(a)   (b)

Fig. 4.52.   Load current detector. (a) General arrangement; (b) circuit connection to logic control.

control circuitry. For a more precise requirement the 4.7 kΩ and the 10 kΩ resistors should be replaced by a potentiometer. As it is, the input signal to the emitter follower will vary between −4.08 and −2.14 V between zero and maximum current. The value of R is arbitrary but is chosen to minimize losses.

In this way the maximum current is never exceeded and allowing for a certain backlash and circuit inductance, the current for the on-off system would be as in Fig. 4.53. For such a controlled system there is no need for a

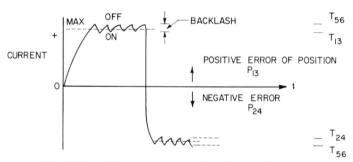

Fig. 4.53.   Constant current for the on-off system.

starter. The inductance of the circuit is enough to allow the switching circuits to act in time to prevent a dangerous current being reached. For a motor with an intermittent positional duty, the maximum current can be greater than full load current.

To minimize losses a differential comparator could be used. This unit compares the voltage at 'a' and 'b' of Fig. 4.54. If 'a' is more positive than 'b' then the comparator produces an output which causes the 'one-shot' multivibrator (*OS*1) to give a pulse. The duration of this pulse is long enough to turn *TH*5 and *TH*6 on. The *EF*1 unit in front of the *OS*1 unit ensures that the differential comparator is not overloaded. The pulse shaper (*PS*1) following the *OS*1 unit reshapes and inverts the signal into the standard d.c. levels (0 or −6 V) at the output.

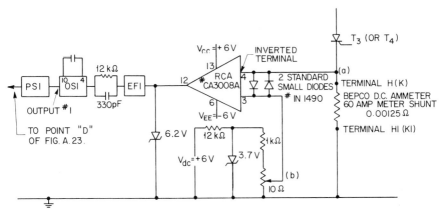

Fig. 4.54.   Current detection using a differential comparator.

4.4. The simple error servo for position control described in Section 4.4.1 is lightly damped. Consequently it has a poor response. Discuss methods whereby the time to reach a required position can be optimized. Show the improvement by analogue simulation.

Optimization. It has been proved experimentally and theoretically that an on-off system with torque switching with the sign of positional error results in a lightly damped and oscillatory system. There are a number of methods to improve the system. Some of these methods are introduced here.

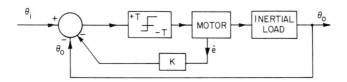

Fig. 4.55.   Positional servo with velocity feedback.

Velocity feedback. If a velocity feedback is added to the system of Fig. 4.33 as shown in Fig. 4.55, the switching of the thyristors and so the motor torque will now depend on

$$Sgn \ (e + K\dot{e})$$

where $\dot{e} = \dot{\theta}_0$, *Sgn* represents the sign (+ or −) of the function and K is the feedback gain. The function

$$e = -\frac{1}{K}\dot{e}$$

is a straight line in the phase plane with a slope $-1/K$.

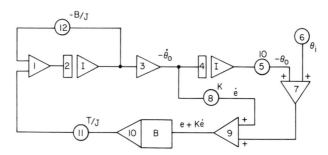

Fig. 4.56.   Block diagram to simulate error and error rate switching from Fig. 4.55.

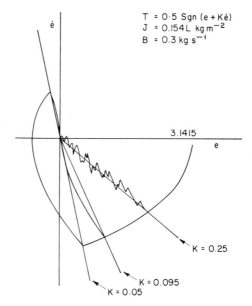

Fig. 4.57.   Positional servo switching on sign of error and error rate.

The system can be simulated by a Pactolus programme again with values used previously. The block diagram is shown in Fig. 4.56, and the results in Fig. 4.57. From these results it is evident that the performance depends on the feedback gain K for a given torque and input. If K is small, the system is still oscillatory. If it is 0.095, and performance is near optimum. If it is large, the output would converge to zero by continuously hunting about the switching line.

Phase advance network. If a phase advance network is added to the experimental system as shown in Fig. 4.58, the output torque will now depend on

$$Sgn\left(\frac{1 + \tau s}{1 + \alpha \tau s}\right)$$

where

τ = time constant of the phase advance damping

α = constant ($\ll \tau$) and

s = Laplace operator.

If the Laplace transform of the phase advance network is expanded as a power series, neglecting terms of α or higher, a non-linear differential equation

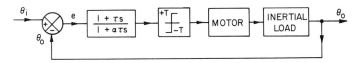

Fig. 4.58.   Positional servo with phase advance network.

is obtained. However, if α is assumed to approach zero as in the ideal case, the switching criterion simplifies to

$$T = Sgn\left[e(1 + \tau s)\right]T_{max}$$

i.e.

$$T = Sgn\left[e + \tau \dot{e}\right]T_{max}.$$

The function

$$\dot{e} = \frac{-1}{\tau}e$$

is a straight line in the phase plane with a slope $-1/\tau$. The system performance would therefore be very similar to that with velocity feedback.

This is one of the simplest methods of implementing optimal or quasi-optimal switching. It is shown by Mills[3] that knowing the servomotor characteristics, a phase advance network may be synthesized such that the switching could be within 1 per cent of the optimum switching time.

Optimal switching. To have an optimal system it is necessary to have error and error rate reaching zero simultaneously. It has been shown in Equation (4.61) that the trajectories of the servomotor in the phase plane are non-linear.

If, however, the trajectories passing through the origin are used as the switching line, that is

$$T = |T| \left[Sgn \left\{ \dot{e} \pm \frac{T}{B} \ln \left(1 \mp \frac{B}{T} \dot{e} \right) - \frac{B}{J} e \right\} \right]$$

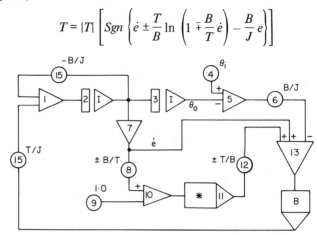

Fig. 4.59. Block diagram to simulate optimal switching.

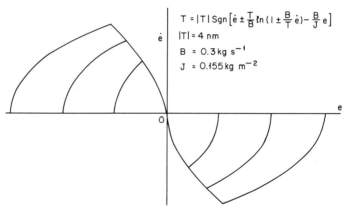

$$T = |T| Sgn \left[\dot{e} \pm \frac{T}{B} \ln \left(1 \pm \frac{B}{T} \dot{e} \right) - \frac{B}{J} e \right]$$

$|T| = 4$ nm

$B = 0.3$ kg s^{-1}

$J = 0.155$ kg m^{-2}

Fig. 4.60. Analogue simulation results of optimal switching.

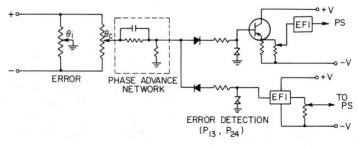

Fig. 4.61. Error detector with the addition of the phase advance network which acts as a switching predictor.

then the system will perform optimally. Zero error and error rate will be reached with only one switching and in minimal time. The experimental system is again simulated on the Pactolus digital analogue simulator, the block diagram is shown in Fig. 4.59 and the results in Fig. 4.60.

Practical optimization by a phase advance network requires only one change in the present control circuit and that is the introduction of the network as in Fig. 4.61.

4.5. Analyse the full wave, single phase converter of the form of Fig. 4.15 to determine the transient load current for a step change of firing angle α for the case when the source impedance is neglected.

$$i(t_n) = \frac{E_m}{z} \left[\sin (\phi - \alpha) e^{-(R/L)t_n} + \sin (\omega t_n - \phi + \alpha) \right] + e^{-(R/L)t_n} I_{n-1}$$

where

$i(t_n)$ = the instantaneous value of current during the nth period
$\qquad (n-1)T_L \leqslant t \leqslant nT_L$
$t_n = t - nT_L$, a time variable during the nth period of the rectified voltage waveform
$T_L = 1/2f$, period of the rectified voltage waveform
z = load impedance
E_m = maximum value of applied sinusoidal voltage to triac 1 or 2
ϕ = phase angle of impedance z
α = firing angle of the triacs
R = load resistance
L = load inductance
ω = angular frequency of the applied sinusoidal voltage and
I_n = load current at the beginning of the nth period of the rectified voltage waveform.

NOTE
Additional problems on page 213

5 Synchronous motor control

5.1. INTRODUCTION

The synchronous motor has found application where a precise constant speed drive was required and especially where a number of machines must run in synchronism. A typical example is in textile mills. Disadvantages such as double excitation (an a.c. armature winding and a d.c. field winding) and no inherent self-starting characteristic has prevented the synchronous machine from becoming a general purpose motor like the induction motor.

The operating speed of a synchronous speed is

$$n = \frac{f}{p} \text{ rps} \tag{5.1}$$

where

    n = rotor speed, rps
    f = supply frequency, Hz, and
    p = number of pole pairs.

A constant frequency supply means that the synchronous motor speed variation occurs in a stepped manner by poles changing. Power electronics adds smooth speed variation to the motor's characteristics. Semiconductor inverter circuits have been described in relation to the induction motor. What is the advantage of a synchronous motor when an induction motor is cheaper to manufacture? Although the induction motor speed need not vary very much, there is still need for a feedback control system for a precise speed. More important is the application of a large number of drives with precise speed requirements which are interlinked, as in a textile mill. Further, it is possible to have a multiload system requiring adjustable speed variation, precisely and in synchronism. Again the open loop, multi-synchronous motors provide the drives and a variable frequency inverter provides the supply.

The synchronous motor, in general, implies a double winding machine. One winding is supplied with a polyphase alternating current for energy conversion and the second winding is for direct current excitation to provide the main magnetic field. Also included in the category of synchronous machines would be one with permanent magnet excitation. Another synchronous machine is the reluctance motor which has a salient pole arrangement and no field winding and yet another is the synchronous induction motor. This is an induction motor with a wound rotor winding whose connections are brought out to slip rings so that direct current can be injected into the rotor to provide an electromagnetic torque at synchronous speed. The hysteresis motor is a permanent magnetic synchronous machine when running at synchronous speed. At other speeds it relies on the hysteresis energy to furnish a driving torque and consequently is only used for small power applications.[1] A final example of a synchronous motor is the inverted d.c. machine. That is, if the armature of a d.c. motor were to be on the stator and the field on the rotor it would be similar to a synchronous motor with one exception. The commutator or frequency changer or better still, inverter, as it would now be called, has its output frequency controlled by the rotor speed and position. Accordingly no stalling occurs as in a conventional synchronous machine but again no precise speed can be obtained without feedback control.

5.2. SYNCHRONOUS MOTOR STARTING

At normal mains frequency, the average driving torque of a synchronous motor is zero at standstill. The rotor might oscillate with a very small amplitude at 50 or 60 Hz but the machine inertia is too great for motor response to cause rotation.

To start the motor the frequency must be low enough so that the current and field changes are in sympathy. That is, synchronism is maintained. Otherwise auxiliary methods of starting must be employed. The first and simplest method must be to add another but smaller induction motor to the load shaft. The synchronous machine could then be run up to near synchronous speed, the synchronous motor would be connected to the supply, and would pull into synchronism. The induction motor could then be disconnected.

Much better methods would be to allow the synchronous machine to start as in induction motor and run as a synchronous motor or to have an induction motor for starting and reconnect it as a synchronous induction motor when running.

5.2.1. An inverter for starting

An inverter which can be controlled to provide an adjustable output frequency is suitable for starting a synchronous motor.

If the frequency of the supply is low enough then the motor can rotate through half a cycle while the current is in sympathy. The torque is then unidirectional. Once the motor has pulled into synchronism at a low frequency, the frequency of the supply can be increased gradually and the motor speed will increase also.

To employ an inverter in place of an induction winding for starting is not economical, but where a frequency changer is also used for speed control, then the method is feasible.

5.3. SPEED CONTROL

Precise speeds are obtained from the synchronous motor and these are given by Equation (5.1). Pole changing, frequency changing and mechanical gear changing are the only ways that the speed can be adjusted. Speed changing by variable frequency inverters using power electronics has been discussed at length in Chapter 3 on induction motors. The same inverters can drive a synchronous motor and here no feedback loop is required for error correction.

A specific example of the application of speed control to synchronous machines will be given. Two solutions are suggested. One is simple and the other is sophisticated. Both methods can be classified as inverters and it is left to the reader to make a comparison. The first example utilizes a d.c. supply and the synchronous machine operates as a stepping motor. The second example relies on a variable firing angle and a constant frequency a.c. supply to simulate a low-frequency output from the thyristor unit. This a.c. to a.c. unit, which does not require a d.c. link, is called a cycloconverter.

5.3.1. A speed control problem (barring a turbo-alternator)

In a power station, when a turbo-alternator is taken off load it is usual for the machine set to be barred. Barring means that the turbo-alternator is rotated at a slow speed to prevent hogging, where hogging is an expression used to describe the distortion of the turbine rotors as they cool down. The possibility of starting turbo-alternators and bringing them back on load is determined by the degree of hogging. This effect is usually minimized by barring to encourage an isotropic temperature distribution.

The simplest and almost universal method of barring is to couple an induction motor through gearing to the main shaft. There are, however, some sets where 'electrical' barring is a possibility. For example, in old sets without conventional barring gear, hogging is usually at a maximum after several hours, and does not reduce sufficiently for the machine to be run up in safety for perhaps twenty-four hours. The lack of availability for such a period or, alternatively, running the machine out of merit to ensure availability has drawbacks in some areas where local power boosting is required for short periods but with short intervals.

'Electrical' barring is possible by using the alternator as a synchronous motor which is supplied with low-frequency power. The low frequency is to provide a low running speed and the power necessary is that needed to overcome friction when running but includes inertia when accelerating. The two very different solutions discussed here are based on a d.c. supply and an a.c. supply. Using the alternator as a stepping motor employs the former and as a conventional motor employs the latter together with a cycloconverter; both have thyristor control.

(a) A thyristor stepping motor

Figure 5.1 shows a simple inverter circuit suitable for low-frequency switching. The low-frequency power is supplied to the motor by sequentially switching the thyristors in the line circuits. The thyristors allow direct current to be injected into one or more phases of the machine at a time. With a fixed sequence of switching the result is an armature field which rotates in steps around the air gap. With the main field excited and if the generated frequency is low enough and the torque high enough, the rotor will be kept in step with the changing armature field position. The machine will act as a synchronous motor without the need for auxiliary starting and the rate of switching each thyristor determines the rotor speed.

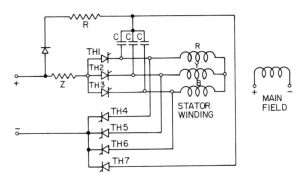

Fig. 5.1.   A low frequency inverter.

The basic circuit arrangement is to use six thyristors (excluding the thyristor $TH7$, the three capacitors and the limiting resistance, R), and to allow current to flow through two phases at a time, say $TH1$ and $TH5$, $TH1$ and $TH6$, $TH2$ and $TH6$, $TH2$ and $TH4$, $TH3$ and $TH4$, and $TH3$ and $TH5$, to form one cycle. Figure 5.2 illustrates the cyclic mmf phasor pattern. This switching sequence, for a given line current, gives the maximum mmf and a 60 electric degree step, which facilitates starting and produces less torque fluctuation than say a 120° step. A 30 electrical degree step could be produced by allowing current to flow alternately in two and then three phases but this would mean pulsating currents, higher currents when the three phases were operative but less active mmf and higher ratings for the thyristors.

The supply to the basic circuit can be direct current, three-phase or single-phase with or without full-wave rectification. None is perfectly suited for this application with thyristors. When the anode of a thyristor is positive with respect to its cathode and a signal is applied between the gate and cathode, the thyristor will switch on and conduct current in the forward direction until that current drops below the holding value, at which point the thyristor will revert to its normal blocking state.

With a single- or three-phase supply the thyristor acts as a half-wave controlled rectifier, so that, when the gate signal has been removed, the current will reduce to zero sometime during the negative half cycle of voltage. That is, under these circumstances the thyristor will turn off naturally by line commutation. To enable the thyristor to conduct over a number of cycles, the gate signal must be applied continuously or as a train of pulses over this period. However, for this half wave supply, the transformer has to be generously rated to prevent saturation. Even though a single-phase transformer may produce some inbalance in the supply, it does mean that, unlike the three-phase transformer, the windings are utilized the whole of the operating time.

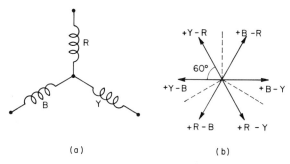

(a)   (b)

Fig. 5.2. Spatial pattern of mmf over one cycle. (a) Winding; (b) mmf cycle.

With direct current or alternating current which has been fully rectified, the current passing through a thyristor will never go below the holding value. This means that a pulsed signal will turn on a thyristor but it must be turned off by forced commutation. The forced commutation of the six thyristors can be accomplished in this practical application by the one thyristor $TH7$, the three capacitors and the limiting resistor. For example, if thyristors $TH1$ and $TH5$ were conducting, a capacitor C would charge up to the line voltage. When the gate signals of the previous thyristors were removed and $TH7$ triggered, the capacitor would discharge through $TH7$ and reverse bias $TH5$. If the charge were great enough, $TH5$ would turn-off, and so would $TH1$. The next sequence of switching would follow.

Some precaution has to be taken, because, if, through some interaction of the circuits, forced commutation is not successful, the next switching operation would short-circuit the supply. Besides fuses an impedance Z in series with the supply and of such a value that it is greater than the impedance of the stator winding would limit the short-circuit current. Any failure to commutate will not produce a dangerously high current and the next switching operation might be successful so that rotation of the alternator is not interrupted. It is possible for the main field winding to take the place of the protecting impedance, thus giving higher efficiency.

The rate at which the thyristors are fired determines the speed of rotation of the turbo-alternator. A programmed sequence of applying gate signals for a 60 electrical degree step of rotation is shown in the diagram of Fig. 5.3, together with the ideal resultant current flowing in the three phases. For half wave rectification the gate signals are continuous, or are pulse trains, over the period of conduction and the thyristor turn off pulse is not required because commutation is natural and is aided by any induced emf in the motor

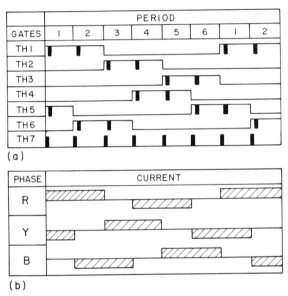

Fig. 5.3. Sequential switching to produce three-phase currents. (a) Gate signals (6 periods per cycle); (b) winding currents.

windings. For the other forms of supply the signals need only be single pulses but because one thyristor is made inoperative every 60 electrical degree step, two pulses must be applied to a thyristor during its 120° operation each cycle.

Figures 5.4, 5.5, 5.6 and 5.7 show 3 kW model results. Although a single-phase supply which is half wave rectified by the thyristors needs least equipment, it does not mean it is the best from the viewpoint of either capital or running cost. The reactance of the winding to alternating current with a d.c. level means higher voltage devices; in the case of the model, the voltage to produce rotation was about five times higher than for the d.c. supply. The increase in the power input to supply the increased iron losses was of the same order.

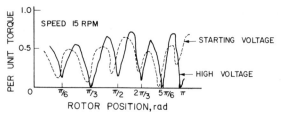

Fig. 5.4.   Torque variation.

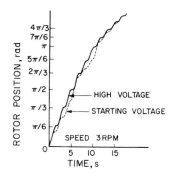

Fig. 5.5.   Position detent at low speed.

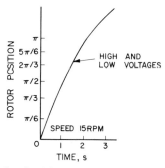

Fig. 5.6.   Position variation (no detent).

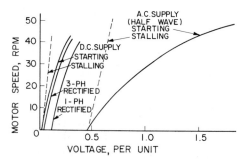

Fig. 5.7.   Starting and stalling voltage.

To overcome the inertia and stiction of the set, higher voltages are required at starting than for running. The associated high currents would also be needed if the speed were so low that the detent of field alignment operated and the effect of applied voltage adjustment would be noticeable, as in Fig. 5.5. For the model, with a switching rate of $\frac{1}{2}$ Hz (15 rpm), a variation of applied voltages did not produce a marked fluctuation in speed over the cycle. Of course, the torque pulsates. Figure 5.4 shows the torque variation over each switching operation but the machine inertia can prevent this being reflected in the rotation and this is revealed in Fig. 5.6.

Higher torques are necessary to accelerate the motor into step for increased speeds. This is shown in Fig. 5.7, based on peak voltage in accordance with thyristor ratings, and for constant field. For the case of half wave rectification, the model pulled into step at frequencies higher than 1.3 Hz, but the lowest speeds for smooth operation and minimum power requirements are well met at much lower frequencies.

(b) A cycloconverter for low speeds

Another way to bar a turbo-alternator by using the alternator as a synchronous motor is to supply it with low-frequency power from a cycloconverter. The cycloconverter transforms a high-frequency supply to a

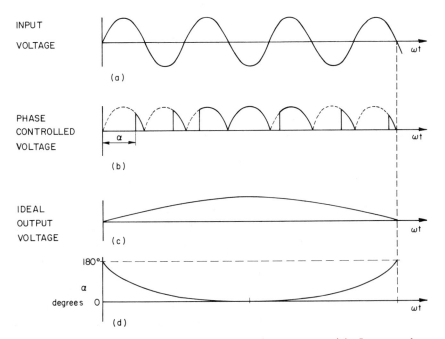

Fig. 5.8. Frequency division using a cycloconverter. (a) Input voltage waveform; (b) output voltage waveform; (c) idealized output; (d) trigger angle waveform.

low-frequency supply without the need to have an intermediary d.c. supply which has been the case for all units up to now. Cycloconverters can be used for any low-frequency application, variable or fixed. They were used first in the 1930's for traction purposes. A.C. series motors have mechanical commutation difficulties at frequencies as high as 50 Hz so the use of the cycloconverter to reduce the frequency to $16\frac{2}{3}$ Hz solved the problem without losing the great advantages of series motor torque characteristics.

In principle an a.c. waveform is available to the input of a cycloconverter as in Fig. 5.8(a). That waveform is not only rectified but it is phase controlled and line commutated. The phase angle α is altered cyclically as shown in Fig. 5.8(b) and (d) so that the ideal output from the cycloconverter (filtered) is that of Fig. 5.8(c). Here the output frequency is shown to be one-seventh of the supply frequency, that is, it is directly proportional to the cyclic change of α.

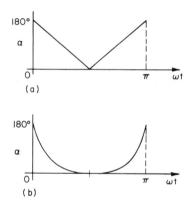

Fig. 5.9.   Voltage control by the adjustment of α. (a) Linear variation of trigger angle; (b) continuous variation of trigger angle.

For a fixed low output frequency the voltage is not problem, but if the application were for an adjustable speed drive where the frequency and the voltage were proportional then voltage control could be through α as well. The cycle of α determines the frequency but it is the function of α with time which determines the total area of the voltage curve over an output cycle and hence the average and rms values. For example, in Fig. 5.9, the function of α in (a) gives a lower voltage than the function of α in (b). However, in phase control of the thyristor conduction, the supply sees a load with a poorer power factor, $\cos \theta$, when α is increased (see Fig. 3.11(d)). It would seem advantageous as far as the power factor is concerned, not to delay α as in Fig. 5.9(a) but to use a pulse modulation technique as shown in Fig. 5.10.

Also to be taken into account are the harmonics associated with the low frequency fundamental of the output. The principle of the method clearly shows that the output frequency can be adjusted from zero up to the supply frequency. In practice the harmonics keep the highest output frequency much below the input frequency. To help keep the harmonics low a polyphase supply is used. A three-phase supply and a three-phase load arrangement is shown in Fig. 5.11. Only one phase of the cycloconverter is shown in full.

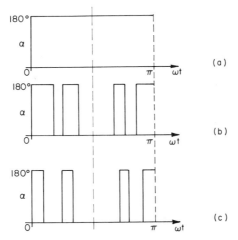

Fig. 5.10. On-off control for good power factor. (a) Zero voltage; (b) low voltage; (c) high voltage.

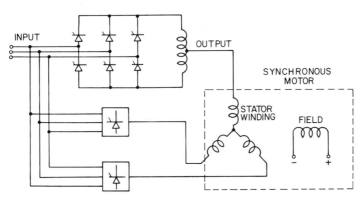

Fig. 5.11.   A three-phase cycloconverter.

The other two are shown in block form. Noticeable is the large number of thyristors which are to be used, that is, six per output phase for a three-phase input.

Fig. 5.12 shows a typical waveform with much less ripple than in, say, the single-phase case of Fig. 5.8. Starting at 0 in Fig. 5.12, the cycloconverter is acting as a controlled rectifier with full conduction. Current flow is into the phase winding of the motor. The phase angle, and hence conduction, is delayed over each successive input cycle until the net output voltage is zero, and then the polarity changes and the cycloconverter begins to invert over a half cycle. Depending on the power factor, $\cos \theta$, of the load, current will then flow from the phase winding of the motor to the inverting cyclo-converter and to the supply. During the negative half cycle of the voltage the phase angle itself goes through a complete cycle of giving a short conduction period, that is α nearly $180°$, increasing conduction of each input cycle successively to a maximum at $0'$ and then decreasing again. Although the voltage ripple superimposed on the fundamental component of low frequency seems a problem, the inductance of the load and line smooths the current waveform. A better waveshape is obtained the higher the number of input phases, but this has to be paid for by the greater number of thyristors and increased control circuitry.

The better waveshape is the advantage over the previous inverter in Section 3.3.1. An attempt is made to synthesize a low-frequency sine wave output

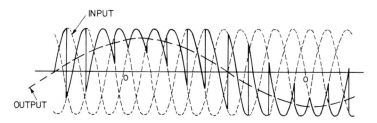

Fig. 5.12. Single-phase cycloconverter output from a three-phase input.

from the cycloconverter whereas the other produces only square waves, which, of course, can be modulated.

Higher frequencies than the input frequency can be obtained but forced commutation would be required.

5.4. SYNCHRONOUS MOTOR EXCITATION

Normally one would not consider excitation as a parameter to control the drive of a synchronous motor. Certainly it is of no use for speed control because the speed is only a function of frequency and the number of poles.

Excitation is useful as an adjustable parameter. Adjustment of the d.c. excitation of the synchronous motor is no different from that of the d.c. machine. This has been discussed in detail in Chapter 4 to include resistance, rectifiers and controlled rectifiers for a.c. supplies, and thyristor choppers for d.c. supplies. It is the application of motor field adjustment and its related problems which will be detailed here.

Power factor correction is one use of excitation control. This is brought about by the ability of the synchronous machine to absorb or supply reactive power. The amount depends on the excitation level. A second use is found in optimizing the design of a machine because on low load, low excitation and on heavy loads, high excitation levels produce savings over a constant high excitation for all loads.

5.4.1. Thyristor automatic excitation control

For constant load conditions it is normal for the synchronous motor excitation to be set at a fixed value. In such a case a reduction in load or a decrease in the applied armature voltage makes the motor power factor more leading. Figure 5.13 shows the case of a reduced load, where the subscript 1 denotes the normal load values and subscript 2 denotes the lower load values.

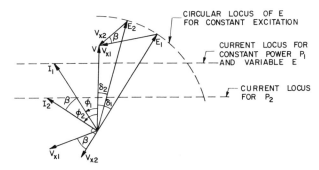

Fig. 5.13. Power factor change with load.

A reduced load means a reduction in load angle from δ_1 to δ_2. This is indicated in Equation (5.2) for constant V, E and X_s. The power equation is

$$P = \frac{VE}{X_s} \sin \delta \text{ per phase} \qquad (5.2)$$

V is the armature applied voltage per phase
E is the armature induced emf per phase
X_s is the synchronous reactance per phase and
δ is the load angle.

Accordingly phasor V_x rotates through an angle β in the phasor diagram and so does the current if the armature resistance is neglected. The power factor becomes more leading. This compensates for a lagging load elsewhere in the system, so it is tolerated but there is no control.

For some synchronous motor applications such as reciprocating compressors, there are occasional peak loads. It is uneconomical to have the motor designed to run continuously with high levels of excitation in order to maintain a stable torque for peak loads. It would necessitate a larger size motor to handle the heat dissipation. Instead, it is advantageous to work at a

lower level of excitation for normal loads and then automatically boost the
excitation for momentarily increased loads. A further step is to be able to
provide a continuously adjustable excitation to suit all loads. The value of the
field current to suit the power could then be a function of the load current
drawn by the armature. That function would depend on the stability and the
value of the power factor, that is the amount of leading reactive kVA desired.
The efficiency of the motor can be controlled, the choice being to work at
maximum efficiency or to improve the system power factor.

A change in load can be rapid so that the excitation control must give a
fast response. This can be provided by a thyristor amplifier, which is shown in

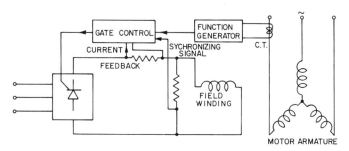

Fig. 5.14.   Thyristor field control.

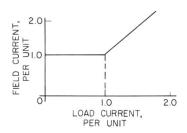

Fig. 5.15.   An ideal function generator characteristic.

block form as a phase controlled, a.c. line commutated rectifier bridge in Fig.
5.14. The thyristor triggering signals are derived from the load current via a
function generator, whose ideal characteristic might be that of Fig. 5.15. The
excitation is kept constant for good power factor conditions until a certain
load is reached and then rises in proportion to the load. To take into account
the non-linear motor magnetization curve and the non-linear relation between
the firing phase angle α and the rectifier output there would be some
deviation, although a field current feedback loop would compensate for this.

During starting, as an induction motor, it is necessary to inhibit the d.c.
field supply and to protect the thyristor rectifier from the high induced emfs
at slip frequency in the field winding. A resistance across the winding
accomplishes both. The voltage across the bridge will not be the open circuit

induced emf, which would necessitate high voltage ratings for the thyristors, but the voltage drop caused by the resulting current through the shunt resistance. Once the machine has run up to speed as an induction motor, the slip is small so the a.c. voltage in the field winding is small. At a particular minimum value, sensed across the shunt resistance, the gate signals can be applied so that direct current can be fed to the field. The motor will then synchronize and the function generator takes control.

(a) Brushless excitation protection during starting

Large synchronous machines have their field windings on the rotor because then there is less power to transport via slip rings. If the synchronous motor is to be brushless, the slip rings have to be eliminated. A typical system is shown in Fig. 5.16. An a.c. exciter is used in place of the conventional d.c. generator

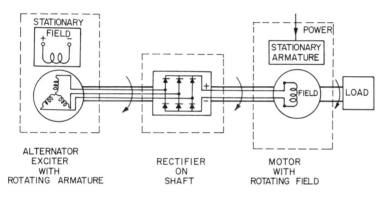

Fig. 5.16.   Static field excitation on the rotor.

or d.c. supply, so that the leads can be taken through the hollow shaft, the a.c. supply rectified and the output connected directly to the field.

Just as with a thyristor bridge, protection must be added to prevent the high voltages, induced in the field winding during starting, from damaging the diode bridge. In practice the Rosenberry circuit of Fig. 5.17 has proved satisfactory. This thyristor circuit is placed between the diode bridge and the field winding of Fig. 5.16.

At the point of starting the a.c. exciter output is zero but there is a large induced emf in the main motor field winding. As the voltage of rail A increases positively, zener diodes Z_1 and Z_2 break down to put thyristors $TH1$ and $TH2$ into conduction. The diode bridge is now short-circuited to prevent voltage damage. Resistance R limits the short-circuit current. When rail B becomes positive, the bridge itself provides the short-circuit and the thyristors turn off. Thyristor $TH3$ is always off during the starting period, because, when rail A is positive, $TH3$ anode is negative with respect to its cathode, and when rail *B* is positive *TH3* gate is negative with respect to its cathode.

The a.c. exciter begins to deliver current as the motor speed builds up. Thyristors *TH1* and *TH2* carry this current until the motor approaches synchronous speed, when the induced emf is too low to break down the zener diodes and allow the thyristors to conduct. At this speed the exciter current, rectified by the three-phase bridge, flows through the motor field winding and the motor pulls into synchronism.

If only one thyristor were used to short-circuit the bridge, it would continue to conduct at synchronous speed because the exciter current would prevent it turning off. With two thyristors, during the half cycle when *D* conducts, there is a voltage drop across *D* of about 1 V. This voltage is sufficient to turn off *TH2* by reverse biasing. As soon as *TH2* blocks, *TH1* also stops conducting and returns to the blocking state. The two thyristors remain in the blocking state during the synchronous running because the breakdown voltage of the zener diodes is designed to be higher than the d.c. excitation voltage.

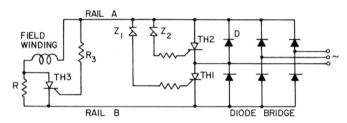

Fig. 5.17.   Motor starting protection.

Once the motor is in synchronism it is quite unnecessary to have *R* in the circuit with its attendant power loss. The resistance is short-circuited at synchronism because both the gate and anode of *TH3* are positive with respect to the cathode so it conducts.

This brushless motor has protection but no adjustable control. Figure 5.14 showed adjustable field control but it was not brushless. A brushless adjustable field control seems possible with a suitable merger of the two systems.

5.5. A SYNCHRONOUS OR A DIRECT CURRENT MOTOR?

The d.c. motor is the most versatile of all motors. If, for some applications, the mechanical commutator of the d.c. motor cannot be tolerated, it is possible to invert the machine. Putting the armature on the stator and the field poles on the rotor means that semiconductor switches can replace the mechanical commutator. To be completely free of brushes and sliding contacts, the field poles have either to be permanent magnets or else excited by another d.c. machine on the same shaft and have an uncontrolled semiconductor rectifier mounted on the same shaft to feed direct current to the pole winding. This is shown in Fig. 5.16. This brushless d.c. excitation is modern practice for large synchronous motors with rotating fields, but there is no reason why it cannot be accommodated for inverted d.c. motors.

For d.c. machines the current must always enter the armature winding at the quadrature axes. Fig. 5.18 illustrates a developed and inverted d.c. motor. A thyristor switching arrangement replaces the mechanical commutator and in the position shown thyristors 1 and 2 must be the only ones conducting. The current distribution will produce a torque on the armature and a reaction torque on the rotor so that rotation ensues. The quadrature axis rotates with the rotor so that to maintain the same constant torque the armature must maintain the same current distribution with respect to the poles. Hence the armature current must always be introduced into the quadrature axis by sequentially switching pairs of thyristors. After one-sixth of a revolution of

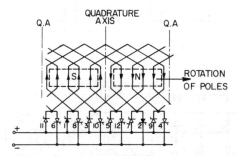

Fig. 5.18.   An inverted d.c. motor with a thyristor commutator.

the machine of Fig. 5.18 thyristors 1 and 2 would be turned off and thyristors 3 and 4 turned on, followed by thyristors 5 and 6 to complete half a cycle.

A large number of thyristors is needed to replace all the actual commutator segments, but there is no need to have so many. Six thyristors would be quite adequate for any winding. That is Fig. 5.18, can be reduced to Fig. 5.19(a) which can be redrawn as in Fig. 5.19(b). It does not appear to be a d.c. motor. However the conventional sequential switching, so that conductors carry current in one particular direction to give unidirectional torque, is still maintained.

To introduce the current to or near the quadrature axis the pole position must be detected. The output of the detection transducers must feed the gate circuits of the appropriate thyristors. These transducers can be mechanical, magnetic, capacitive, radioactive or optical. They enable the switching rate, as well as the sequence, to be that required for the armature field to stay in step with the rotor. An important factor, if the motor is to be self-starting, is that the sensing transducer must be capable of knowing the pole position without an external power source, and when stationary. Figure 5.19(b) could be described as a synchronous machine and indeed it is to a certain extent, except that it has been given the name d.c. machine because of the nature of the supply. The mechanical commutator was the machine's own frequency changer. The thyristor inverter has the same function. So here as a d.c. motor, the rotor controls the armature field rotation to be in step. Hence, if the load is excessive the speed of the rotor just reduces until the electromagnetic and mechanical torques balance one another. During starting there is the same need to limit the current in the armature as in conventional machines, voltage being constant.

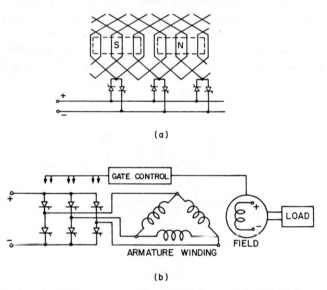

(a)

(b)

Fig. 5.19.   The brushless d.c. machine. (a) A reduction of thyristors; (b) the winding rearranged.

This sequential switching of currents from a d.c. supply, in the stator winding, produces a rotating field pattern. Actually there is some resolution and the field pattern travels around the air-gap in discrete steps. The greater the number of coil elements and the faster the switching, the more uniformly the field pattern appears to rotate. The steps are usually 60 electrical degrees in the configuration of Fig. 5.19(b).

In this way the stator winding of Fig. 5.19(b) can be looked upon as universal. That is, it can be used for any of the machines, d.c. synchronous or induction motor type. The d.c. and the synchronous motors would have the same rotors. In the d.c. case the rotor controls the rate of armature switching and ensures current injection at the quadrature axis. In the synchronous motor the armature controls the rotor so that the rotor locks in and follows the armature field, and, unlike the d.c. motor, if the load is excessive, the synchronous motor stalls. With a cage rotor the machine becomes an induction motor, the speed of which is nearly proportional to the switching rate. The thyristor inverter has tended to unify the electrical drives. Even the inverter has a basic configuration. It is the thyristor switching modules which now fit the machine to the load characteristic rather then vice versa. Another important point is that the inverter has made it possible for the machines, if not strictly commutatorless, at least to be free from sliding and mechanically switching contacts.

REFERENCES

1. Roters, H. C. (1947), 'The hysteresis motor', *A.I.E.E. Trans.* **66** 1419.

BIBLIOGRAPHY

Power applications of controllable semiconductor devices (1965), I.E.E. Publication, No. 17.

Griffin, A. W. J. and Ramshaw, R. S. (1965), *Thyristors and their applications,* Chapman and Hall, London.

Rosenberry, G. M. (1960), 'A new brushless d.c. excited rotating field synchronous motor', *Proc. A.I.E.E. Applications and Industry,* 136.

Edwards, J. D., Harrison, E. H. and Stephen, D. D. (1966), 'Thysyn motors', *A.E.I. Engineering,* **6**, 36-39.

Ramshaw, R. S., Griffin, A. W. J. and Lloyd, K. (1965, 1966). 'A brushless adjustable speed motor for extreme environments', *Control pt. I,* **9**, (90) 669-672; *pt. II,* **10** (91) 40-44.

Wilson, T. G. and Trickey, P. H. (1962), 'D.C. machine with solid state commutation', *Electrical Engineering,* **81** (11) 879.

Nishimura, M., Murakami, Y., Sakuma, N. and Kuroyama, T. (1969), 'A pulsewidth-controlled cycloinverter', *Electrical Engineering in Japan,* **89** (10).

St. J. Lamb, C. (1963), 'Commutatorless alternating – voltage fed variable speed motor', *Proc. I.E.E.,* **110** (12) 2221.

Gallagher, P. J., Barrett, A. and Shepherd, W. (1970), 'Analysis of single-phase rectifier thyristor-controlled load with integral-cycle triggering', *Proc. I.E.E.,* **117**, (2).

Power semiconductor application (1972), IEEE Press.

Appendices

Logic circuitry for inverter control

The three-phase inverter chosen is of the McMurray type which is described in Section 3.3.1(c)(i). The purpose of the logic is to switch the bridge thyristors sequentially to produce an a.c. output from a d.c. input. Protection of the thyristors from overcurrent conditions is also provided by the logic circuits.

Figure A.1 shows the bridge inverter which employs auxiliary thyristors for impulse commutation. Thyristors 1 to 6 are the load carrying thyristors. They

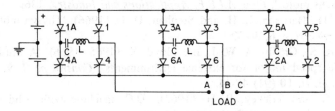

Fig. A.1. Three-phase inverter bridge.

are numbered in their firing sequence. The commutating thyristors are numbered $1A$ to $6A$.

When the load thyristors are turned on and off in the correct sequence, the voltage waveforms at the three output terminals, A, B and C are shown in Fig. A.2. The thyristor gate pulses are also shown. At any time three thyristors are on. In one cycle of the output there should be six switching operations of the load thyristors and six of the commutation thyristors.

In each phase of the inverter there are two load carrying thyristors connected in series. Only one of them should be on at any time. The logic circuit must ensure that one of them is prevented from conducting when the other is on. For example, in phase A $TH1$ should be on only when $TH4$ is off. Accordingly the gate pulse to $TH1$ should be applied when $TH4A$ has successfully turned off $TH4$.

At the start, the correct thyristor must be triggered on to ensure proper sequential switching in order to obtain a cyclic output. In the event of an overload all the thyristors must be turned off.

190

From these general requirements a logic circuit can be designed. One such design is illustrated in block form in **Fig. A3**.

The logic circuit should provide six gate pulses to the commutation thyristors *TH1A* to *TH6A* in sequence, as shown in **Fig. A.2**. A six position

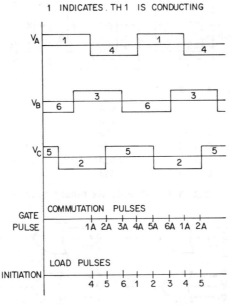

Fig. A.2.   The inverter output voltages and thyristor gate pulses.

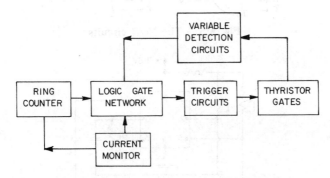

Fig. A.3.   Block diagram of logic design.

ring counter can be built in to provide this sequence of pulses. This is formed from a modulo six binary counter and *NOR* gates. The six-position counter gives a repetitive waveform which has six distinct states. The *NOR* gates decode this to provide the necessary gate pulses for the commutation thyristors.

Three logic modules are used in the modulo six binary counter. They are shown connected in Fig. A.4. The gate pulses, which are generated when the three outputs of the modules take on different states, are also shown in the same figure. These modules are of the *J-K* flip-flop type.[1]

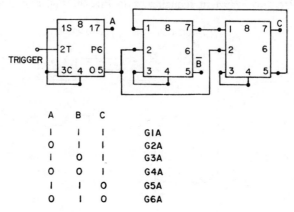

A	B	C	
I	I	I	G1A
O	I	I	G2A
I	O	I	G3A
O	O	I	G4A
I	I	O	G5A
O	I	O	G6A

Fig. A.4.　Modulo six binary counter.

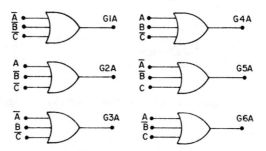

Fig. A.5.　The *NOR* circuits.

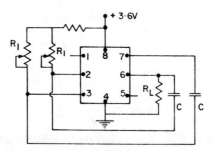

Fig. A.6.　An astable multivibrator.

To obtain *G1A* to *G6A*, the gate pulses to the commutation thyristors, six *NOR* circuits are used as shown in Fig. A.5.

The trigger pulses to the counter can be obtained from an astable multivibrator module as shown in Fig. A.6. A variation of *R* changes the frequency of the train of pulses. A large inverter can be used to obtain squarer pulses for better switching characteristics.

The next function of the logic circuitry is to provide gate pulses to turn on thyristors 1 to 6 in the sequence shown in Fig. A.2. In any one phase, the gate pulses for the two current carrying thyristors have to be provided in such a way that both of them are not turned on simultaneously. Thus in phase A, $G1$, the gate pulse to $TH1$, should be generated only when $TH4$ has turned off and $G1A$ is not present. Therefore, $G1$ can be expressed as $\bar{T}_4 \cdot \overline{G1A}$ where T_4 designates the state of $TH4$ conducting. This can be obtained from a *NOR* gate with inputs $G1A$ and T_4. There should be a detection circuit to obtain T_4. Similar functions for $G2$ to $G6$ can be obtained. They are

$$G1 = \bar{T}_4 \cdot \overline{G1A} \quad \text{or} \quad \overline{T_4 + G1A}$$

$$G2 = \bar{T}_5 \cdot \overline{G2A} \quad \text{or} \quad \overline{T_5 + G2A}$$

$$G3 = \bar{T}_6 \cdot \overline{G3A} \quad \text{or} \quad \overline{T_6 + G3A}$$

$$G4 = \bar{T}_1 \cdot \overline{G4A} \quad \text{or} \quad \overline{T_1 + G4A}$$

$$G5 = \bar{T}_2 \cdot \overline{G5A} \quad \text{or} \quad \overline{T_2 + G5A}$$

$$G6 = \bar{T}_3 \cdot \overline{G6A} \quad \text{or} \quad \overline{T_3 + G6A}$$

The circuit for generating the pulses $G1A$ to $G6A$ and $G1$ to $G6$ could be as in Fig. A.7.

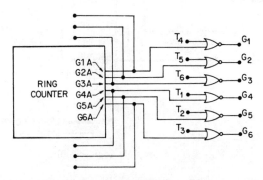

Fig. A.7. Thyristor gate pulses.

Such a circuit will not be adequate for starting the inverter. As seen earlier, three thyristors are on at any time. Since the ring counter always starts with $G1A$, the inverter should start by firing thyristors 4, 3 and 2 (see Fig. A.2). But in order that the capacitors in the commutation circuits have the correct polarity, thyristors $6A$ and $5A$ should be fired together with $1A$ before 4, 3 and 2 are fired. Thus, at start, *G5A* and *G6A* are made 'on' before the switch is turned to run. A switch position reset is provided between off and run position which ensures this.

In Fig. A.8 the reset voltage of 3.6 V is applied to two *R-S* flip-flops *BS2* and *BS3*, which turn on *G5A* and *G6A*. *G1A* is provided by the ring counter. *BS2* and *BS3* are reset by *G2A*. Thus these are on only for the first 60°. The reset pulse also resets the ring counter. In the run position, the ring counter starts with *G1A* and proceeds to *G6A* and back to *G1A* and so on. At the

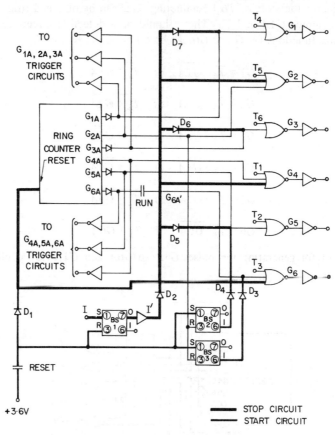

Fig. A.8.   Complete logic circuit.

instant of switching to the run mode, *G1A*, *G5A* and *G6A* are on, and so *G1*, *G5* and *G6* cannot be on. *G2A*, *G3A*, *G4A*, T_5, T_6 and T_1 are off and so *G2*, *G3* and *G4* will be on. After 60°, *G5A* and *G6A* will be removed, *G2A* will be on and *G1A* off. *TH2* will turn-off and *TH5* will turn-on. The firing will then proceed in the correct sequence.

To stop the inverter, thyristors 1 to 6 should be turned off. It is sufficient if thyristors 1, 3 and 5 are turned off. In order to stop, *TH1A*, *3A* and *5A* should be fired. Thus *G1A*, *G3A* and *G5A* are 'on'. This is achieved by the application of the reset voltage through $D1$ to $G1A$, $G3A$ and $G5A$. At the same time, this voltage makes $G1$ to $G6$ go to zero. The reset position thus provides stop also. There is one difficulty however. To stop, $G3A$ is made 'on'. $G6A$ has to be made 'on' for starting. If both thyristors $3A$ and $6A$ are made on, there will be a short-circuit. To prevent this, a contact is provided in the switch which is open in the reset mode and closed only in the 'run' mode. The voltage from $BS3$ is connected to $G6A$ through this contact and so $G6A$ will be on only in the run mode when $G3A$ will be off.

Overcurrent protection is also included in the logic circuit. When an overload occurs the thyristors are turned off as in stop. In order that the circuit may not turn on again before the fault is cleared, the overcurrent detection voltage is applied to a bistable circuit which applies a voltage to $G1A$, $G3A$ and $G5A$ and also turns $G1$ to $G6$ off. In Fig. A.8, $BS1$ will be set to 0 at pin 7 when an overcurrent occurs. The amplifier inverts it and this voltage is applied through $D2$. $BS1$ can be reset by manually turning the switch to reset.

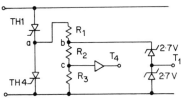

Fig. A.9. Detecting state of thyristor.

For proper operation of this circuit, two variable detection circuits are necessary. One is to detect T_1 to T_6 and the other for overcurrent. The circuit can be operated without these detection circuits but with a fixed delay instead of detecting if a thyristor has turned off. Application of a voltage to terminal 1 of $BS1$ to simulate overcurrent conditions turns off the inverter.

Two circuits are suggested for detecting these variables. Figure A.9 shows a circuit for detecting when one thyristor is off.

$$\text{When 1 on, 4 off,} \quad V_a = 230 \text{ V}$$
$$V_b = 5.5 \text{ V}$$
$$V_c = 3.0 \text{ V}$$

$$T_1 = 1 \text{ and } T_4 = 0$$

$$\text{When both 1 and 4 are off,} \quad V_a \simeq 115 \text{ V}$$
$$V_b \simeq 3 \text{ V}$$
$$V_c \simeq 1.5 \text{ V}$$

$$T_1 = 0 \text{ and } T_4 = 0$$

$$\text{When 1 off and 4 on,} \quad V_a = 0$$
$$V_b = 0$$
$$V_c = 0$$

$$T_1 = 0, T_4 = 1$$

For overcurrent detection, a small resistance can be put in the d.c. bus. The voltage across this resistor is connected to *BS1* through a zener diode and resistance as shown in Fig. A.10.

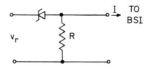

Fig. A.10.   Overcurrent detection.

APPENDIX II

Logic circuitry for bidirectional converter

The logic control unit of Fig. 4.21 must maintain three steady-state conditions and allow transfer between them as shown in Fig. A.11.

Since a minimum time is allowed for the transfer between states, a forced driving function must be used. Therefore, the states of Fig. A.11 are expanded

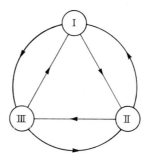

I : ZERO CURRENT IN COIL

II : −30 A CURRENT IN COIL

III : 30 A CURRENT IN COIL

Fig. A.11.   Transfer between states.

as shown in Fig. A.12. This Mealy state diagram has seven stable states, each of which are explained below:

  I   Zero current flows in the coil and no triggering pulses are applied to the triacs;

  II The 'forced driving' phase angle ($\alpha \sim 1°$) is applied to the triac turn-on in order to cause positive current to build up rapidly in the coil;

 III While in this state, the positive current regulator is in operation and the current is held at 30 A;

 IV The 'forced driving' phase angle ($\alpha \sim 178°$) is applied to the triacs in order to cause the positive current to decay rapidly in the magnet circuit;

V The 'forced driving' phase angle is applied to the triacs in order to cause negative current to build up rapidly in the magnet circuit;

VI While in this state, the negative current regulator is in operation and the current is held at −30 A;

VII A 'forced driving' phase angle is applied to the triacs in order to cause the negative current to decay rapidly in the coil.

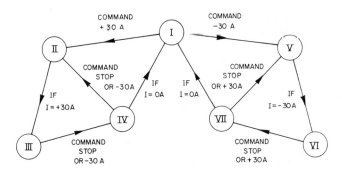

Fig. A.12. Expanded states for forced driving function.

The outputs of the logic control unit are characteristic of the controller state which is summarized in Table A.1.

Table A.1. Controller States

State	Force 30 A ($\alpha \simeq 1°$)	Force zero ($\alpha \simeq 178°$)	Positive regulate	Negative regulate	Triac pulses for positive current	Triac pulses for negative current
I	NO	NO	NO	NO	NO	NO
II	YES	NO	NO	NO	YES	NO
III	NO	NO	YES	NO	YES	NO
IV	NO	YES	NO	NO	YES	NO
V	YES	NO	NO	NO	NO	YES
VVI	NO	NO	NO	YES	NO	YES
VII	NO	YES	NO	NO	NO	YES

The logic circuit signals required at the logic circuit control terminal are T_A, T_B and T_C where

T_A = 1 means that the positive 30 A order is active,

T_B = 1 means that the negative 30 A order is active and

T_C = 1 means that zero current order is active.

The logic circuit also requires input signals from the current detection circuit so that the controlling signals to the triac switches can be determined.

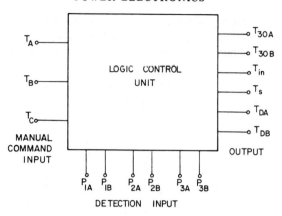

MANUAL
COMMAND
INPUT

OUTPUT

DETECTION INPUT

Fig. A.13.   Logic control unit block diagram.

Figure A.13 shows the logic circuit requirement where the logic symbols for current detection are represented by

P_{1A} = 1 means positive current flows ($i > 0$)
P_{1B} = 1 means reverse current flows ($i < 0$)
P_{2A} = 1 means positive 30 A flows ($i \geqslant 30$ A)
P_{2B} = 1 means reverse 30 A flows ($i \leqslant -30$ A)
P_4 = 1 means no current flows ($i = 0$)
      $= \overline{P_{1A} + P_{1B}}$ (P_4 logic unnecessary)

P_{3A}, P_{3B} = 1 means positive, reverse 35 A flows respectively. The logic unit output feeds into the firing angle α control circuit. Logic output symbols are represented by

T_s = 1 makes the firing angle $\alpha = \alpha_s \simeq 1°$
T_{in} = 1 makes the firing angle $\alpha = \alpha_{invert} \simeq 170°$
T_{30A} = 1 makes the firing angle $\alpha = \alpha_{30} \simeq 70°$ (for positive 30 A regulation)
T_{30B} = 1 makes the firing angle $\alpha = \alpha_{30} \simeq 70°$ (for reverse 30 A regulation)
T_{DA} = 1 means pulse to a particular gate for forward current and
T_{DB} = 1 means pulse to a particular gate for reverse current.

The block form of the logic circuit is depicted in Fig. A.13.
Integrated circuit Resistor Transistor Logic elements are used throughout this sub-system. An element contains a pair of dual input positive logic NOR gates in a single package. These elements are used to construct the circuit of Fig. A.16 by realizing the equivalence of Fig. A.14.
When two logic NOR gates are combined as in Fig. A.15, they form a bistable or flip-flop. The R-S flip-flop whose truth table is also shown is convenient for changing an order to a new state. A capacitor and resistor are added to the reset gate so that when power is initially applied the reset gate R goes to the H state.

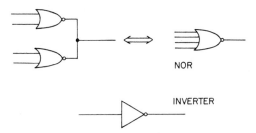

NOR

INVERTER

Fig. A.14. *NOR* circuit equivalence.

The logic operation functions are

$$T_S(\text{on}) \quad = 1 = \overline{(P_{1A} + P_{1B})} \times (T_A + T_B) = 1 = \text{set}$$

$$T_S(\text{off}) \quad = 0 \text{ if } T_C + P_{2A} + P_{2B} = 1 = \text{reset}$$

$$T_{in}(\text{on}) \quad = 1 = T_C + P_{1A} \times T_B + P_{1B} \times T_A$$

$$T_{in}(\text{off}) \quad = 0 = \overline{(P_{1A} + P_{1B})}$$

$$T_{30A}(\text{on}) \quad = 1 = P_{2A}$$

$$T_{30A}(\text{off}) = 0 = T_C + P_{1A} \times T_B$$

$$T_{30B}(\text{on}) \quad = 1 = P_{2B}$$

$$T_{30B}(\text{off}) = 0 = T_C + P_{1B} \times T_A$$

$$T_{DA} \qquad = P_{1A} + \overline{(P_{1A} + P_{1B})} \times T_A \quad \text{and}$$

$$T_{DA} \qquad = P_{1B} + \overline{(P_{1A} + P_{1B})} \times T_B$$

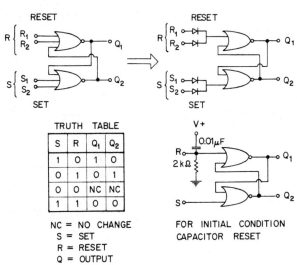

S	R	Q_1	Q_2
1	0	1	0
0	1	0	1
0	0	NC	NC
1	1	0	0

TRUTH TABLE

NC = NO CHANGE
S = SET
R = RESET
Q = OUTPUT

FOR INITIAL CONDITION
CAPACITOR RESET

Fig. A.15. *R-S* flip-flop.

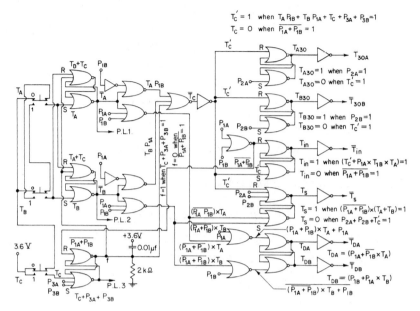

Fig. A.16.   Logic circuit.

The complete logic circuit is shown in Fig. A.16.

The pulse generator is shown in Fig. 4.20. The secondary voltage v is much greater than the zener voltage of 3.3 V so that fluctuations of the power supply have a minimal effect on the output firing angle α. The output of the pulse generator is fed to the current direction control circuit of Fig. A.17.

The current detection circuit of Fig. A.18 and the regulating circuit of Fig. A.19 complete the details of the converter control circuit whose block diagram is depicted in Fig. 4.21.

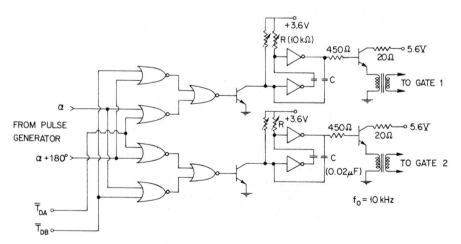

Fig. A.17.   Current direction control and firing pulse modulator.

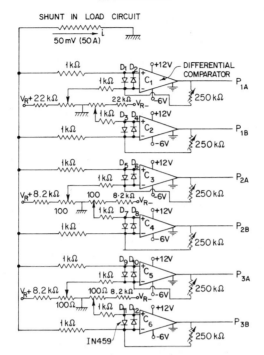

Fig. A.18.   Current detection circuit.

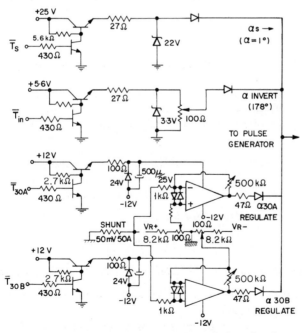

Fig. A.19.   α step change and regulating circuit.

APPENDIX III

Logic circuitry for on-off servo

The variables for the thyristor bridge circuit have been defined in Section 4.112 of Chapter IV and the logic functions stated in Equations (4.69), (4.70) and (4.71).

The switch functions can be determined by constructing a truth table. This is done by considering all possible permutations of the variables and then logically the designer determines what the output should be for each set of inputs. A more elegant method is to use Karnaugh's map for minimization (see Fig. A.20). The map is essentially a truth table but it is presented in such a way that minimization becomes simpler, for four or at the most five variables. In this case there are six variables (T_{13}, T_{24}, T_{56}, P_{13}, P_{24}, and C), from which three switching functions are to be derived. For one of the functions one variable may be eliminated, while, for the other two, the Karnaugh map is modified as a simple means of representation of the truth table and the resulting functions, if necessary, can be simplified by Boolean algebra.

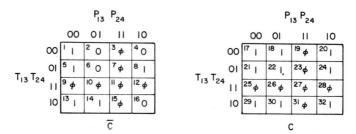

Fig. A.20.   Karanaugh map for triggering $TH5$ and $TH6$.

The input variable T_{56} may be deleted when determining the switching function for thyristors $TH5$ and $TH6$. The state of the two commutating thyristors, on or off, is dependent only on the other variables and not on itself.

In the figure,   0 is false or negative state
1 is true or positive state and
∅ is a state either 0 or 1

From the map the switching function is

$$T_{56} = C + \bar{P}_{13} \cdot \bar{P}_{24} + T_{13} \cdot P_{24} + T_{24} \cdot P_{13}$$

which simply means that thyristors $TH5$ and $TH6$ should be triggered on if

(a) the current has exceeded the allowable maximum or
(b) there is no positional error or
(c) one set of load carrying thyristors is on but the positional error is such that the other set should be on.

The detailed derivation of the equation is as follows. Take any four variables A, B, C and D, then examine the map in Fig. A.21 where the values of A and B are given by the heading of the column, and C and D are given by the row designators. All possible states of the four variables are represented by the various cells. The states of adjacent cells, either horizontally, vertically or end to end differ in the value of only one variable and it is this property that makes the Karanaugh graph so useful. This example shows that '1' is entered in the map corresponding to four conditions determined by the states of the variables whose transmission is '1'. The four entries are then grouped into the cell groups (dotted). By examining each of the groups the transmission is evidently

$$T = B \cdot \bar{C} \cdot \bar{D} + \bar{A} \cdot B \cdot D.$$

It is seen that a third group can also be formed, (shown in solid line), but it would be redundant as all the transmission terms have already been included.

In using the Karnaugh map much labour is saved by recognizing certain patterns of entries and grouping them into sub-cases as in the example. A

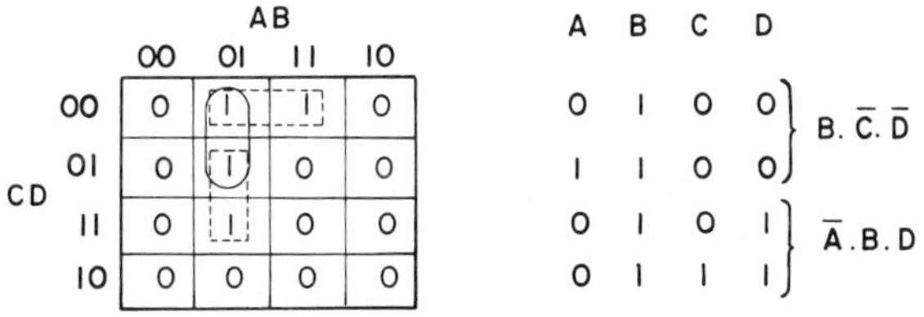

Fig. A.21.   Example of a Karanaugh graph.

sub-cube is defined as a set of cells within which one or more variables have constant values. Thus a group of two cells forming a sub-cube, as in the example, will have three variables constant with one variable taking both possible states. So for a two cell sub-cube one variable can be eliminated. Similarly, for a four cell sub-cube, two variables can be eliminated and for an eight cell sub-cube, three variables can be eliminated.

Referring again to Fig. A.20, the five-variable function is mapped as two four-variable functions. The left map contains entries for which 'C', the current, has exceeded the limit and the right map contains entries for which the current is below limit.

The simplest required transmission is obtained by

(a) considering all the entries in the right hand map to be 1's so there is only one variable that does not change its state and that variable is C
(b) considering all the entries in the first column of both maps as 1's, so that the variables which do not change the states are $\bar{P}_{13} \cdot P_{24}$
(c) considering the entries of cells 10, 11, 14, 15, and 26, 27, 30, 31, as 1's, so that the variables which do not change the states are $T_{13} \cdot P_{24}$, and
(d) considering the entries of cells 7, 8, 11, 12, and 23, 24, 27, 28 as 1's, so that the variables which do not change the states are $T_{24} \cdot P_{13}$.

All the entries which must be 1's in both maps have now been considered and so the simplest transmission for T_{56} is

$$T_{56} = C + \bar{P}_{13} \cdot \bar{P}_{24} + T_{13} \cdot P_{24} + T_{24} \cdot P_{13}.$$

For the remaining two switching functions, all six variables must be considered. The Karanaugh map cannot be used but is modified to represent the truth table. The truth tables representing triggering of $TH1$, $TH3$ and $TH2$, $TH4$ are shown in Fig. A.22(a) and (b) respectively.

$T_{13}\ T_{24}\ T_{56}$

$P_{13} P_{24} C$	000	001	011	010	110	111	101	100
000	0	0	0	0	ϕ	ϕ	0	0
001	0	0	0	0	ϕ	ϕ	0	0
011	0	0	0	0	ϕ	ϕ	0	0
010	0	0	0	0	ϕ	ϕ	0	0
110	0	0	0	0	ϕ	ϕ	0	0
111	0	0	0	0	ϕ	ϕ	0	0
101	0	0	0	0	ϕ	ϕ	0	0
100	1	0	0	0	ϕ	ϕ	0	0

(a)

$T_{13}\ T_{24}\ T_{56}$

$P_{13} P_{24} C$	000	001	011	010	110	111	101	100
000	0	0	0	0	ϕ	ϕ	0	0
001	0	0	0	0	ϕ	ϕ	0	0
011	0	0	0	0	ϕ	ϕ	0	0
010	1	0	0	0	ϕ	ϕ	0	0
110	0	0	0	0	ϕ	ϕ	0	0
111	0	0	0	0	ϕ	ϕ	0	0
101	0	0	0	0	ϕ	ϕ	0	0
100	0	0	0	0	ϕ	ϕ	0	0

(b)

Fig. A.22. Truth tables to determine switching functions for (a) T_{13} and (b) T_{24}.

By ignoring the possible 1's in columns 5 and 6, the transmission of the signal for triggering $TH1$, $TH3$ and $TH2$, $TH4$ are respectively

$$T_{13} = P_{13} \cdot \bar{P}_{24} \cdot \bar{C} \cdot \bar{T}_{13} \cdot \bar{T}_{24} \cdot \bar{T}_{56}$$

and

$$T_{24} = \bar{P}_{13} \cdot P_{24} \cdot \bar{C} \cdot \bar{T}_{13} \cdot \bar{T}_{24} \cdot \bar{T}_{56}$$

The above simply means that

(a) the current must be below a maximum value
(b) all thyristors are in a blocking state
(c) for T_{13}, positional P_{13} exists but not P_{24} and vice versa for T_{24}.

It should be noted that theoretically it is not possible to have both P_{13} and P_{24} error at the same time. In practice, unless the detection circuits are properly calibrated, both errors may appear. Hence it is necessary to have both P_{13} and P_{24} terms in equations.

The switching functions are depicted in the block diagram of Fig. 4.38. However, the actual control circuitry used in the positional servo considered here incorporated Philips Circuit Modules.[3] Due to their loading characteristics the circuit was assembled as shown in Fig. A.23.

There are seven types of modules used in this design. They operate at supply voltages +6 V and −6 V and have switching speeds of 100 kHz.

$EF1$, $EF2$ represent two types of emitter follower. The $EF1$, with its high

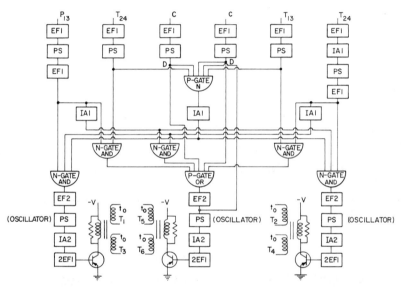

Fig. A.23.   Block diagram of actual control circuitry.

input impedance and low output impedance, is used as the first stage after a detection circuit to prevent loading. It is also used as a power amplifier. The $EF2$ is specially designed to amplify the weak output signals originating from a diode gate circuit.

$IA1$ and $IA2$ are amplifiers. The former is used to perform an inverting or NOT function while the latter serves the same purpose but has the advantages of appreciable power gain to amplify the weak output signals originating from a diode gate circuit.

PS is a pulse shaper with similar operating characteristics as a Schmidt trigger. A d.c. input signal, exceeding the input triggering level of the unit, is reshaped and inverted into the standard d.c. level (0 or −6 V) at the output. It is therefore used for d.c. level detection following the initial emitter follower circuits to reshape the input signals. The unit can also operate as a relaxation oxcillator whose pulses are amplified and isolated by a pulse transformer to trigger the thyristors. The oscillation frequency is controlled by the value of a capacitor. An OV input on any one of the input terminals will stop the oscillation.

Two gates, a positive P gate with a +6 V supply and a negative N gate with a −6 V supply can be employed to perform logic 'AND' and 'OR' functions.

Table A.2   Truth table of gating modules

Input signals, V			Output signals, V	
A	B	C	N-GATE	P-GATE
−6	−6	−6	−6	−6
−6	−6	0	0	−6
−6	0	−6	0	−6
0	−6	−6	0	−6
0	0	−6	0	−6
0	−6	0	0	−6
−6	0	0	0	−6
0	0	0	0	0

The operation of the gates is most readily illustrated by the truth Table A.2. Thus the function of the gates are

(a) a N-gate performs 'AND' operation on −6 V inputs and 'OR' operation on OV signals.

(b) a P-gate performs 'AND' operation on OV signals and 'OR' operation on −6 V signals.

REFERENCES

1. Fairchild, (1966), 'Using the JK flip-flop in small modulo counters', *Semiconductor Application Bulletin App. 120.*
2. Morris, N. M. (1969), *Logic circuits,* McGraw-Hill, U.S.A.
3. Bulletin − Philips Circuit Blocks.
4. Wickes, W. E. (1965), *Logic design with integrated circuits,* John Wiley & Sons, London.

Additional problems for Chapters One, Two, Three and Four

1.1. Since the thyristor is a fast acting switch, it can cause the load voltage to be applied at any point on the waveform. Further, the thyristor can control the number of cycles of the waveform that appear at the load. Consequently in the control of power there can be a deformation of the desired sinewave. In a.c. applications it is often necessary to know the RMS value of a distorted waveform, while in d.c. applications the average value of the waveform is important.

In the following calculate the RMS and average values of the current waveforms.

(a) A sine wave $i(t) = 100 \sin 377t$.

(b) A full sine wave rectified, where the first half cycle is described by $i(t) = 100 \sin 377t$.

(c) A half sine wave rectified, where the first half cycle is described by $i(t) = 100 \sin 377t$.

(d) A phase controlled sine wave $i(t) = 100 \sin 377t$, where the trigger angle $\alpha = 90$ degrees for both positive and negative half cycles. This is made possible by having a triac or two parallel opposed thyristors.

(e) A sine wave $i(t) = 100 \sin 377t$ with on/off integral cycle control as in Fig. 1.3 with 3 cycles on, 2 cycles off, 3 cycles on etc.

(f) A rectangular wave, with positive and negative half cycles having an amplitude 100 A and a frequency 60 Hz.

(g) A triangular wave, with positive and negative half cycles having an amplitude 100 A and a frequency 60 Hz.

Answers:

(a) $I_{rms} = 70.7$ A, $I_{av} = 0$

(b) $I_{rms} = 70.7$ A, $I_{av} = 63.6$ A

(c) $I_{rms} = 50$ A, $I_{av} = 31.8$ A

(d) $I_{rms} = 50$ A, $I_{av} = 0$

(e) $I_{rms} = 54.8$ A, $I_{av} = 0$

(f) $I_{rms} = 100$ A, $I_{av} = 0$

(g) $I_{rms} = 57.7$ A, $I_{av} = 0$

1.2. Thyristors can chop, rectify and invert a supply voltage waveform. In order to analyse the effect of waveform adjustment it is common to split the waveform into a fundamental waveform plus its harmonic components. The following are examples of this harmonic analysis.

Obtain the amplitudes of the fundamental and harmonic components (up to the 7th harmonic) for the following two cases.

(a) A rectangular wave, with positive and negative half cycles having an amplitude I amperes and a wavelength 2π radians.

(b) A fully rectified sine wave, whose first half cycle is described by $i(\theta) = I_m \sin \theta$.

Hint:

$$\text{If } f(\theta) = a_0 + a_1 \cos\theta + b_1 \sin\theta + a_2 \cos 2\theta + b_2 \sin 2\theta + \ldots\ldots$$

$$a_0 = \frac{1}{2\pi} \int_0^{2\pi} f(\theta) d\theta, \ a_n = \frac{1}{\pi} \int_0^{\pi} f(\theta) \cos n\theta \, d\theta,$$

$$b_n = \frac{1}{\pi} \int_0^{\pi} f(\theta) \sin n\theta \, d\theta$$

Answer:

(a) $i(\theta) = \dfrac{4I}{\pi}\left(\sin\theta + \dfrac{1}{3}\sin 3\theta + \dfrac{1}{5}\sin 5\theta + \dfrac{1}{7}\sin 7\theta \right)$

(b) $i(\theta) = \dfrac{2I_m}{\pi} + I_m \left(\dfrac{2}{3}\cos 2\theta + \dfrac{2}{15}\cos 4\theta + \dfrac{2}{35}\cos 6\theta \right)$

CHAPTER 2

2.5. In a half-wave controlled rectifier circuit as shown in Fig. 2.21 the firing angle α can be varied in order to alter the average voltage across the load. However harmonic components are present and these can give rise to increased losses and both oscillating and braking torques in rotating machines.

Obtain the amplitudes of the harmonic components of the load voltage if the supply voltage is sinusoidal when the firing angle $\alpha = 90°$

Answer:

$$v_L = \frac{\hat{V}}{2\pi} - \frac{\hat{V}}{2\pi}\cos\omega t + \sum_{n=2}^{\infty} \frac{\hat{V}\left(\cos n\pi + n \sin n\frac{\pi}{2}\right)}{\pi(1-n^2)} \cos n\omega t$$

$$+ \frac{\hat{V}}{4}\sin\omega t + \sum_{n=2}^{\infty}\left[\frac{-n\hat{V}\left(\cos n\frac{\pi}{2}\right)}{\pi(1-n^2)} \right]\sin n\omega t$$

2.6. A d.c. source of 100 V supplies a purely inductive load of 0.1 H. The controller is a thyristor in series with the source and load. From the response of this simple thyristor circuit find the minimum width of the gating pulse to ensure thyristor turn-on. The specification for the thyristor gives the latching current to be 4mA.

Answer: 4 µs

2.7. Consider the circuit as shown in Fig. 2.28. Let the only protection be the R and C elements and Let L, C_1 and R_1 be removed. A d.c. source of 100 V supplies a purely resistive load of 20 ohms. A diode is connected across the resistance R, whose value is 10 ohms, such that the anodes of the diode and thyristor are connected together.

Consider that the thyristor has just been turned off. Find the minimum value of C so that the thyristor will not turn on again due to dv/dt breakdown. The junction capacitance of the thyristor is 20 pF and the minimum value of the charging current required to turn on the thyristor is 4 mA.

Answer: 0.025 µF

2.8. A simple thyristor circuit consists of an a.c. source, with $v = \hat{V} \sin\omega t$, and a single thyristor controller in series with a resistive load. The thyristor conducts current when its anode voltage is positive; that is when $\omega t = 0$ to π, $\omega t = 2\pi$ to 3π, etc. The thyristor is fired at an angle α, where $0 \le \alpha \le \pi$, and conduction occurs over the period α to π for each positive half cycle, since the current is in phase with the voltage for a resistive load.

Show that the output voltage across the load is a variable d.c. voltage whose average value is

$$V_{av} = \frac{\hat{V}}{2\pi} (1 + \cos\alpha)$$

2.9. A voltage source $v = 100 \sin 377t$ supplies a resistive load of 100 ohms through a thyristor, which performs half-wave controlled rectification. Calculate the average power in the load, if the thyristor firing angle is fixed at 45 degrees with respect to the supply voltage waveform.

Answer: 22.7 W

2.10. In the circuit related to problem 2.8 the load is changed to become inductive, L, and resistive, R, and the thyristor is fired at $\alpha = 0$ radians. The steady-state current will lag the voltage.

While the current rises to a peak value the source supplies energy to R and L. From the current peak to the time the voltage crosses zero, the source supplies energy to R and energy is being extracted from L (to reduce the flux linkage). Finally from the time of zero current voltage crossing to zero current the energy extracted from the inductance (to bring the flux linkage to zero again) goes to R and the supply.

Find the non-zero, instantaneous value of the load current.

Answer:
$$i(t) = \frac{\sqrt{2}}{R}\, \hat{V} \sin \frac{\omega t}{2} \cos \frac{\omega t - 2\phi}{2},$$

$$\tan \phi = L/R.$$

2.11. For thyristor turn-off the current through the device must be reduced to zero momentarily. This can be achieved by storing energy in a capacitor by means of a resonant circuit, blocking further oscillation by means of a diode, and thus preparing for the capacitor to discharge and reverse bias the thyristor.

Fig. 2.24 shows the basic circuit for reversing the polarity of the capacitor, which has been charged up to a voltage of 100 V for the initial conditions. With the thyristor TH1 switched on at $t = 0$ find the instantaneous value of the current through L at any time t and determine the voltage waveform across the inductance.

Answer: $i(t) = 0.577 \sin 577t$ for $0 \leq t \leq \pi/\omega$ where $\omega = 577$ rad/s.

2.12. A thyristor is a switch. Load circuits comprise a combination of R, L and C elements. Consequently it is natural to want to find the transient response, when a supply is suddenly connected to a load by means of a switch or thyristor.

Consider the following two cases.

(a) A battery in series with a thyristor, a resistance R, and inductance L and a capacitance C.

(b) A battery in series with a thyristor, an inductance L and a parallel combination of a resistance R and a capacitance C.

For these cases determine

(i) The parameter relations for the underdamped conditions,

(ii) the resonant frequency in terms of the parameters and

(iii) the current waveforms when the thyristor is switched on.

Answer: (a) (i) $R < 2\sqrt{L/C}$, (ii) $\omega_0 = \frac{1}{2}\sqrt{(4/LC - R^2/L^2)}$

(b) (i) $R > 0.5\sqrt{L/C}$, (ii) $\omega_0 = \frac{1}{2}\sqrt{(4/LC - 1/C^2R^2)}$

2.13. A triac controls the power to a load comprising a resistance of 10 ohms and an inductance of 0.0265 henrys. If the supply is 110 V rms at 60 Hz and the triac is fired at $\alpha = 75$ degrees in both half cycles, calculate the instantaneous value of the load current.

Answer: $i(t) = 11 \sin(377t - \pi/4 + 1.31) - 5.5 \exp(-t/0.00265)$

2.14. Consider the circuit associated with problem 2.13. Find an expression for the instantaneous value of the current in the circuit for any firing angle α.

Answer:

$$i(t) = \frac{\hat{V}}{[R^2 + (\omega L)^2]^{1/2}} \sin(\omega t - \phi + \alpha) - \frac{\hat{V} \sin(\alpha - \phi)}{[R^2 + (\omega L)^2]^{1/2}} \exp(-Rt/L)$$

2.15. Consider a 3-phase, half-wave, controlled rectifier, whose firing angles of all 3 thyristors are set at $\alpha = 0$ radians.
   If the 3-phase voltages are

$$v_1 = \hat{V} \sin \omega t$$

$$v_2 = \hat{V} \sin(\omega t - 2\pi/3) \text{ and}$$

$$v_3 = \hat{V} \sin(\omega t + 2\pi/3)$$

Calculate the average voltage output for a resistive load.

Answer: $0.827 \hat{V}$

2.16. Consider a case of parallel capacitance turn-off as illustrated in Fig. 2.25. Let the load resistance be 5 ohms and the applied d.c. voltage be 120 V.
   Calculate the minimum value of C if the manufacturer's specified turn-off time of the thyristor for forced commutation is 15 μs. What is a suitable value of R, if the thyristor TH1 is pulsed on every mullisecond.

Answer: $3 \mu F$, 55Ω

2.17. Consider the circuit shown in Fig. 2.28, without the components, L, C_1 and R_1, and with the addition of a diode across R, such that the diode and thyristor anodes are connected. The d.c. voltage supply is 500 V and the load resistance is 3.5 ohms. Let the diode forward voltage drop be assumed negligible. The junction capacitance of the thyristor is 20 pF and the maximum forward dv/dt withstand of the thyristor is 180 V μs^{-1}.
   Calculate the minimum value of C to prevent premature turn-on when the supply circuit-breaker is closed. What is the purpose of the resistor R and how would its value be determined?

Answer: $0.8 \mu F$

2.18. A series resonant turn-off circuit is depicted in Fig. 2.23(b). Describe the action of turn-off. Show mathematically that the current through the thyristor, and the voltage across the thyristor are as shown in Fig. 2.23(c) over the period from the time when the thyristor is fired to the time when the thyristor begins to turn off.

2.19.
   (i) How would you find the limiting dv/dt of a thyristor?

(ii) Describe the firing sequence of a 3-phase inverter.
(iii) What is the purpose of having parallel operation of thyristors?
(iv) What care must be taken when paralleling thyristors?
(v) Explain the use of a free-wheeling diode.
(vi) How would you use a power semiconductor switch to control the speed of an induction motor?
(vii) How would you use a power semiconductor switch to control the speed of a d.c. motor?
(viii) What do you understand by thyristor turn-off?
(ix) What is the turn-off time of a thyristor?
(x) Which is greater, the latching current or the holding current?
(xi) Why must the thyristor be protected against a rapid rise of current during turn-on?
(xii) What is the approximate limit of di/dt during turn-on?
(xiii) What form of protection is used to limit di/dt?
(xiv) How does the thyristor differ from the triac?
(xv) What are the gating differences of the thyristor and the triac?
(xvi) Why have thyristors in series?
(xvii) What form of protection do series thyristors need?
(xviii) What advantage does the disc type thyristor have over other types?
(xix) What advantage does a cycloconverter have over other inverters?
(xx) What disadvantage does a cycloconverter have over other inverters?

CHAPTER 3

3.6. Consider the inverter shown in Figs. 3.19(c), 3.20(a) and 3.21 and make the simplifying assumption that the inductance L has an infinite value. The load is 30 ohms resistive (R_L) and $n = 1$. Determine the maximum thyristor turn-off time for satisfactory inverter operation if the commutating capacitor C has a value 0.18 μF.

Answer: 15 μs

3.7. Consider a single-phase inverter configuration as shown in Fig. 3.18(3) with the addition of an inductance L in series with the battery and a commutation capacitor C in parallel with the load resistance of 30 ohms. If the inductance is considered infinite to maintain a constant battery current, what is the value of C for successful inverter operation, when each thyristor has a turn-off time of 30 μs?

Answer: 1.44 μF

3.8. Consider the three-phase inverter as shown in Fig. 3.29 and the output voltage as shown in Fig. 3.30. By Fourier analysis determine the amplitudes of all harmonics up to and including the fifth of the line voltage output.

Answer: $\dfrac{\sqrt{6}}{\pi} V, 0, 0, 0, \dfrac{\sqrt{6}}{5\pi} V$

3.9. Consider the three-phase inverter as shown in Fig. 3.29. If the load is an induction motor, what effect will the fifth harmonic of line voltage have upon the performance of the machine?

CHAPTER 4

4.6. A d.c. series motor is controlled by a thyristor chopper circuit, which is fed from a 600 V d.c. supply. Estimate the chopper pulse frequency to limit the armature current excursion to 20A (the difference between maximum and minimum values), when the ratio of time on to pulse period of the load thyristor is 0.5. The total load circuit inductance is 0.1 H and the resistance can be neglected.

Answer: The average value of the motor voltage to the supply voltage is

$$\frac{V_m}{V} = \frac{t_{on}}{T} = 0.5, \text{ where } t_{on} = \text{time of pulse and } T = \text{pulse period}$$

Therefore $V_m = 0.5 \times 600 = 300V$

The difference between the average voltage and the peak voltage of the pulse is associated with the establishment of flux. That is

$$V_l = L \ di/_{dt} = L \ \frac{\Delta ia}{\Delta t}$$

since the current rise and fall is linear.

$$V_l = V - V_m = 600 - 300 = 300 \ V$$

and $\Delta i_a = 20 \text{ A.} \qquad \Delta t = t_{on}$

∴ $t_{on} = \Delta t = \dfrac{0.1 \times 20}{300} = 6.67 \ ms$

But $\dfrac{t_{on}}{T} = 0.5$

∴   Pulse frequency $= \dfrac{1}{T} = \dfrac{0.5}{t_{on}} = 75$ pulses per second.

4.7. Consider the oscillation chopper circuit of Fig. 4.26 and let the load be a d.c. motor with negligible armature resistance. What is the ratio of pulse time to pulse period, when the switching frequency is 200 Hz, the armature inductance is 10 mH, the measured current excursion is 10 A and the d.c. supply voltage is 200 V.

Answer: 0.9 or 0.1

4.8. An a.c. supply, $v = 100 \sin 377t$, is connected in series with a resistance, 10 ohms, a thyristor and a 50 V battery, whose anode is connected to the thyristor cathode. Compute the average value of current in the circuit, if the thyristor is fired by a continuous d.c. signal.

Answer: 1.095A

When the thyristor firing angles are $\alpha = 80°$, the coasting period is observed to be $\pi/2$ radians. Find the speed drop between conduction periods.

Answer: 6.3 rpm

4.9. A 1-phase, half-wave controlled rectifier is fed from a 110 V rms, 60 Hz supply and provides a variable d.c. voltage at the terminals of a d.c. motor. The thyristor, which comprises the controlled rectifier, is triggered continuously by a d.c. signal. The resistance of the armature circuit is 10 ohms, and, because of fixed motor excitation and high inertia, the motor speed is considered constant so that the back emf is 55.5 V.

Calculate the average value of the armature current, if the armature inductance can be neglected.

Answer: 2.49 A

4.10. Consider the same circuit as in problem 4.9. The d.c. motor is changed to one where the armature resistance can be neglected but the inductance plays a fundamental role. The specification of the separately excited motor is that at a full-load torque of 31.42 newton metres the speed is 600 rpm, and the total moment of inertia is 0.05 kg m^2.

When the thyristor firing angle $\alpha = 0$ find the speed dip between conduction periods if the observed coasting period is about π radians.

Hint: Consider steady-state operation. Conduction begins as soon as the applied voltage becomes greater than the back emf. During the conduction period electrical energy flows into the armature to produce an electromagnetic torque. The ensuing acceleration gives an increase in the speed.

Conduction ends when the net flux linkage is zero again and the inductance has returned its stored energy to the circuit. There follows a period of motor coasting, when the load energy is taken from the kinetic energy of the motor, and the speed drops. The cycle then repeats. For steady-state operation the speed rise will equal the speed dip. Consequently to find the speed excursion it is simpler to consider the coasting period, because there are no electrical variables to consider. Hence the problem can be tackled as follows:

(i) For the coasting period solve the dynamic equation of motion.
(ii) Determine the mechanical time constant.
(iii) Determine the period of the electrical supply.
(iv) Compare (ii) and (iii) and hence linearize the equation for speed obtained in (1).
(v) Make numerical substitutions to find the speed change.

Answer: 50 rpm

4.11. Consider the same circuit specification as in problem 4.10 with the additional information that the armature resistance is 2 ohms, the gross load torque is 0.6 times full load value, for which the thyristor firing angle is 90 degrees. It is observed that under these conditions the coasting period is 240 degrees and the armature constant is 3.142 volts per radian per second.

Determine the average speed of the motor and the speed excursion as a percentage of the average speed.

Answer: 102 rpm, 11.1%

4.12. A single-phase, full-wave thyristor bridge controls the speed of a d.c. motor, which has constant and separate excitation. The a.c. supply feeding the bridge is 120 V rms at 60 Hz. The motor rated speed is 600 rpm at a full-load torque of 31.42 N.m. An added mechanical load, whose inertia is 0.15 kg m^2 imposes full-load torque at rated speed. The motor inertia is 0.05 kg m^2.

When the thyristor firing angles are $\alpha = 80°$, the coasting period is observed to be $\pi/2$ radians. Find the speed drop between conduction periods.

Answer: 6.3 rpm

4.13. A 3-phase, half-wave bridge comprising three thyristors is fed from a 277 V rms, line to neutral, 60 Hz supply, and provides an adjustable d.c. voltage at the terminals of a separately excited d.c. motor. The motor specifications are

$$R_a = 0.02 \text{ ohms}, L_a = 0.001 \text{ henrys}, E_a = 1.2 \, \omega_m$$

and full load $I_a = 500$A.

Find the firing angle α so that the motor operates at full-load current and at the rated speed of 200 radians per second (ω_m).

Assume continuous conduction and neglect the thyristor forward voltage drop.

Answer: $\alpha = 40°$ where $\alpha = 0$ corresponds to $\omega t = 30°$

Index